100 THINGS
SEAHAWKS FANS
SHOULD KNOW & DO
BEFORE THEY DIE

100 THINGS SEAHAWKS FANS
SHOULD KNOW & DO
BEFORE THEY DIE

John Morgan

TRIUMPH
BOOKS

Library of Congress Cataloging-in-Publication Data

The Library of Congress has catalogued the previous edition as follows:

Morgan, John, 1982–
    100 things Seahawks fans should know and do before they die / John Morgan.
        p. cm.
    ISBN 978-1-60078-399-9
    1. Seattle Seahawks (Football team)—Miscellanea. 2. Seattle Seahawks (Football team)—History—Miscellanea. I. Title. II. Title: One hundred things Seahawks fans should know and do before they die.
    GV956.S4M67 2010
    796.332'6409797772—dc22

                                                                    2010017780

This book is available in quantity at special discounts for your group or organization. For further information, contact:
    Triumph Books LLC
    814 North Franklin Street
    Chicago, Illinois 60610
    (312) 337-0747
    www.triumphbooks.com

Printed in U.S.A.
ISBN: 978-1-60078-958-8
Design by Patricia Frey
Photos courtesy of AP Images unless otherwise indicated

To Mary, Jerry, Jan, and Graham Chant, for giving me a home when I had no home, and giving me a family when I had no family.

Contents

Introduction

Sometime spring of 2007, I read the NFL's report about concussions and head injuries with the intention of writing a post about how the NFL could improve player safety. My idea was to softly fuse the helmet with the shoulder pads since much of a helmet's protective power derives from its ability to spread force over a larger surface area, but players must be able to pivot their necks. It was the off-season, so shoot me.

When the dire, life-deranging effects of continual blows to the head were finally revealed and publicized, I, as someone who had played organized football, someone who loves sports, and has championed its meritocratic nature; as someone who prizes toughness and sacrifice of the non-brain, strictly mechanical bits of the body, I was horrified and disgusted. Discouraged. For the second time in seven years, I was on the verge of swearing off football entirely.

But I had time, and what promised to be among the most exciting seasons in Seahawks history to look forward to. As muses go for this pseudo-jock, pretend intellectual, there's few better. But I wrote and spat, wrote and spat, sequestering all those false starts to a file entitled Purgatory. Little came of weeks of writing, and I wasn't sure any part of me wanted to be a sportswriter anymore. What's the upside? Become Bill Simmons? Peter King? I didn't want that and I couldn't possibly be that. I wasn't even entirely sure I wanted to watch football. However much I loved it, loved the Seahawks, it seemed ever more clear to me that the NFL was entangled in an evil they couldn't end.

August 9, what counted as middle of the night for us and which was really late morning, I got the call. That call at that time of day you intuitively know, can almost hear in some impossible to describe change in the timbre of the ring, is worse than bad, which can only mean crisis. I shot out of bed and ran to the phone jack in our kitchen and answered and heard an unfamiliar voice. It was a little brassy, not anxious nor eager but arrested, flat, and measured. His sentences short and declarative, but not clipped.

It had gotten worse the night before, her headache painful enough to be frightening, and she was speaking nonsense. The headache—she had it all weekend, just a dull headache mostly, but persistent. Then her words became jumbled and almost randomized, but her eyes glassy and vibrating with panic, spoke of a mind trapped by a malfunctioning mouth. Life-saving fear, gut fear awakened her, and she awakened Pete, her husband. Pete said write on this, on the back of this envelope. Probably some junk mail or a bill. "Take me to the hospital," it said, maybe, Pete didn't say. He didn't want to go. He feared hospitals; feared maybe the confirmation of crisis, too. But my mom is stubborn, tough—willful and able to get her way even deprived of speech.

They took the Banfield, arrived at the hospital. I don't know what the ER looked like that morning, but I know ER waiting rooms. Strange people with familiar faces, huddled in small groups, looking wounded, defensive, afraid, and ashamed. Watching television. Or I guess. How vivid really was my imagination that morning as Pete continued sharing a string of facts, all but the only important one. Did they make it through triage? I asked, ever the pedantic boob. Pete said my mom spoke her gibberish and the doctors, now alarmed, ending their shifts and all but out the door, fast-tracked her for surgery.

She has bleeding on the brain.

She's alive.

She'll be out of surgery by two.

We said "good-bye" or something equivalent, and I set down the phone. Ordered apart from her, powerless and arrested waiting, my mom...I softly drew my finger across the touch pad of my laptop and went to ESPN.com, Field Gulls, and Advanced NFL Stats. I read football, football, football, maybe some

Mariners. I later read *Crime and Punishment* and *Nova Express* by her bedside, some Bertrand Russell, probably. It inevitably finds its way wherever I go. But for every 10 words of literature, I surely read 100 words about the zone read and Christine Michael and Nick Franklin and Percy Harvin's hip ligaments and C.J. McCollum. I read about sports. I busied myself with thoughts about sports. I survived the most desperate, powerless, and panicked morning of my life through caring about the lives of strange people, of strange talents, that do not even know me to not care about me.

Why?

Origin stories are seldom interesting or revealing. Among sports fans, team affiliation is typically determined through geography, family, and plain ol' dumb luck. Had I not been born in Tacoma, had I learned to read on something other than the World Book Almanac and supermarket-bought copies of *Funk & Wagnalls New World Encyclopedia*, had Ken Griffey Jr. not debuted when I was six, had our one white-trash splurge been wave runners instead of cable television, had my father not been a Junior Olympian, had my mother not been going to school throughout my childhood, had my brother and I not been latchkey kids…maybe I would love paleontology, psychology, Scientology but not sports. It was sports that captivated me.

I knew Magnus ver Magnusson and Magnus Samuelsson and remember distinctly the new joint he put into the humerus of Aussie Nathan Jones. I knew Martina Hingis, my favorite, and preferred women's tennis with its emphasis on volleys and rallies and backhands and forehand winners, over men's tennis and the dirge-like, monotonous Thwump-ahh-thwump-Ahh of players trading aces. I remember the inside-baseball quality to anchor interactions on live *SportsCenter* and distinctly remember Stuart Scott calling out another anchor's Q score in that always awkward but fun and spontaneous few seconds that abutted the show. Rich Eisen, his partner, looked over at him with such shock and disgust, I just had to know what a Q score was.

Who knows why, who cares how, with every second of life spent on sport, it becomes an unchangeable part of who I have been and ineffable part of who I am. There is no reliving my childhood. There is no reliving this past second spent writing. I have spent the better part of three decades loving athletic competition. There is no more reason to regret it than deny it. And when life caught up with me, and I suffered the very dear cost of loving someone, and I began to feel those emotions of such an intensity that they are not felt over a day, week, month but years, we talked sports. We talked stupid, irrelevant sports, sports, sports.

Pete talked Aaron Hernandez, and so did my grandma…kind of. She's doubly alone now since my grandfather's stroke: alone in their home, alone beside his hospital bed. She lives in New Hampshire, and I call her using my phone card, and we talk never often enough, and our talks are sad, repetitive, and often bitterly wistful, but she knows I love sports, and she tries to meet me halfway.

Sometimes, though, it is hard to try and tease out what about sports and the Seahawks matter. It's a day-to-day thing. It's something I can share with strangers. It's a bridge to conversation. It's a place of respite from the serious and the corrupted. But mostly it's just something that grew into me, the way a place does, or a time period does without us even knowing. It's 30 years part of who I am now. I know sports. I know the Seahawks. Billions of little organic fibers of me are dedicated to trivia and formations and sensations of loss and hope, and something you learn during tragedy is you never stop being you. The worst happens, and you're no different. And I was no different.

Then I stopped writing. I just couldn't do it…not again…not another anonymous stranger insulting my family because he didn't like my writing, my tone, my opinion. It's not me…I wasn't hurt from the comments, but the arrogance, meanness, and entitlement that surely inspires someone to "troll."

Shortly after that, I lost my shit. Not writing, no longer able to invest anything in sports, the sadness of life, the calamity, and helplessness of living, the haunting knowledge that this foundering trauma, which almost killed my mom, that it was the seamy story of every hit, every hard collision, that my hobby was compelling beautiful young men of grace and spirit to destroy their brains, to plunge themselves permanently into the nightmare I could hardly stomach seeing my mom suffer momentarily.

And then I got help. My mom, she's recovering.

In 2014 I am watching the best, most thoroughly likeable and enjoyable Blazers team of my lifetime. And the Seahawks are Super Bowl champions. Life is oddly devoid of taught editing and tension stings. You won't anticipate the resolution because the story's nearing two hours. And you will find something you love, and it will be foolish, unjustifiable, a love lived moment to moment— desultory, cheap sometimes, unrewarding often, with no prove-it moments of swallowing the hemlock, and a dubious payoff, at best. Only ever the moment to moment to moment to moment unceasing love, in those boring moments we look back to as bliss.

The Russell Wilson Era

"Remember when" is the lowest form of conversation.

—Tony Soprano

Nothing's so morbid as nostalgia. Nothing cheapens now like constantly comparing the hot instantaneous to the baby blue confabulations of the past. Now Seahawks fans are luckier than most to have been so cursed, blighted, beaten up, and deprived. Entering the 2013 season, the twin peaks of Seahawks fandom were Laura and Maddy: massacred by an inhuman monster (the Raiders playing "Bob") in the 1983 AFC Championship Game and suspiciously wrapped by plot convenience in Super Bowl XL. This legacy is an acquired taste. Very Seattle.

There's no anchor in the past to cheapen by comparison the future, no perfect season or Steel Curtain Defense, no Bill Walsh, Bart Starr, no moldering glory days to haunt this franchise. I've a friend who relates with grief the day his voice changed. His life is a series of irretrievable losses. Say what you will about a Kurt Cobain childhood, it smothers nostalgia in the crib. Seahawks fans are optimists. Seahawks fans are futurists. They haven't a choice. First quarter in the roll or last in the pocket, this next will be their high score.

But a few years ago, during the ruinous transition from Mike Holmgren to Jim L. Mora, from the 16 megapixel photos of pinpoint slants and off-tackle run blocking as delicate as ballet to another early morning sprint up Tiger Mountain, from passing glory teased but never quite achieved to the mortal threat of incompetence with tenure.

A screaming comes across the sky

—Thomas Pynchon

Named Russell Wilson. First, though...

A friend of the devil is a friend of mine

—The Grateful Dead

During the winter of 2009, the Seahawks cleaned house, disposing both what was dear (Matt Hasselbeck, Lofa Tatupu, and Walter Jones) and what had rotted deep in the crisper drawer (Jim L. Mora, Tim Ruskell's stuff). For the second time in his role as team owner, Paul Allen put a dent in that towering vat of gold doubloons he swims in and spits out, all artfully (arcfully even) from his yellow duckbill and hired a big, fancy, high name value head coach. This time it was Pete Carroll. Someone described Allen and Carroll's arrangement as Allen providing Carroll with a golden parachute. Impending and soon to be very severe sanctions were hanging over Carroll's former employer, the USC athletics program. A promotion and a pay raise is a nice way to jump ship. It's ridiculous how little I care about that today and yet how funny it still is.

Carroll developed a highly specialized defense, Carroll redacted those clauses in the Seahawks player acquisition manual which emphasized duty, rectitude, and Christianity, and scribbled in talent, talent, and talent.

But the team didn't really take off. It finished 2010 7–9 with an improbable and spirited playoff run. It finished 2011 7–9 with one Tarvaris Jackson starting at quarterback. (Two Tarvaris Jacksons, standing too close, are known to cause a singularity.) Carroll had stumbled into the same trap of their own making defensive-minded head coaches so often stumble into: he could build a great defense, but because of that great defense, his teams were too good to finish with a bad enough record to select a franchise quarterback. And, it seemed,

In just the second year of the Russell Wilson Era, the franchise quarterback helped bring a Super Bowl championship to Seattle.

his talent evaluation was not keen enough to find that franchise quarterback by some other means. See: every quarterback pre-Wilson.

This is hardly a new story. Since the turn of the millennium, 11 of the 14 Super Bowl champions have been defense-first teams. And those teams were all gifted an improbable talent at quarterback. Tom Brady was a sixth-round pick. Ben Roethlisberger and Joe Flacco were selected at 11 and 18, respectively. New York landed Eli Manning after Manning refused to play in San Diego. (That trade, by the by, landed the Chargers Philip Rivers, Shawne Merriman, and Nate Kaeding.) The Tampa Bay Bucs traded *two first-round picks, two second-round picks,* and eight million smackeroos for Jon Gruden and his amazing powers of quarterback necromancy. Brad Johnson went from Brad Johnson to Super Bowl champion Brad Johnson because of Gruden's unholy arts.

But how? How would Seattle beat the system? How would Carroll overcome this Chinese finger trap—by pulling harder? Surely by pulling harder. No. This would require subtlety. Some ability to see an inefficiency, talent where others saw only limitation. This would require some football taboo being broken. This would require new ideas, a new way of seeing the gridiron, a keen sense of what really and truly makes a great quarterback great.

This would require Matt Flynn.

A fluttering whirs incomplete.

Seattle signed Flynn to be their starting quarterback March 18, 2012.

A screaming comes across the sky.

And six weeks later drafted one Russell Wilson.

There's much in the rest of this book about what exactly Russell Wilson the player is, and there's more than enough choking the media about who exactly Russell Wilson the person may be. But let me explain why I call this, beginning in 2012 and extending onward to some time not yet known, the Russell Wilson Era.

The most valuable baseball player of all time is, you guessed it, Frank Stallone. That is to say, Babe Ruth. At his peak, Ruth was worth about 13 wins a season. That's about 1/12 of a baseball season. Absurdly valuable but not enough alone to make the Yankees consistent World Series champions. Baseball's like that. According to three different methods picked because value in basketball is still somewhat controversial in its determination, LeBron James peaked at 20–30 wins. That is a quarter to more than one-third of a season, and this is why having a player like James or Michael Jordan or Magic Johnson or Larry Bird or Bill Russell, etc. is pretty much a guarantee of contention and, most likely, of one day winning a championship. Not always, but probably.

Football stats do not allow for this kind of precision, but a quick analysis by statistician Brian Burke allows us to ballpark the value of someone like Russell Wilson. Comparing Aaron Rodgers and his longtime backup Flynn, and using the simple metric of adjusted yards per attempt (AY/A) (which is: yards + 10 x TDs) + (-45 x INTs / attempts), Burke determined Rodgers was worth about four wins more than Flynn. Flynn may or may not be "replacement value," but he's close enough for our purposes. That, too, is a quarter season's worth of wins. (And if Flynn is above replacement value, which he very well may be—no shame in losing out to Russell Wilson—Rodgers too may be worth five or more wins, a third of a season!)

Which is to say should Wilson eventually develop the kind of value of Rodgers, Seattle has its very first MJ: that player so incredibly valuable, he alone makes his team a perennial contender. Were he paid a baseball-equivalent wage ($5 million to $6 million per win above replacement and those wins one of 162), Wilson would be worth $200 million to $300 million *a season*. Maybe you think that's crazy. The Seahawks franchise was valued by Forbes at $1.08 billion, which is why a great player is often called "the Franchise." Four wins take a below-average team and lets it squeak into the playoffs. Four wins take an average team and turns it into a potential No. 1 seed. Four wins take an above-average team and turns it into a young dynasty.

2 Your 2013 Super Bowl Champion Seattle Seahawks

I fell back first to the couch, rapt in maniacal laughter. It was over. It was over. It wasn't over, but it was all over but the crying. The discouraged tears of the crushed. The sweet sadness and relief of the victorious. The Seattle Seahawks would be Super Bowl champions. The Seattle Seahawks were Super Bowl champions. The Seattle Seahawks were Super Bowl champions but for 34 minutes of play clock. The Seattle Seahawks, my Seattle Seahawks, our Seattle Seahawks, the city of Seattle's often embarrassing, ever discouraging, always hope inspiring, Seahawks would become the 48th Super Bowl champions.

Seattle wouldn't win a great Super Bowl. Not a Super Bowl for the ages. The Seahawks would not win on a last-minute drive or by preventing a fourth-quarter score. There would be no iconic tackle, catch, or fumble. The Seattle Seahawks would score on a safety 12 seconds into Super Bowl XLVIII, the earliest score in Super Bowl history, and never relinquish that lead. No team in Super Bowl history had ever beaten a team so quickly as Seattle beat the Denver Broncos.

It was a blowout.

The blowout is all that is right and good in sport— not because we seek blowouts, not because a closely fought, last-second win would not have been more exciting, more engaging throughout, better for Denver fans, better for neutral fans, but because without the blowout, the late rally that comes up short, the grinding affair that's close but boring without the possibility that our expectations can be disappointed, our expectations cannot be fulfilled.

The blowout is dangerous. The blowout is radical. The blowout is Bambi starving after his mother dies. The blowout is Luke missing the exhaust port. The blowout is Walter White succeeding, surviving, and living happily with his family, unpunished by the angry hand of his creator, a living testament to the earthly triumph of evil. The blowout is casting a 12-year-old in the role of Lolita. It doesn't pre-screen its results or seek approval from its producers. It doesn't negotiate with Peyton Manning's agent. It's not approved for younger audiences. It begins. It progresses. It becomes Cinderella for one, Kafka for the other.

Oh oh oh, except one slight detail, one little deviation—Kafka starts low and bottoms out almost immediately. There's almost mercy in Gregor dying, eh? There's no flatline, no variations on a theme of otherwise undifferentiated suffering. No toying, no bullying, no sadistic but sanitary, safe-word forgotten, period of divine domination. Nope. Nope.

We need to win and be beaten. We need, even experienced vicariously, the sensation of glory, of having our hearts ripped out, and desolation, and piqued hopes dashed, and damn right that surge of hope answered—our hopes fulfilled! But were every win or loss close and down-to-the-wire and decided at or near the final play, it would quickly become tedious and stagey and render most of the game irrelevant. No we need the purifying blast of a whoopin.' Given or received and Lo! these are Pete Carroll's Seahawks: given.

As little by little all is swallowed by some corporate entity, and the regressing pull of the mean renders sensitivity and true oddness and sophistication taboo, sport defies the market-driven need for all to be content and no one happy.

So the Seahawks won. The Seahawks won! And many were disappointed. Many a Super Bowl Sunday was ruined. There would be no "The Catch." But I gotta think, I gotta, gotta think Seahawks fans wouldn't have it any other way. It was fun. It exorcised the demon of XL. It was unique and fair—a true battle of skill and talent versus immeasurably greater skill and talent. Even perhaps the beginning of a dynasty—who knows? But most of all, it was ours. It was this team, our guys, whooping Broncos ass for 60 minutes without a second of letup, until that Lombardi Trophy couldn't be torn away by ten Bill Leavys and a black hole.

3 Blue Hypergiant: Walter Jones

On Stars

A star floods space with photons. Stars of sufficient luminosity and that are sufficiently close can be seen, some even in the tangerine and mauve of the sky above the *urbs*. The closest visible star in the night sky, Alpha Centauri, is 4.37 light-years away. For us to be able to see Alpha Centauri, it must put out photons in every direction, filling a theoretical sphere 2,054,976,356,000,000,000,000,000 square miles in volume. And despite the vast amount of space traveled and the incomprehensibly vast amount of space infiltrated by Alpha Centauris light, the star is then only visible to the naked eye if it is sufficiently bright. Those photons, over four years old, emanating from a giant but relatively small point 25.7 trillion miles away and growing ever more diffuse as the tiniest divergences in angle are magnified billions of miles by billions of miles, had to have been so numerous, so densely packed, as they emanated from that distant star (stars, actually), to be spread across the cosmos yet still sufficiently dense to be seen from Earth.

The modern usage of "star" to mean "lead actor, singer, etc." originated in 1824, 14 years before Friedrich Bessel first measured the actual distance of a star from Earth. It's not hard to understand the intended analogy. But as the word becomes steeped in cliché, cheapened by overuse, and the once strikingly apt metaphor is

Walter Jones, the Seahawks' best-ever player and probably the greatest left tackle in NFL history, blocks a Raiders linebacker during a blowout 31–3 loss at Oakland–Alameda County Coliseum in October 2000.

forgotten, and "star" becomes synonymous with celebrity, it has become easy to forget what it means to be a star. It is an incomparable acknowledgment of magnificence, significance, and grandeur.

A pop celebrity like Justin Bieber is not a star. A better analogy would be: Bieber is a virus. He is a terrestrial phenomenon. Of the set of all people that know of Bieber, the subset of people that know and like Bieber is dwarfed by the subset of people that know and dislike or just don't care about Bieber.

Walter Jones is a star. While everyone that knows of Jones may not equally appreciate his extreme luminosity, few could ever dislike him. He achieved his status not through infiltrating the memories of the unsuspecting and adulterating normal human impulses for his own gain but by simply doing his job well. Doing his job with such grace and power, such proficiency and ease that it was something to behold. Somewhere on some Earth-like exoplanet, the light from his 2004 season is just reaching the eyes of some barely sentient race. And they are awed.

Nebula

Jones spent two seasons at Holmes Community College in Mississippi before transferring to Florida State. There are people that call themselves "humble" and there are the truly humble, who carry the foundering insecurity of rejection and the scars of their hard-scrabble ascension for the rest of their lives. In his acceptance speech for the Pro Football Hall of Fame, Jones said he wanted to make it into the NFL to "play in this game to say I could play in this game." That's humble.

Protostar

Jones only played one season of Division I football. Typically, that makes a player *seem* risky. No analysis I know of has ever tested the supposed risky versus safe distinction assigned to NFL Draft prospects and so I am most dubious. Aaron Curry, for instance, was said to be safer than Ralph Nader's car, a real surefire talent. Some players bust. Curry combusted. But whatever the truth, the semblance of risk still seems to matter to decision makers. And safer talents like Mike Williams are drafted higher than head-cases like Randy Moss.

Luckily for Seattle, Dennis Erickson, Randy Mueller, and Bob Whitsitt were interested in big action and bold moves. And Jones was proving himself a workout warrior. He ran a 4.75-second 40 at the 1997 NFL Combine. That became a kind of suffix. He wasn't the best offensive tackle of his class. That was Orlando Pace, who went first overall to the St. Louis Rams. That designation of second-best became a kind of prefix. Second-best left tackle prospect, Walter Jones, who ran a 4.75/40 in the 1997 NFL Combine, was drafted sixth overall by the Seattle Seahawks.

The sixth overall pick in the NFL Draft is hugely expensive: both in salary and what's called opportunity cost. In the late '90s, rookie contracts hadn't exploded, but the salary cap was commensurately smaller. A top 10 pick is a vital resource granted only the lowliest of teams. Bad teams build from them. Bad teams are sunk by them. Good teams have built from them. Their ranks are a who's who of great all-time players: Peyton Manning, Bruce Smith, John Elway, Kenny Easley, Eric Dickerson, Lawrence Taylor, and on and on.

Seattle had two picks in the first round after trading Rick Mirer to the Bears. (*Yes,* Chicago sent a first-round pick to Seattle *for Rick Mirer.*) The Seahawks had moved up to No. 3 to draft Shawn Springs and wanted to maneuver up to No. 6 to nab Jones. It would be costly, and ownership was in flux. Peter King related the fateful conversation that brought Jones to Seattle: "Aware that anti-Seahawks sentiment at the state capital was running high, Whitsitt warned his boss, 'You could be out of this in three days. Dennis and Randy think they can move up and get this great tackle, but it could really push your costs up. If they get Springs and this tackle, it could cost $13 million in signing bonuses alone.'"

"What did we say when we got into this?" Allen replied. "If we're involved, we're involved. Are we still involved?"

"Yeah," Whitsitt said.

"Then we have to do it," Allen said.

Paul Allen was in, and with his backing, Seattle was about to add its best player ever.

Seattle had spoken with the Jets about trading for New York's sixth overall pick. The deal was: No. 6 for No. 12 and the

Seahawks' third- and sixth-round picks. It fell through. The Jets backed out and instead traded with Tampa Bay. Seattle was sure Tampa had moved up to draft Walter Jones, but general manager Rich McKay, Tim Ruskell's then-boss and mentor, called Seattle and offered to trade back. Somehow, the pick had become cheaper in translation. Seattle packaged the 12th overall pick and a third-round pick for the sixth overall. The sixth-rounder they kept as a result became Itula Mili.

Star Birth

Knowing only Jones' career as it actually happened, speculating about disastrous possibilities that could have been may seem morbid, but it allows us to relate to Seahawks fans of 1997. We now see Walter Jones's development from draft pick to promising rookie to stalwart superstar anchoring the offensive line to Hall of Fame-bound legend and greatest Seahawk of all time as fated. But in the summer of 1997, Jones was an expensive, seemingly risky player, that played a less-than prestigious position (or, at least, not very flashy and easy to underestimate). His rookie season would add another alarming phrase to the bunch: often injured.

Jones missed two games in September with an ankle injury. He missed two games in November with an injury to the other ankle. I am sure some people were pretty concerned. This was a fan base that had endured the soap-operatic saga of Kenny Easley, his chronically-injured ankle, the terrible toll of painkiller abuse and how it ended his career and almost ended his life. Easley hadn't developed his problem ankle until later in his career, but once injured, he had little recourse but rest and large doses of painkillers. Imagine the panic had we known that a kidney condition kept Jones from taking strong painkillers.

The injuries proved to be aberrant. Jones would not miss another game because of injury until injury ended his 2008 season and, with it, his career.

Jones made quarterbacks better and running backs great. He helped 41-year-old Warren Moon improbably make a Pro Bowl in 1997. Jones blocked for Trent Dilfer's best years as a pro. He helped a sixth-round pick develop confidence and lead the Seahawks to their first Super Bowl.

Moon was a mad bomber. Jones made practical the five- and seven-step drops that a deep passing game relies on.

Dilfer had scattershot accuracy and more arm than he knew what to do with. By eliminating drive-killing sacks, giving Dilfer a clean pocket to step into, and fighting off defenders that might otherwise panic Dilfer and scare him into poor reads or inaccurate throws through bad mechanics, Jones helped make Dilfer something he had never really been: consistently above average.

But his best work was saved for his best, and in some ways, most needy quarterback: Matt Hasselbeck.

Star

The differences between a typical left tackle and a legendary tackle are both great and subtle. Few fans train their eyes on the position, preferring, most naturally, to follow the ball carrier and the "action." We usually notice an offensive tackle on two occasions: the chagrined, bent, and idle pose taken by a beat blocker. This is colloquially known as the "Winston Justice"—referring both to the man and the moral concept of fairness as applied to overhyped clods. The Winston flashes before an end or linebacker explodes into the quarterback.

The other is rare and sweet. Walter Jones made half a career out of locking down and driving back ends. Week 2 of the 2005 season, he drove Patrick Kerney like a plow, tearing open a hole for Shaun Alexander to jog through. Jones' dominance was cartoonish at times. He could drive an end into a linebacker and create a time-based sculpture, *Pile: Portrait of Man Defeated.*

Hasselbeck needed a run game. Mike Holmgren, who ran a classic Walshian West Coast Offense, spread the field horizontally and set up the run with the pass. This compensated for the two great deficiencies of a weaker-armed quarterback: the deep pass and negotiating the condensed and claustrophobic confines of the red zone.

Hasselbeck wasn't a garbage deep passer. Despite his below average arm strength, he had touch and accuracy. But unlike a true great deep passer like Russell Wilson, you wouldn't want Hasselbeck to throw a deep pass anywhere near double coverage. What might seem like an insignificant difference in speed 10 or 15 yards down the field becomes significant when a deep safety has that extra second or so to break on a pass 30 or more yards down the field. Hasselbeck was at his best sustaining drives with quick, precise short and intermediate throws. Jones so excelled at winning his matchup that slants were rarely ever batted down, and not until the Seahawks line crumpled did you see Hasselbeck double clutching the ball, shifting this way and that in the pocket, looking for the right combination of open receiver and throwing lane. If Hasselbeck could complete the short passes, keep Seattle in good down and distance, and convert third downs, Jones and eventually Steve Hutchinson could clear out the front seven for Touchdown Alexander to cash in.

Helium

For his excellence, Jones wanted to be paid. Mike Holmgren and later Bob Whitsitt complicated the situation and pushed it to the brink. Seattle franchised Jones in 2002. He wasn't happy. He held out through training camp and into the season. Finally, he signed and reported before Week 3. It became a yearly tradition. Seattle would not extend a long-term contract that satisfied Jones; the Seahawks would franchise Jones to retain him, he would hold out through training camp, then return for the season. It became a joke. Jones was nicknamed "the Franchise."

Hypergiant

Holding out didn't hurt his play. He established himself as a perennial Pro Bowler and, along with Pace, put left tackle on the map. The position became a respected building block, and linemen's salaries skyrocketed. Nowadays left tackles are more highly valued than running backs. If salary is the measure, in 2009 the top five offensive tackles were more highly paid than the top five corners and the top five wide receivers, and were behind only defensive ends and quarterbacks. Left tackle has become a building block, but also a position of superstars. Fans talk up big blocks and pancakes. They brag about footwork and drop steps.

Flashier moments earned Jones a reputation among fans, but every-snap steadiness and consistency earned Jones a position among the greatest offensive tackles to ever play. He allowed zero sacks in 2004. Zero. Jones had it all. He could move, he could control, he could pull and wage total war on a defense. He was a superstar and a lunch-pail player. Jones kept it simple, yet astonishing. For 12 seasons, he broke huddle, took his position on left end at left tackle, put his hand down, sprung up, and blocked out the sun.

Supernova

Thanksgiving of 2008 was Jones' last game. He had been ever so slowly declining, but as with the truly exceptional, it could be hard to tell because he was still so good. But the best must beat the best. Jones could shut down pedestrian ends and withstand even the very good, but that day and against DeMarcus Ware, Jones' decay and vulnerability were exposed. He allowed $2 \times \infty$ more sacks in that one game than he allowed in all of 2004. Ware was in the midst of his greatest season and would finish with 20 sacks. It was two Hall of Fame talents, at different points in their career, one just hanging on, the other establishing his legacy.

So like a supernova did Jones end it all. His body broke in a flash. And all he was spread every which way to help foster the stars of tomorrow. It was a sad end, as endings always are, but a glorious end.

4 XL 1: Kickoff

Super Bowl XL. Ford Field, Detroit. Seahawks versus Steelers. First quarter, kickoff...

Josh Scobey secures it just inside the 3, then stutter-steps, sprints behind up-man Maurice Morris. XL is on; Seattle ball. The Seattle machine, all short routes and pull blocks, pistons made of linemen, gears made of wide receivers, is easing into first. First snap, three-step drop, Matt Hasselbeck to Darrell Jackson for a too-easy seven yards. The Seahawks will punish soft coverage until stopped. Then we'll beat you over top.

Mike Holmgren has a plan, and it's working. For the first series, Jackson is unstoppable. Another pass launched before Jackson can finish his cut. Reception. Holmgren gets the MVP involved. Shaun Alexander charges behind Sean Locklear, cuts in, puts a hand on Chris Gray's hip, and the two jog for eight. Jackson again, running an out, and it's another easy first down as Hasselbeck rainbows it in. Holmgren envisions a masterpiece, and his medium is offensive linemen. Ryan Hannam then Walter Jones then Steve Hutchinson pull sequentially and fan toward the sideline. Shame Alexander only runs for one before collapsing on the ball.

"Could this be real?" I'm standing. I'm shouting at the TV set. I'm shouting at my girlfriend's parents' TV set.

SEA!—HAWKS!

No. Nononono—not yet. Incomplete. It's third-and-9. It's third-and-9. Seattle sets three wide, split backs, and Pittsburgh responds with a 3-3 nickel. This is the game? It feels like the game. It's the first quarter. It's the first quarter. It feels like the whole game in the balance.

Snap.

Locklear and Gray pop; Lock slanting in while Gray slides out to contain the edge rush. Clark Haggans stunts in and tears through the inside shoulder of Locklear. Steelers swarm the edge, and Hasselbeck can feel it all closing in. He's hardly through his seven-step drop before he's attempting to step up, step out of pressure; steps into a sack by Haggans instead.

Okay. Okayokayokayokayokay. So high and now so low, but it was a good drive, and we can pin 'em back. Pin 'em back, Rouen. Pin 'em—ah, crap. Touchback.

The crowd is roaring. Al Michaels says it's 80 percent Steelers fans. They cheer their team right into a false start. Hahaha. Backed up—get after it, D! Chuck Darby slices in and falls behind the line. That's bad. Leroy Hill knifes in and wraps, stopping Willie Parker for no gain. Is that Lofa Tatupu appearing from the pile? Putting a shoulder in? Damn right. *Ta! Tu! Pu!* And there he is again, charging hard from the third level and blowing up the Steelers screen. How you like third down, Pittsburgh? Uh-huh. False start, again. That's another five. Okayokayokay. Yes. Yesyesyes. It's third-and-19. Seahawks rush three. Bryce Fisher edge rushes to perfection and nearly sacks Ben Roethlisberger at the 1. Ben scrambles, slides into a charging Tatupu for 10. Punt time. That's the D. That's the D that made the difference, that got us here.

Punt. Warrick, headliner of D-Jack's draft class but a castoff now, motions hook and ladder then shimmy-shakes for minus-2. A lot of noise and little production, that's Peter Warrick.

Matt Hasselbeck drops back to pass during an early drive near midfield in Super Bowl XL against the Pittsburgh Steelers.

Let's power this up. Power it up. Put it away. *Seahawks! SEA!*

Alexander motions from the backfield to wide left. Yeah, that's not fooling anyone. Hasselbeck takes the snap and pitches to Mack Strong. Hannam cut blocks. Jones straight abuses Joey Porter. Hope you weren't planning on participating in this play, Joe-Joe. Strong starts his giddy-up but is tripped up by Kimo von Oelhoffen. Shoot. Shoot. If they awarded yards for execution…Morris motions wide. Jones smacks around Kimo this time. Hasselbeck surveys, sees nothing, tucks and runs for nine. That's right, improvise. Show those quicks. Make them respect the legs, Matt.

My heart barely beats before Hasselbeck finds Jackson for 10 and the first. Drive alive. Madden is prattling about Holmgren never wanting Alexander to be the lone back. Seattle breaks three wide, split backs. Morris motions wide, leaving Alexander as the lone back. Haggans charges, Alexander "blocks," curls, and "receives." Bobble, bobble, and not even the presence of mind to drop the ball before falling to the turf for a loss of two. Damn it. Damn it, Shaun. Damn it. Where have your hands gone, Shaun? Damn it. Away from the action, Robbie Tobeck is making sure a Steeler remembers him. We scrap in Seattle, too. This ain't Rams football. This ain—

Okay. Okay. Hasselbeck to Bobby Engram for six. We're back on that brink. It's third down. Here we go. Here we go. Hasselbeck drops, targets Jackson, and connects for 18—

Holding? Bunch a damn bull. Wait, no, that's holding. Gray stabs an arm under James Farrior and clotheslines the charging linebacker. Argh.

That's bad. Third-and-16. Drive has a sword hanging right over it. A steel sword. Heh. *Er.* Seahawks break three wide, two on the left, and the Steelers counter with a wacky 3-2 look. Get that crap out of here, Lebeau. Hasselbeck drops, Steelers rush three, Hasselbeck launches and...*noooooooooooooooooooooooooooooooooo!*

Dropped. Hasselbeck's pass falls between Jackson and Joe Jurevicius and nearly into Ike Taylor's mitts. But he drops it. Confusion. Route confusion or something.

Punt.

Hines Ward motions wide left into the left slot. He's trying to draw Marcus Trufant into the pile and thus create a short edge for Willie Parker. Seahawks read it, strong safety Michael Boulware runs down to cover Ward. Dude's gonna be good. Kid has all the tools. Snap. Parker blasts left, attempts the edge but is dropped by a charging Trufant. Attaboy.

Steelers pick up six on the next attempt. Shoot. Still, third down, third down, get them off the field. Hawks rush four, and Roethlisberger targets Ward slicing through a disorganized zone.

The pass drops in low and incomplete. Two Pittsburgh drives. Two three-and-outs.

SEA!—FENSE!

Ball back in the good guys' hands. Ball back where it belongs. Seahawks line surges into the Steelers' front three, and Alexander runs for an easy four. Seahawks pick themselves up and set. Hasselbeck takes a three-step drop and zips it to Jackson. He has inside position on Taylor, receives and burns by him. That's good for 20. Reset. Reset. Hasselbeck drops back, sits in a comfy pocket, and finds Vicious coming back on a hook route. Joe extends his long arms away from his frame and pulls in the catch. Quietly, Mack Strong makes the play. Seattle's line pushed hard left, and only Strong was left to pick up blitzing linebacker Haggans. He engages and runs Haggans around the pocket, never dropping his block for a second and keeping Hasselbeck free of pressure.

Seahawks are driving, on the 16, about to punch it in and pull away in the first. Okay, not pull away, but establish that vital early lead. And then pull away! I'm standing. My future wife has abandoned the insanity for someplace quiet. She's about to hear my anguish pour through the walls.

End of the first quarter...to be continued.

The Many Brilliancies of Steve Largent

Since his retirement, Steve Largent's three major records—receptions, receiving yards, and receiving touchdowns—have all been bested. His record in receptions has been bested 19 times. His record in receiving yards has been bested 11 times. His record for receiving touchdowns has been bested five times and tied once, by Tim Brown.

Breaking Largent's record is not a key to Canton. His receptions record is now little more than a signpost in a good wide receiver's career. Recently retired receivers Derrick Mason, Muhsin Muhammad, and Hines Ward all passed Largent, and only Ward has any shot at the Hall of Fame. And Ward would enter because of his team's success rather than his own.

Even his more sterling record—receiving yards—was quickly eclipsed by contemporaries like Henry Ellard and James Lofton. Lofton was inducted into the Pro Football Hall of Fame, but after five years of eligibility. Ellard is still very much on the outside looking in.

Largent is perhaps the greatest beneficiary of the Mel Blount rule. Largent was always an adept route runner who had deceptive speed, but in the bruising mid-'70s pass environment, he struggled to get open. He had 87 receptions in his first two seasons, despite starting 27 games. He caught 71 in 16 games in 1978. Only two strike-shortened seasons stopped him from surpassing 60 the next 10 seasons. It's easy to see his place within league history without denying his steadily fading place on the record books. Couple his fast-sinking achievements with his known tools deficiencies, and it creates a warped portrait of the player. Make no mistake, Largent was great, just maybe not great in the way some Seahawks fans want him to have been.

Largent was a great value and great story. Seattle acquired him for an eighth-round selection. The Houston Oilers saw him as too small and too slow and planned to cut him. Seattle acquired him, played him in Week 1, and Largent caught five passes for 86 yards and never looked back. Apart from being an underdog, he was handsome and white in a sport that was steadily not, and at a position that was almost exclusively black. Maybe it didn't matter.

It did matter that he was the first star on an expansion team that not only lacked stars, but much of anything to root for. His quick success earned him a spot on the All-Rookie team. His third season, he went from good to great, and the Seahawks followed, posting their first winning record. He had refined his style. His yards per reception were dropping, but his receptions skyrocketed, and so did his value.

Largent was a possession receiver before that took on pejorative connotations. And as atypical as he was when he was drafted, he unwittingly became the prototype for the modern receiver. In the run-first game that had dominated the NFL before 1978, running was the backbone of an offense, passing a high-risk/high-reward means to cash in. Coaches said, you run to pass, and play-action was a staple of every offense. Largent was not fast or tall, but reliable. He ran precise and deceptive routes and caught whatever came near him. In many ways, he was the forerunner for Jerry Rice, and Rice a continuation of the prototype Largent had developed.

See, Rice wasn't fast either. Yes, he was athletic, but athleticism wasn't his calling card. Rice was a receiver you could run an offense through. Unlike Largent, he had a coach who embraced that. Rice became the embodiment of the new NFL, where passing would rule, but Largent was the prototype.

The skills he possessed, even today, define truly valuable receivers. Descriptions of Largent are full of apologies. Even his Hall of Fame profile is overrun with excuses and qualifiers. It starts, "Steve Largent, a 5'11", 187-pound wide receiver with only average size and speed but armed with exceptional determination and concentration…" As if, after all these years, coaches and voters are still scratching their heads—*how the hell did that guy beat us?*

I won't argue his determination and concentration, but it's a little insulting to the hundreds of corners, safeties, and linebackers to argue Largent was simply more determined. No, Largent was better. He was an innovator. Instead of outrunning his opponent,

Steve Largent, the prototype of the modern-day possession receiver, heads to the end zone on a touchdown reception during a preseason game against the Minnesota Vikings in 1986.

instead of outmuscling, outjumping, out-whatever, he beat them through skill. He read secondaries like Fischer read a board, and struck mercilessly at weaknesses. Whereas most receivers must run a clean, accurate route with little to no variation from the play call (so as to avoid chaos or, worse, an interception), Largent was often trusted to determine his own route.

Think of third and five, if you will. Third-and-5 is a typical and typically neutral down, which favors a pass play but does not require it. Now picture Largent split wide right; picture a defense, for the sake of ease, picture two safeties deep, man coverage. That

23

would be an uncommon but not nutso defensive play call. Now Largent and surely Dave Krieg know that among the easiest ways to beat two-deep, man coverage, especially when the line to gain is close, is a simple slant route. But that coverage may not be clear while the two are in the huddle. So there's Largent split wide right and Krieg maybe eyeballing him—the two conducting that non-verbal communication great teammates perfect. Snap. Slant. Catch. First down.

Largent honed every route to be indistinguishable from another. This requires coordination, practice, and a great deal of discipline. He caught everything, earned trust with every quarterback, became a master of detail and bedeviled opponents by attacking vulnerabilities they had never considered. We, in our need to oversimplify and compartmentalize, think of such awareness, acumen, discipline and will as skills rather than talents, but there's a fine line between the two. Think how completely our impression of Largent changes if we say that he was not skilled at being fast but exceptionally talented at playing wide receiver.

Maybe it's the insecurity of being great but never sensational, of being Hank Aaron instead of Mickey Mantle, but Seahawks fans struggle to make Largent somehow more than he ever was, and in so doing, diminish him. Largent was a first. Maybe he couldn't play in the modern NFL, but if he couldn't, it is because he helped make it. After Monet, every failed portrait artist became an Impressionist. After Largent, every slow receiver with smarts and great hands became a possession receiver.

Or maybe he'd be great? The legacy or maybe better said the lineage of Largent is stronger than ever. Contemporary skilled, less talented in those abilities we call "talent," receivers like Wes Welker and Doug Baldwin still flourish. Most are as underestimated as ever. Most teams still overcompensate to stop deep passes. Most scouts foolishly prioritize speed, size, and leaping ability over the component skills/talents of a great wide receiver.

The lessons of Largent are hard learned, it seems, but the value of a receiver that can catch, catch, catch, and convert third downs, is greater than ever.

The records fade. The name-value of Largent has perhaps dropped. But the way he played the game has never before looked so brilliant in retrospect.

6 XL 2: Second-Quarter Mania

Super Bowl XL. Ford Field, Detroit. Second quarter…

Robbed. Door kicked in, drawers rifled through, heirlooms stolen, violated, robbed. The Seahawks were robbed of a touchdown. Did Darrell Jackson extend his arm? Maybe. Okay, certainly. And did that action create separation between him and defender Chris Hope? Yes. Yes. But was it really severe enough to warrant a penalty? Of course not. Right?

My lunatic fan brain accepts no quarter. The officials are compromised. Cull the lot.

I am enervated with frustration. Seattle's drive slumps. Mike Holmgren burns a couple plays running the ball. Shaun Alexander strings the run wide, then wider, then out of bounds. Kimo rides Walter into Shaun on second down. It is third-and-23. Third-and-not-worth-trying. Third-and-don't-screw-up.

Seattle splits four-wide, two a side, and Pittsburgh responds with a 3-3 nickel. Hasselbeck receives the snap, drops five, pump fakes over the middle, and launches hard toward the end zone! D.J. Hackett is isolated in the corner. The kid with hops. The Seahawks' now and future secret weapon. He stops, soars, but mistimes his leap and is falling as the ball arrives. Rookie Bryant McFadden swats it away. Time for Brownie. Josh Brown nails it to put Seattle up three.

That word, *ambivalent*, I feel it. It isn't ambivalent, *meh*. Or ambivalent, *yeah!* But ambivalent, what? Would a Super Bowl win's good be better than a Super Bowl loss's bad? It was like Pascal's wager. If I believed in this team until now, whether I could know if they would win today or not, I could achieve the only satisfactory end: a win I never doubted. Right?

The Seahawks were the third team in history to prevent its opponent from achieving a first down in the first quarter. Al Michaels told me that. So maybe three wasn't so bad. Seattle was shutting down the Steelers' offense. It was winning drives even if it had only three to show for it.

My little pep talk is halted by the resumption of play. Pittsburgh returns it to the 20 and sets two wide, two tight on the opposite side. Seattle is in a base 4-3. The receivers are bunched. For some reason this concerns me. D.D. Lewis is turned around and upside-down covering Cedrick Wilson on a simple curl route, but Lofa Tatupu storms downhill and forces the incompletion with a hard shoulder tackle.

Jordan Babineaux tips away a bomb to Hines Ward, and the Steelers are buried under third-and-long. Yes? Yes. Yes! Defensive football. It's…unexpected. It's…taking a while to embrace. It's… *awesome*. I'm standing again. I'm shouting weird things at the TV. Sentences peppered with Seahawks and the unknown names of Steelers' mothers and ancestors. A guttural "SEA!" erupts from my lungs, and I know this isn't making a strong impression on the future in-laws, but I'm damned if I care.

Pittsburgh is four-wide, shotgun. Seattle is in a 4-1 dime package. Seattle stunts its line: Darby around the blind side and Wistrom up the gut forces Roethlisberger to scramble. Tats breaks coverage and truncates Ben's scramble. He stops, plants, and fires deep. The ball rainbows errant over Tru in lockdown coverage on

Nate Washington. Seahawks force another three and out. I'm not drinking but I'm plenty drunk. It's all irrational and reactive and incomprehensible and impassioned. It's fandom at its fringes.

Chris Gardocki outpunts his coverage, and Warrick receives and breaks free to his right. *Go. Go. Go.* Thirty-four yards— *Oh! No!*

Flag. Frickin' Pruitt. Frickin' Pruitt. Frickin' officials.

Chris Gray fires forward, and Alexander runs for five. Hass overshoots Engram high and to the right, and it's third down. Seattle splits four wide, two a side, and the Steelers show a 3-3 before settling into a 4-2 nickel. An NFL game has about 11 minutes of actual game action, leaving hours of agonizing anticipation. Lot of life's best things are like that. What'd that junkie say? All pleasure is only relief?

Snap. Pitt sends five, retreating the right end into coverage. Chris Hope fires through the interior, and before Mack Strong can engage and pancake the chump, Hasselbeck is on his horse, rolling to his left. He strikes to Joe Jurevicius on an in, and it's good for 15 and another heartbeat in my strangled chest.

Hutch fires out and owns Larry Foote on an otherwise unremarkable run. Alexander trips in the hole and falls forward for three. He nets five off right tackle. This time Steve Hutchinson loses his block, and James Farrior slices in for the stop. It's third, but it's manageable. It's third, but it's not a crisis third. It's third, but Hawks only need two to convert.

Ryan Hannam motions right to create trips off right tackle. Steelers are in a 3-4. Hasselbeck drops five steps and waits a beat before zinging to Jerramy Stevens. Stevens is free after running a post corner toward the right flat. He catches, plants two feet, and begins to turn before Hope punches the ball free with hard, helmet-first tackle. It's a clear fumble but not called, and I'm caught between praising the Lord and damning the devil. Goddamn, Stevens. Goddamn you! Thank you, merciful God. But damn,

Stevens. Damn his hands. Damn his illegitimate children, should he have any. Damn. Damn. Damn. Thank God that wasn't called.

Every moment hangs like a flare. Tom Rouen's punt hangs high and expertly drops and bounds up at the 1. Scobey is in position to down it, but looks disoriented, punches the air, whiffs, and the ball tumbles past for a touchback. I damn his mother. I do. Then I forgive. Then I ball my fists. Then I sit.

"And Jerome Bettis is in the game for the first time!" The crowd explodes.

Ben runs play-action then rolls right. Bryce Fisher alone reads the action and pursues Roethlisberger into the right flat. Ben eyes Hines Ward and flings it wild out of bounds. Marcus Tubbs pursues Bettis and drops him after two. Little known fact about Jerome: he sucks. What's that, you say? He doesn't? In fact, he's Hall of Fame bound? Oh, no. No. No. He's worthless.

I pull myself back from the brink. Maybe I don't care too much, but these conversations would seem saner if they involved two people. I think.

Seattle has forced third-and-long, and, swallowing my consuming hatred for the Bus for a second, I recognize this is a good thing. This is an essential thing. Pittsburgh fans four wide receivers tight. Seattle responds with a 3-2. LeRoy Hill is in a sprinter's stance, barely hiding his blitz, and the rookie is unprepared for the snap. His blitz fails, and he's barely to the line when Ben fires toward Antwaan Randle El. Ah, hell. Trufant closes and bats the ball loose, but El recovers and runs away and past the magic yellow line. Nearing a great play, Trufant breaks cover and allows the first. Tatupu cuts across to make the clean-up tackle. Balls. Ball almost loose, but recovered, balls on your mother, brother. Argh.

All but Marquand Manuel break contain, and the Steelers punish Seattle's aggressive defense with an end around to Hines Ward. I'm sitting. Manuel is sitting. Manuel is injured. Manuel is Seattle's back-up free safety, pressed into action after starter Ken

Hamlin's season ended on the other end of a street sign. Third-string safety, that's encouraging. In comes Etric Pruitt.

Steelers break, I don't know—two wide? Seahawks something-something. Some guy runs behind the line before the snap. Lofa is slapping hips and getting the linemen over the proper gaps. Like it matters. Here goes nothing. Ben fakes play-action. Rolls. Underthrows! Boulware's on his horse! He's under it! Jumps!

Yes! Interception!

Michael Boulware is running "over" coverage but reads Ben's pathetic wobbler right out of his hand and breaks contain to play the ball. It's all expert stuff. Awesome. Stupendous. I didn't say *stupendous.* I said something *cool,* like, "Bad. Ass." That play was bad. Ass. Boulware is a badass. Seahawks! Seahawks! Seahawks! Seahawks gonna be badass champions of the world. *SEA!*

To be continued…

7 The Promise of Mike Holmgren

Head coach is the closest most of us will ever relate to a famous football professional. We can relate to businessmen even if their business is a bit specialized and odd. But among the men stalking the sidelines, controlling the action through action or instruction, we can imagine ourselves in the head coach's place: calling the play, going for it on fourth, heartbroken/cringing, happily awaiting the Gatorade shower. Yeah, a lot of us mucked it up in the trenches, threw a moonraker spiral that dropped over the receiver's right shoulder, intercepted a pass and didn't realize it until we were burning the return, did something heroic, did something natural that's unnatural, were great for a second and got it. Got what it's like to be a great athlete. But as we aged, we lost that. Away from organized sport, watched as our bodies declined. Became just average guys.

And so the head coach, scrawny and short, tall and rotund, sunken-shouldered and glowering—that's us. Our window into the world of professional football. We can decide whether to go for it or kick the field goal. We can watch the clock and plan timeouts. We can know when it's time to drop the veteran down and start the rookie. We can feel the thrill of the perfect play call. We can be the coaches we admire, like we could never be Kenny Easley, Shaun Alexander, or Earl Thomas.

Mike Holmgren was the second great head coach in Seahawks history. Like Tom Flores, his greatest triumph came before joining the Seahawks, but like Chuck Knox, he brought glory to a team without much. *Hope.* That dangerous word.

Seattle acquired Holmgren the way any benighted franchise acquires talent above and beyond its standard: with a truckload of cash and promises of unprecedented power. Holmgren had built a consistent contender in Green Bay. That's not the truth-truth, but sometimes unvarnished facts deceive. Ron Wolf, Brett Favre, Reggie White, even, we now know, one John Schneider helped build the Packers into a consistent contender—a run of contention that didn't vanish when Holmgren left town. But Holmgren was the embodiment of that organization. He brought to Seattle a piece of the most accomplished team in the history of American football.

January 9, 1999. After a stinging Packers wild-card loss to the San Francisco 49ers, Mike Holmgren signed an eight-year, $31 million contract to become Seattle's head coach and executive vice president. He would make the meal and pick the ingredients. He was the Man or, as he would come to be pejoratively known, "the Big Show."

The Holmgren hire can be appreciated in a factual sense. Holmgren was a gifted disciple of Bill Walsh, and Walsh was the

Head coach Mike Holmgren stands on the sideline before the kickoff of a preseason game in August 1999, his first season with the Seahawks after guiding the Green Bay Packers to two Super Bowls and one championship.

most revered coach in football at the time. Walsh's ideas were powering many of the best offenses in football, including the still potent 49ers (and long after Walsh had retired), the then current Super Bowl champion Denver Broncos, and Holmgren's own Super Bowl XXXI–champion Packers. Holmgren had served as quarterbacks coach and offensive coordinator of the 49ers during their dynasty and had earned a reputation as a quarterbacks guru. He molded Brett Favre into a young legend and before him had coached Joe Montana and Steve Young. Many had thought Young was a failure and fantastic bust before joining San Francisco. He was later inducted into the Pro Football Hall of Fame.

Or the Holmgren hire can be appreciated for what it really was: a promise from new owner Paul Allen that rebuilding was over and the Seattle Seahawks would again be a relevant football team.

Montana was Montana when Holmgren was still coaching at Brigham Young. One could argue Montana was Montana when Holmgren was still an assistant coach at Oak Grove High School. Young was an achievement, but whose? Walsh casts a long shadow. Coaching for him did not mean adopting his greatness. Nor does coaching Favre give Holmgren a piece of Favre's greatness. Coaching is like that: esoteric. We appreciate it from the outside, from the results, but we rarely know exactly what a coach does, if their decisions are correct or if their and their team's successes or failures happen independent of their actions.

Holmgren could have failed. He could have failed to bring to Seattle the greatness that had to that point defined his professional career, as many high-profile coaches have done after changing teams. Paul Allen did not ensure Seattle success. He ensured Seattle relevance. He ensured that Seattle would not just be relevant in the Pacific Northwest, but that the Seahawks would fight hard to be the best team possible.

Holmgren did not fail.

8 The Rise of Matt Hasselbeck

"Dil-fer! Dil-fer!" roared from the seats of Husky Stadium. It was a bad day to be Matt Hasselbeck. It probably ranked alongside that day he first noticed his forehead waging an inexorable campaign on his hairline. It was a bad season to be Matt Hasselbeck. He was later benched in favor of Trent Dilfer.

What If? Umm...Maybe Not

One of the great what-ifs we will never know is how good Seneca Wallace could have been if he played receiver. Mike Holmgren thought he could be special. Matt Hasselbeck said he wore out the Seahawks corners in practice. His slant-and-go route in the 2005 NFC Championship Game is still the thing of legends. He didn't just shed Ken Lucas like dirty laundry, he caught an underthrown pass by pinning it against his left shoulder.

The truth is, while Wallace maybe could have been a great receiver, we can never be sure or even really believe it was likely. In 2008, when Seahawks receiver was the most dangerous job in football and Seattle was signing street free agents, Holmgren finally swallowed his orthodoxy and took a risk by playing Wallace as a returner and receiver. Well, he tried. Wallace injured himself during warm-ups. It's a reminder that receiving in practice involves a lot fewer bone-jarring tackles.

Seahawks Nation apologizes.

If Bobby Engram was Mike Holmgren's masterstroke as a general manager, Matt Hasselbeck was his single most important move. It was an inside deal. Seattle acquired Hasselbeck for the NFL equivalent of a bag of chips—and not fancy, small-batch, kettle-cooked chips—no, no, the kind that succeed based on shelf placement and an association with one's childhood. I'm talking Cool Ranch Doritos—off-brand. Seattle traded its No. 10 overall pick and a third-round pick to the Green Bay Packers for Matt Hasselbeck and the No. 17 overall pick. As fate would have it, that 10th overall selection turned into megabust Jamal Reynolds. Seattle's pick turned into Steve Hutchinson. No adjectives necessary.

Hasselbeck had the rare honor of starting his first year under Holmgren. Holmgren was always a veterans-first coach, and the team had signed Dilfer in the off-season. Dilfer had the musk of winner about him after riding the Baltimore Ravens' historically good defense and special teams to a Super Bowl victory. But while Holmgren loved veterans, he loved his guys even more, and Hasselbeck was definitely one of his guys. Holmgren scored, finding Hasselbeck in the sixth round of the 1998 NFL Draft. He had cut Hasselbeck in favor of Rick Mirer, but after trading Mirer to the Jets for what would become a fourth-round pick, (No, seriously.) Hasselbeck was signed off the practice squad.

Hass was a bit buried in Green Bay. A little-known Mississippian who never got hurt, Brett Something, never got hurt, or got hurt but emasculated his rivals with unprecedented toughness, or played through pain, warriored up, and, most importantly, just had fun. Out there. Just had fun out there. Which didn't allow Hasselbeck to have any fun. Out there. He might have been having a blast from the bench.

Holmgren fleeced his former home and brought the best quarterback (pre-Russell Wilson) in Seahawks history to Seattle. That was March. Holmgren reassured his new quarterback of the future by signing Trent Dilfer. That was August 3. At the time, Holmgren downplayed the significance of signing Dilfer by saying, "We have young quarterbacks, and I've been looking for a veteran quarterback. It has very little to do with Matt Hasselbeck. Matt's our quarterback." And he would continue to be Seattle's quarterback for, oh, about eight more weeks.

Mike never lost faith in Hasselbeck, but we can be forgiven if he was the only one. It was Dilfer mania in Seattle after he replaced an injured Hasselbeck. Seattle upset Jacksonville and Denver at home. Of course, "upset" is a matter of perception. Jacksonville was a year removed from a 14–2 season and thus had the luster of a contender. By 2001 they were a mediocre team that finished 6–10. Denver had finished 11–5 in 2000, but would finish 8–8 in 2001. Dilfer had won against teams Seattle could be expected to win at home against. And he had played decent football against defenses that weren't.

But fans in the stands are essentially a seated mob, and though Hasselbeck returned and performed ably against a stifling Dolphins

Matt Hasselbeck lets fly in the second half of Seattle's 24–21 overtime win over the New York Giants on November 27, 2005. Hasselbeck's long, uphill struggle to be the No. 1 quarterback culminated in the team's drive to Super Bowl XL.

pass defense, the Seahawks still lost. They lost Hasselbeck's next start, too. Washington was an even better pass defense, and Seattle was playing on the road.

"*Dil!—*"

Seattle snuck out a win against Oakland, but Shaun Alexander and his 266 yards starred.

"*—Fer!*"

Trent knew something about winning. He knew it involved outscoring one's opponent. In Baltimore this involved handing off to Jamal Lewis and watching from the sideline as his defense committed sanctioned homicide. Occasionally, Dilfer would grab the ball by its laces side and attempt to "spiral" the ball forward, but this radical practice was discouraged by head coach Brian Billick. Too risky. Football players are not awarded style points.

How this could possibly translate to Seattle is better discussed by the mob. I think they might respond with a hearty:

"*Dil!—*"

Hasselbeck suffered a separated left shoulder in Week 14, and after weeks of bad play, bad sacks, and losing, Holmgren started Dilfer in his stead. Seattle won each of its next two games. The Seahawks finished 5–7 in games Hasselbeck started. It finished 4–0 in games started by Dilfer.

"*—Fer!*"

XL 3: Dangerous Words

Super Bowl XL. Ford Field, Detroit. Second quarter (continued)…

I spoke dangerous words. Dangerous, regrettable words. I saw my girlfriend and said, "We might win this."

What could I do? Tension had ebbed. I was smiling. I was sinking into the couch.

The kid had stepped up, reached out, and plucked perfection from the sky. Michael Boulware. Former linebacker. Former human being. Ascension to godhood. Bless you.

Seattle takes the ball, has the lead. Shaun Alexander blocks, and there isn't a surer sign of triumph. Hasselbeck rolls right and finds Bobby Engram curling back to the ball. It's easy. Three easy yards. Not flashy or big, but productive. Enough to keep the Seahawks rolling. Alexander runs behind right guard, and though Mack Strong loses his block, Shaun coasts for an easy four. Easy. Easy.

36

It's third down. Third-and-manageable. Third-and-easy? Third down, nevertheless. Third down, and I am edging up, getting up, tensing up, standing up, and balling my fists. Seattle splits three wide, split backs. Pittsburgh is in a 3-3 with Troy Polamalu edged up, playing a hybrid linebacker/defensive back. Snap. Alexander throws a good block. All right. Strong runs left and quick curls. Reception. Turn, run, tackled over the marker. First—

But it's a bad spot! That's a bad spot. *That's a bad spot.* (It really was a bad spot.)

Seattle is short. A fraction of a ball's length, a third maybe, the space between the laces and the point, but short. Michaels and Madden are talking temptation, the temptation to go for it, but the need to punt. They mention momentum. Seattle has it, but would give it away if they couldn't convert. The Seahawks are on their own 26, and a failed conversion almost guarantees the Steelers a field goal. That's the lead, damn momentum, that's 21 minutes of winning football given up. So Holmgren makes the obvious call. The right call.

It really was a bad spot.

Tom Rouen of unfortunate name and coming infamy, kicks it low and short, and El, Antwaan Randle, fields it with bad intentions. Niko Koutouvides knocks him airborne, and a wave of blue bats him hard and into the ground like an Ichiro single. It's good, but it's not good. It's scary. All that smiling, and now I feel like a fool. Seattle barely touched it before giving it back, and the hard realization dawns that nothing is even half done.

It's Tatupu-Hill on the next two plays. Lofa hitting Willie Parker behind the line, and LeRoy finishing the job. Lofa smacking down the fullback and LeRoy knifing in for the tackle. Love these kids. Listen to me. Love 'em.

Steelers continue their customary strategy of run-first, pass if they must. Seattle has forced them into another third-and-long. Pittsburgh spreads four wide receivers tight, two on a side. The

Kill the Ref

Seahawks fans would be less sensitive about spotty officiating if it had not become part of their team history. Super Bowl XL was not even the first time Seattle suffered a phantom touchdown scored by a quarterback.

Seattle was still in the 1998 playoff hunt. They were up 31–26 with 20 seconds to play against the Jets at the Meadowlands. The Seahawks had forced fourth-and-goal. That is when Vinny Testaverde ran a quarterback sneak that was stopped visibly short of the goal line. However, head linesman Earnie Frantz declared it a touchdown. Making matters worse, the crew then convened and, rather than overturn a categorically bogus call, confirmed the ruling. Seattle lost 32–31 and missed the playoffs by one game.

The play became an embarrassment for the NFL. Unlike XL, there was no ambiguity, replay showed Testaverde down well short of the goal line. The league responded by voting instant replay back into place, but the damage was already done for Seahawks fans and coach Dennis Erickson. Erickson was fired that off-season.

formation looks like wings or a crescent. Roethlisberger is in shotgun. Seattle responds with six defensive backs, Tatupu, and four down linemen.

Fisher pressures, and Seattle looks golden, but Ben evades and flips to a *wide-open Hines Ward!* Ward continues running toward the right sideline then redirects upfield for 12 before Marcus Trufant tracks him down. How was that? Where was that? How did that happen?! Replay shows Trufant getting picked on the left and Ward streaking free underneath. Tru recovers, but after the fact.

It's the Steelers' second third-down conversion of the game, but it feels like Armageddon. I'm gripping. I'm pissed. I'm scared again, and it can't be reasoned away. Parker runs for one. Wistrom raps from under the pile. Cedrick Wilson exploits the seam and receives for 20 in front of Trufant. Roethlisberger pumps and delivers, but it tumbles harmlessly from Ward's fingertips. Catch, and it's a touchdown. Dropped. A funky screen pass to Bettis is brought back on offensive pass interference. The penalty du jour.

It's second-and-20, and I'd feel good but I don't. Wistrom, all eleventy billion dollars of him, flies around left end and drops Ben for eight. It's third-and-28, and I'd feel confident but I don't. Pittsburgh empties the backfield. Seattle rushes three. Wistrom bends around left tackle Marvel Smith, clubs down Smith's arms, and flashes free before Ben steps up. That puts Smith smack in the middle. It's worrisome. It gets worse. Roethlisberger runs toward the left flat. Wistrom attempts to separate but falls on his face. Roethlisberger sees this and stops, plants, surveys, and fires toward Ward. Ward is running away from Boulware. He catches for 37. *He catches for 37!* The drive isn't alive, it's amuck. Steelers on the Seahawks' 3.

I collapse into a sit. The next two plays happen. I notice, but I don't. Seattle hasn't folded, but...

It's third-and-short, and I want to care so much I begin to again. It's third-and-short, but Seattle has stood tall, defended their end zone, recovered, and attacked. Bettis is in. I hate his face. I hate his beard. I hate his eyelashes. I hate "the Bus." I hate Detroit for birthing him. I want this play not to end with a stop, but a fatality.

Pitt plays three tight ends, two backs in an I formation. Seattle has five down linemen and three linebackers. It's smashmouth football. A battle of wills. And while I sit back, Seattle muscles up. It's third down, and I don't need to try to care. I can see the whole ballgame in this snap.

Ben takes the snap, motions pitch to Bettis, keeps. Bus flies forward and blocks out Tatupu; Roethlisberger leaps, stretches, falls. Short? The line judge runs up the goal line and suddenly, for no apparent reason, raises his arms: touchdown.

It can't believe it. It's reviewed. I don't see it. It's being reviewed. I don't see it break the plane; D.D. Lewis drives him back. I feel worried excitement. I don't know the right call. Does he break the plane? Can we know? Why the hell did Mark Perlman rule it a touchdown? Now it can't be overturned. It's not overturned. Touchdown. Play confirmed. I'm freaking out.

Seattle pieces together a miserable two-minute drill, and I'd be damned if I noticed a second of it. Didn't Darrell Jackson break the goal line before he stepped out? This isn't right. The pass-interference penalty from earlier that cost Seattle a touchdown seems sinister in retrospect. That was a huge swing. Why rule it then?

A drive happens. It's fractured and futile and flashes before my eyes, but not remembered. The Seahawks stall, needlessly burn clock, kick, miss the field goal.

It's halftime. That spot and those holds and that touchdown. Ford Field is caving in on us. I pass Alanya a look that says this isn't normal anger. This isn't consolable anger. This is stay-the-hell-away rage. I'm pacing. I'm plotting. I'm, I'm, I'm—

To be continued...

10 Chuck Knox

I had heard about Seattle's rain, its gray, its dreariness. I had read about it being so far from civilization that back in the 1800s businessmen on the East Coast would ship women out there by boat so the lumberjacks would have someone to talk to. It sounded like the perfect place to get my kind of job done.

—Chuck Knox

I admit it. I not only do not hold most NFL coaches in particularly high regard, I think many are little more than meddlers who attempt to force a system on players often completely incompatible with that system. Many coaches are vengeful, cutting kickers after missing one crucial field goal. They have favorites and arbitrary standards for what is good football and what is not. They were raised on football, and that can give them a limited scope on life. Jack Patera was known to deny players water during practice, and that practice has since killed. Some overvalue practice and play clearly overmatched players because that play is assignment correct. They have doghouses, and their doghouses are built on sand.

Had I been cognizant during the tenure of Chuck Knox, I doubt I would have appreciated him very much. He favored running the ball at the very eve of the passing revolution. That earned him the name "Ground Chuck." I would have choked on those words. He was swaggering and opinionated and old-school fiery—which is to say he could and would get righteously pissed—and was more than a little stuck in his ways.

Yeah, I'm the last person who should write an appropriately gold-tinged and fawning retrospective on Chuck Knox. But I must, and I'm sure Chuck would have none of my sniveling. Would he?

No, he would not. See, Chuck was Greatest Generation. He forged steel. His father was a steelworker and beat hell out of his son. His father was an Irish immigrant with a drinking problem, and as Knox put it, "His pride put him in constant need of a fight to prove himself. But he didn't know who or how. So he fought me."

It was regular Horatio Alger bull, but real. And so it was dirty and fraught with lucky breaks and near misses. Chuck coached high school and built the Ellwood program. He became an assistant at Wake Forest and then Kentucky. He was hired to coach offensive line under Weeb Ewbank with the Jets, left New York in 1967, and so doing missed his only chance to win a Super Bowl ring.

All that struggling and overcoming made him relatable. He had an ease and confidence found only in those who have consistently overcome. Knox was hard, but he cared. He did that most essential thing that any great coach must do, he motivated.

The AP named Knox Coach of the Year in 1973. He took a team that finished 6–7–1 in 1972 and turned it into an instant Super Bowl contender. The Rams won 12 games in 1973 and finished in the playoffs every one of Knox's five years. Despite all that, he warred with owner Carroll Rosenbloom. Two strong men, two old football minds, destined to battle from the start. Knox took a million-dollar offer from Ralph Wilson and signed to coach the Bills.

Buffalo became a home. Chuck failed to turn around the Bills his first year as he had done with the Rams, but he did eventually. In his third year, Buffalo broke into the playoffs, and Knox won his second Coach of the Year.

Knox was successful, but he was never very popular with his bosses. Rosenbloom thought "Ground Chuck" was boring and unimaginative. Maybe he was right, but running reigned in the early '70s, and Knox brought the Rams unprecedented success. Just not a Super Bowl. Wilson thought Knox spent too much. No owner in NFL history rivaled Wilson for sheer cheapness. (As professional football in the ever shrinking city of Buffalo has become less and less practical, and more and more based on little but inertia and the stubbornness of its owner, that stinginess has become ever more necessary, and ever more crippling to the Bills' chances of contention. I cannot fathom the desperation Bills fans must feel, and I'm a Mariners fan. On the eve of his final year under contract with the Bills and at an impasse in negotiations, word found Seahawks general manager and interim head coach Mike McCormack that Knox wanted out of Buffalo. He opted out, signed with Seattle, and the rest, the rest is Seahawks history.

* * *

In his first season, and with Seattle closing in on a victory, the Seahawks began to edge the sideline, ready to run onto the field and celebrate. Knox was worried that if Seattle incurred a penalty for rushing the field, that the opponent would get another play. I'll let him tell the rest:

> I screamed, "Get back! Get back!" I saw a huge body run past me, and out of instinct I turned and slugged him. It was Mike Tice, a tight end about a foot taller than me and 50 pounds heavier. I landed my punch directly in his gut. He doubled over. I looked up to see a couple pairs of eyes get like fried eggs. Everybody shut up and ran back. Once Tice caught his breath, he stumbled back, too.
>
> "Coach," he said, gasping, "you almost knocked me out!"
>
> "No, I didn't," I told him. "If I had wanted to knock you out, I would have used my right."

What makes me want to look back at this grizzled old survivor, loved by his players, sympathetic, successful, successful in Blue, and want to judge him? Want to discredit him? Modern arrogance, I guess.

Knox was wholly and beautifully of his time, and because of that, Ground Chuck and Hard Knox is exaggerated by some, and held up by others as some lost Golden Age. Truth is, Chuck was never the hardass so many wanted him to be.

One of his first moves upon signing with Seattle was to provide water for players during practice. Crazy, huh? That sounds less like the school of Hard Knox and more like rational, respectful management. He had what he called an "open door–closed door policy." His door was always open to anyone, and when that person entered, the door closed behind him. Not for some epic shout-off or act of intimidation, but to ensure privacy.

Knox was old-school, but not the caricature often portrayed. He feared heights. The press compared him to General Alexander Haig, continuing the worn but persistent football/war analogy. It's a stupid analogy. Knox wasn't compelling young men to die for the abstract concept of country. He was compelling rich young athletes to perform seven-on-seven drills. And he did so through a system of fines, not fear.

Knox removed contact from practice, instituted "thump" drills. He thought pitting his own team against itself only doubled the chance of injury. How practical; how sensible. He embraced a style of football that reigned in the '70s, and as the complexion of football changed, his offenses became less potent. But he constructed a heck of a defense.

Knox was known for his aphorisms, which makes for good print, and compared to Patera, the media found him warm and approachable. He had a TV show and a radio show. He made the hard decision to start Dave Krieg after Jim Zorn flatlined. The two would never admit it, but I think they were kindred spirits in a way. Krieg started for Milton College. He went undrafted but stuck with Seattle. Milton would close permanently before Krieg ever started. Two Midwest guys who took the long path to success, Krieg and Knox shared a language of experience.

Knox grew up in Sewickley, and he grew up poor. He was born into the kind of life sociologists deem a vicious circle: poor, abused, not well educated, and with little choice but to give his children the same. Knox worked 19 years to become a head coach in the NFL, and I'm sure there were countless times a bad break or a bad decision could have derailed him. For every one Chuck Knox, there were so, so many like him that never made it, that we'll never know. But for each like him that followed, at least the life of Chuck Knox proved great achievement was possible.

He brought success to the Rams but was fired for being too conservative. He brought respectability to the Bills but couldn't squeeze out a new contract. He lucked into Seattle, and Seattle lucked into him. He finished out with the best winning percentage in franchise history, gave Seahawks fans a time to be proud of, a period of hope and prosperity, and maybe Knox didn't win the right way—certainly not the modern way—but he won.

I can respect that.

11 XL 4: Disintegration

Super Bowl XL. Ford Field, Detroit. Halftime...

I walk outside. Alanya hesitantly follows. She lights a cigarette. I don't smoke but take a couple nervous drags, anyway. I give her the lowdown. Somehow things crystallize in the retelling. It doesn't feel like Seattle is losing, but it sure feels like Seattle will lose.

I walk in. Steve Young says something about Seattle not getting the calls. It feeds an ugly, suspicious notion that is growing, branching out across my brain. I am starting to pace and then stopping. Starting long enough to know it's foolish, creepy. Stopping only long enough to feel compelled to begin again.

It's Steelers ball to start the half. Al Michaels mentions that Marquand Manuel is out for the game. Etric Pruitt is now Seattle's surviving free safety. This is bad.

Ben Roethlisberger takes a three-step drop and slings it toward Hines Ward running a curl in the right flat. It's underthrown, but Ward slides to get under. He drops it. Cool. It's a subtle reminder nothing is done, nothing is decided. Seattle is containing the run. Roethlisberger is struggling. The Seahawks offense has been inches away. Pittsburgh aligns three wide receivers left, tight end right in a peculiar unbalanced formation. Seattle counters with nickel. Before the snap, Ward motions right.

Things start to unravel in a hurry. Kendall Simmons and Max Starks blow back and turn Rocky Bernard. Starks pulls forward and

Seahawks cornerback Kelly Herndon (31) intercepts an errant Ben Roethlisberger pass intended for Cedrick Wilson near the goal line and runs it back for a big gain in Super Bowl XL.

engulfs Lofa Tatupu. From the left, Alan Faneca is pulling around and through the right hole. He pancakes LeRoy Hill. Seahawks are dropping fast, and Willie Parker is just entering the hole. Michael Boulware sprints from the third level but over-pursues left.

Oh. No.

Parker hits the hole. The right is cleared out. Pruitt attempts to fly over from the deep left, but he takes a bad angle. Parker, fast. Willie Parker jogs into the end zone. He doesn't look fast at all. I don't feel angry. Quite worse. I feel defeated. It's too decisive, too fast, and maybe it's the nicotine, but I feel light-headed. ABC shows replays, but there is not much too see. Everything breaks down. Bernard is bullied and turned, and then it's all giant offensive linemen engulfing spritely linebackers.

Seattle ball. Alexander juggles, drops. Morris receives. Mack Strong runs past Troy Polamalu for the first. Alexander breaks it wide for 21. Hannam, Engram blocking like champs. Seattle sets two wide, Jerramy Stevens tight right, I formation. Pittsburgh counters with a vanilla 3-4 look. Stevens angles right to avoid the jam and then streaks free up the seam. Hasselbeck motions play-action, plants, hits Stevens in the hands—*dropped!* No. *Nooo!* Dropped. Again. Dropped.

The line slides right, and Alexander runs straight past the exposed left edge. It's a good run. I don't care. It's a good run.

Pittsburgh sends the safety blitz, and Strong misreads, blocks left. Hasselbeck throws a desperation fade toward Darrell Jackson, but Jackson gets spun around, can never find the pass, and it drops into the right flat, incomplete.

Brown misses the field-goal attempt.

Steelers take the ball with good field position and proceed to begin to put the game away. Ben hits Ward for 15. Bus runs for six. Incomplete. Tatupu and Pruitt blitz, but Ben finds Ward springing free for 16. Ward pushes off Herndon so hard that Herndon is sent reeling backward. It's ugly and unfair and unflagged, but I'm flagging, and it doesn't feel outrageous so much as inevitable.

Bus runs opposite a blitz for 12. That's embarrassing. Bus dodges right for four. Pruitt is rah, rah, slapping his big gloved hands together. It stinks of overcompensation. Boulware pops through a blocker and hits Bettis for no gain. It's third down, baby. Third down. And I am not optimistic.

Pittsburgh calls a timeout, retakes the field in a confusing and unorthodox formation. *That's bad*, I think. It starts with two wide receivers right, a tight end and slot back left, and a running back deep, but motions the back into the left flat. Empty backfield.

Seattle is in a 4-2 nickel. Verron Haynes' motioning attracts Tatupu, and he follows him into the flat.

Snap.

Seattle collapses the pocket around Roethlisberger, and he lobs a floater right.

Herndon breaks underneath. Intercepts it! Intercepts it! Intercepts it! Sprints down the right flat. Looks free to the end zone. Has Blockers. Has Blockers. Bernard is to his right, but, but...Crap. Pulls up with a hamstring. Bryce Fisher is pacing Herndon and cuts in front to *throw Ben Roethlisberger to the turf.* But he cuts off Herndon, and the return is stopped.

So what?! I'm I'm—

Yes!!

HAHAHAHAHA.

Oh, my, oh, my God. *Yes!*

It's like, it's not over, and it's not won, but suddenly, it's not lost, either. Herndon, you glorious bastard. Andre Dyson goes down, and you show up like a mother.

Alexander cuts back left for four. Engram runs an angle route, but the ball eats him up and bounces away incomplete. Jackson runs a post, picks out Polamalu, and Hasselbeck throws a perfect touch pass even Stevens can catch. He hauls it in, cradles it in the end zone, *touchdown.*

We were on the brink. We were done. We were within seconds of falling behind 14, maybe 18. But Herndon and Hasselbeck, and now it's 14–10. I'm a little giddy and a little exhausted, and a little wary to celebrate.

To be continued...

Et Tu, Hutch?

We at Guard and Guard pride ourselves in the perfect production of perfect football guards. Our products match their time period and our buyers' needs without flaw.

In the era of barnstorming we made Walt Kiesling. He was big, indefatigable, tough, and master of such contemporary tools as the strike, wedge, and eye gouge. We used state-of-the-art pneumatics to power his punishing piles of pummeling punches. Powered his motor with leaded petrogasoline and set his chronometer to Swiss time.

For George Halas we produced our first and only biomechanical model: the Dan Fortmann 5000. Fortmann had the fresh face, smarts, and underdog grit of an American GI, and as our brave soldiers fought trench to trench and island to island, Fortmann fought in the trenches on an island.

We do not just build at Guard and Guard. We retrofit. Weeb Ewbank sent us Jim Parker in summer of '62, and we started right away dismantling his tackle machinery and refitting him for guard play. We installed an atomic hand punch, jet-powered uncoiling action, high-fidelity sonar, and a positive attitude toward authority.

We built Tom Mack tough and Russ Grimm technical. We built Larry Allen to giant proportions for Jimmy Johnson, and Johnson was so happy he had us build his entire offensive line. We built every great guard in American Football history, every enshrined guard and every Canton snub. We built each with only one goal, to make them better than any guard we had made before.

So when Mike Holmgren contacted us in the winter of 2001, we knew our challenge was very great. Holmgren wanted the build, breadth, and agility of the best tackles, but the tenacity and fight of the meanest centers. He needed feet and vision like a running back, but the gifted hands and coordination of a wide receiver. He needed the head of a quarterback and the heart of a fullback. He needed our newest to be quicker, more agile, stronger, and more precise than any guard we had made before, and he was.

And he was Steve Hutchinson.

* * *

What a great way to remember Hutch. He was—is, too. Steve Hutchinson is one of the greatest offensive guards to ever play football. Wherever he's played, that team's running game took off. He blocked for the last years of Ricky Watters and helped make Shaun Alexander. He traveled to Minnesota and made Chester Taylor a name, before maybe making Adrian Peterson an all-time great. What a great way to remember Hutch, if only I could.

Hutchinson is undoubtedly one of the greatest Seahawks to ever live. It pains me to write that, as it surely pains most Seahawks fans to read it. As I write this, the former Seahawk, former Viking is now retired. I am sitting here, editing this, listening to "Night on the Sun," editing my own damn words, and yet still startled to learn in 2009, Hutch became more Viking than Seahawk. His final totals: 68 starts with Seattle, 89 starts with the Purple. Which is part of why Steve Hutchinson is a great player, a great all-time Seahawk, and a great villain.

Seattle acquired Hutch with the draft pick it acquired in the Matt Hasselbeck trade. It was a good day to be Mike Holmgren. It was a better day to be a Seahawks fan.

Guard is an atypical selection so early in the draft. Coaches see it as an inferior position to offensive tackle, but Hutchinson was a rare talent at guard. He started 45 games for Michigan State and is reported to have not allowed a sack in his final two seasons. Hutch was a strong pass protector, but it was his elegance and versatility at run-blocking that made him so special.

He was great, truly a peer of Fortmann, Grimm, and Allen, a seven-time Pro Bowl selection and a six-time first-team All-Pro. But Hutch got away, and the blame can be spread around. Tim Ruskell risked losing him for the sake of relative pennies. As blind as Holmgren could be to the importance of defense, Ruskell could be equally blind to the importance of offense. Otherwise he wouldn't have risked such an astounding talent, even if the risk of losing Hutch was, to Ruskell, an unknown unknown. The Vikings will forever be detested even if it's somewhat unclear exactly who designed the poison pill. It could have been Hutchinson's agent, Tom Condon. If it was his agent, he did it serving Hutch. Arbiter Stephen Burbank betrayed the intent of the transition tag and defied the league by honoring the clause. All deserve some portion of our immense enmity, but only Hutch really betrayed us.

Steve Hutchinson wanted out of Seattle. Prior to his signing with the Vikings, the Seahawks had finished their most successful season in franchise history. He was paired with a legendary left tackle, Walter Jones, blocked for an MVP running back, Shaun Alexander, and played for a coach who appreciated him as much as any coach could: Mike Holmgren. But Hutchinson still wanted out, desperately. Whether he conceived the ploy or not, he approved of it, and accepted a lengthy and surely frustrating process that could have failed, because he did not want to be a Seahawk anymore. Seattle offered to match the contract, even restructured Jones' contract to negotiate the poison pill, but it didn't matter. If you believe in team and loyalty, and that if a team wants you and is willing to do anything to succeed with you, you stick with them, then only one person truly deserves the blame for the loss of Steve

Hutchinson: Steven Hutchinson. He did not want to be a Seahawk anymore, and no matter what Ruskell missed, or Condon schemed, or Burbank decided, that is why Steve Hutchinson will enter the Hall of Fame a Viking.

What a poisonous thought, yet how curative an anti-venom is winning a Super Bowl.

* * *

A weird little postscript appeared on my Twitter feed partway through the 2013 NFC Divisional Round Game against the Saints. Seattle was barely edging out the Saints, and as a Seahawks fan, it was hard not to feel royally frustrated with the play-calling of offensive coordinator Darrell Bevell. Now, armchair criticism of play calling is a foolish endeavor. I liken it to the person watching two superior chess players. That person fidgeting, stifling his suggestions, and finally just blurting out all the moves each player has missed. Typically, this observer is so far out of the loop, the tremendous tactical coup he thinks he sees is in fact a foundering blunder. So Bevell's clockwork run-run-pass play calling seemed *prima facie* stupid, but I bit hard on my tongue before crying bloody murder. Hutchinson, who worked with Bevell in Minnesota, including the season Bevell took over play calling from head coach Brad Childress, didn't feel such compunctions. And he tweeted out: "If Seattle wins it's because of D. Offensive game plan is horrible." And then, much more pointedly "Just because ur the coordinator of a playoff team, doesn't mean you should be a HC somewhere else. Some shouldn't be coordinators to start."

It was an odd little window into the lives of two Seahawks. One of great talent and one of great achievement, one beloved but disloyal and one modest but a Super Bowl champion. It was a hell of a nasty thing to do, but maybe Hutch was right. Or maybe all our kvetching was little but competition neglect given voice.

Anyway, as a football player, Steve Hutchinson could be beautiful. It's too bad guard and guard didn't box him back up when the blocking was done.

Oh, and his Twitter handle: poisonpill76.

13 Tez

The shortest path to the quarterback is a straight line. But that path is blocked. When that path is taken by Cortez Kennedy, it has to be double- and triple-blocked.

I could write this entire book about Tez, his dominance, how teams had to commit two and three linemen just to stop him, and how he made even miserable surrounding talent look good. If you never saw him, imagine barrel-chested Red Bryant, the impossibly thick lower half of Brandon Mebane, the springy athleticism and explosive power of Michael Bennett, and the first-step quickness of Chris Clemons. Take those attributes, fuse them into one player, and then give him the standout size and physical presence of someone like Haloti Ngata. That was Kennedy. Or at least the parameters, if not the player.

Football is a game of yards, but fundamentally it's a game of time, space, and overwhelming force. Some of the greatest plays occur nowhere near the ball carrier, and some of the greatest players do not tackle, intercept, or sack, but make or wreck schemes, force double teams, take away the deep pass, or force the safety out of the box. Earl Thomas, for instance, had a sensational season in 2013 and very much deserved the Defensive Player of the Year award over Carolina middle linebacker Luke Kuechly. Kuechly's win was yet another triumph for WYSIATI (What You See Is All There Is, a common kind of cognitive bias). Because while Kuechly tackled and tackled and tackled, all visible in the infuriatingly small strip of space 10 yards on either side of the line of scrimmage that television broadcasters deign the viewing audience to see, Thomas did something much more valuable. He played such a terrific deep center that despite Seattle's heavy reliance on man cover, teams rarely ever attacked the Seahawks defense deep. Thomas was indispensable to the best defense in football. His talents and abilities made that defense possible. Kuechly farmed stats—a good player but hardly essential.

Tez was essential. Like all the greatest interior defensive linemen, he was above all else a great presence. Like Thomas, it wasn't always about what Kennedy did but what opposing offenses couldn't do or what they had to do to stop him.

Somehow I don't think Tez would appreciate a long, fawning expository breakdown of his career. He was all about the shortest path to effectiveness. He was all about efficiency and domination. Instead, let's just consider his inhuman 1992. That was the season that Cortez Kennedy won Defensive Player of the Year. Seattle finished 2–14. The offense was historically bad. It was starting a Stan Gelbaugh, a Kelly Stouffer, and sometimes even a sentinel known as Dan McGwire. It was "Raiderized," and in early '90s lingo that meant "crappy."

The Seahawks line was decrepit. Joe Nash and Jeff Bryant were both 32. Nash would struggle on for a few more seasons of mediocre play. Bryant was a year from retirement. On his right was Tony Woods. Woods was a run-of-the-mill, undistinguished end who stuck and stuck, but never did much. Kennedy was in the center, playing the one-tech. He was like a red giant in some cold, empty solar system.

Nash and Bryant were undersized artifacts from a formerly good defense. They were great players, but they were not the kind

Cortez Kennedy, "Tez," became one of only three players to be named NFL Defensive Player of the Year while playing for a losing team, in 1992.

of talents that you imagine aging gracefully. Tez had 20 pounds on any of his linemates and was expected to anchor, give the interior ballast, substance.

The Seahawks were outscored 312–140. Game after game, the defense was battling against its own offense. The offense was last in yards, last in points, and last in first downs. That translated to short fields, clock-killing drives, and little rest between series. Any human defender couldn't hope to stand out on such a miserable team.

Tez did not stand out. No. He stood atop the corpse of the Seahawks offense and dominated. He had 14 sacks. Fourteen. He had a sack in 11 games. He was unstoppable. Crazy enough, sacks were not even his game.

He was named the NFL Defensive Player of the Year. He became only the third player ever to win that honor on a losing team, and the other two, Reggie White and Lawrence Taylor, played for teams that were each only a game short of .500. The why is both simple and complex. Most basically, players on losing teams rarely get recognition. Whoever actually is the best, national awards are more for honoring the most noteworthy. Pro Bowls and MVPs and Defensive Player of the Year are awarded to the best players among the best teams.

It wasn't just that, though. Defense depends on offense. Taylor played in close games. Only two were lost by eight points or more. He was able to get his 7.5 sacks because he faced quarterbacks who had incentive to risk a sack if it meant making a play. Not surprisingly, five of his 7.5 sacks came in games won by the Giants.

Tez dominated against teams that had every reason to run, check down, or throw it away. The Seahawks were behind so often, for so long and without any hope of recovery, they actually faced the least number of passing attempts in the entire NFL. A team that couldn't create a drive with God's hand still somehow got off the field on defense.

Canton is obsessed with team achievements and statistics. It only sees Kennedy as a very good player who peaked early, but never played for a very good team. That is stupid. He was great, singularly and incredibly great. Kennedy was not just one of the greatest defensive tackles of his generation, he was one of the greatest defensive tackles to ever play. His 1992 is every bit the achievement of Peyton Manning's 2004, Jerry Rice's 1995, or Chris Johnson's 2009. He transcended his team. He deserves a transcendent honor.

Finally, in 2012, Kennedy was enshrined in the Pro Football Hall of Fame. He thanked his dad. He thanked his mom. And he thanked his teammates at Northwest Mississippi Community College. He thanked a lot of people and said all the right things, ending with a very Russell Wilson-like "God bless America, and God bless the Seattle Seahawks!"

14 The Modest Champion

Matt Hasselbeck always seemed a hair away from greatness. He could squat where legends lived. His Northwest pale complexion, nasally voice, and subtle jaw line gave him the look of a sidekick rather than a leading man. Brett Favre looks carved from marble. Hasselbeck has an oval face that wore frustration better than triumph.

Frustration followed him into his second season in Seattle. His uneven performance had lost him the starting position to Trent Dilfer. It must have been jarring to go from sixth-round pick buried behind Favre to quarterback of the future to Dilfer's backup in less than a year. There was pride in being Favre's backup. That position could describe almost any quarterback in the league. It had once described Mark Brunell, and Brunell became a Pro Bowl starter. There was pride in being a starter. A starter could fail, but he was always the man. Everyone on any football team anywhere knows their starting quarterback. He is the nucleus of the team. The leader.

There was no pride backing up Trent Dilfer. Even in his Super Bowl–winning season quarterbacking the Ravens, Dilfer earned titles like "game manager" and "worst starting quarterback to ever win a Super Bowl." It was not like Dilfer had arrested the position from Hasselbeck through eminent skill, either. Look at Football Outsiders DYAR rankings for 2001, and you will find Dilfer wedged between Ryan Leaf and Rob Johnson.

Dilfer was at an age, and the Seahawks had the kind of surrounding talent that, had he been able to stay healthy, he could have taken the starting position and run away with it. What a horrible thought. Human frailty saved Seattle from human fear, and Mike Holmgren's plan to start the proven veteran ended temporarily when Dilfer sprained his MCL in the Seahawks' first preseason game. Hasselbeck did not win the position back. In fact, his preseason was lousy and plagued by the same problems that resulted in his benching the year before. He was not confident in Holmgren's system and could not execute it at game speed. Suddenly, Hasselbeck was not just being outplayed by Trent Dilfer, but every quarterback to don the blue. Aged Mark Rypien, Jeff Kelly, and Ryan Van Dyke had little trouble besting Hasselbeck's five interceptions and seven sacks in just 54 drop backs.

He carried that momentum into the season. Quarterback rating thought Hasselbeck was an All-Pro, but quarterback rating spits some funky opinions. He threw for 155 yards in 32 attempts, a very Dilfer performance, and after matching touchdowns in the first quarter, Oakland ran away with it the second. They built a 28–7 lead that Hasselbeck was powerless to overcome.

So it was back to the bench and back to backing up Dilfer in Week 2. Dilfer did what he always did: put up a palatable stat line while doing little to help his team win. Much to the shock of people

Hasselbeck and that Clown from Carolina

In the 2005 NFC Championship Game, Matt Hasselbeck faced his former head coach at Boston College, Dan Henning. Hasselbeck had had a bit of a rocky relationship with Henning. He benched Hasselbeck and questioned his leadership. He thought Hasselbeck was too subdued. Hasselbeck retorted, "You should wear big red shoes and a big red nose because you are a clown!" Get him, Matt.

It's fitting then that Hasselbeck found his perfect match in Mike Holmgren. The Big Show was a big dog, and I think he preferred a quarterback who followed more than led. I wonder if Henning felt pride or anguish watching Hasselbeck tear through his Panthers. I imagine pride.

who buy into garbage stats like quarterback record, the quarterback who never did anything to win, but won anyway, started losing. This is where I would like to write that Hasselbeck rode in on a horse named Destiny and finally seized the position from Dilfer.

Instead, Dilfer suffered a torn Achilles tendon and was placed on injured reserve. The infallible coaching hierarchy, determined by skill, unadulterated by favoritism or superstition, was again fixed through injury. This time, though, when Dilfer went down, Hasselbeck stepped up. The accuracy that had always enticed now paired with confidence in the system, and everything Holmgren could have hoped for from Matt began to show itself. He was making quick decisions and trusting his arm. (What a weird thing we say "trusting his arm," like it's not a part of the person. But any athlete of any caliber knows, sometimes our arms and legs are like faulty tools. We tell it "throw there," "kick there," but our motion is subtly askew, like miscalibrated machinery. That tiny terrible defect apparent as ball errs wildly away from where we aimed.)

Dilfer could have never led the 2005 Seahawks to the Super Bowl. Hasselbeck was probably the most irreplaceable part on that team—as a quarterback typically is. Alexander got the record and the MVP, and because of that, Steve Hutchinson and Walter Jones were finally recognized as the best guard and tackle playing in the NFL, but great running teams come and go. The Seahawks were a great team. They had the best offense in the NFL by DVOA, a balanced offense, but their passing game was more than twice as valuable per play as their run game.

It was not a great receiving corps. Joe Jurevicius was a thirty-something journeyman receiver. Much is made about Jerramy Stevens' talent, but his value was locked into his position rather than his play. When Seattle set with a tight end off right tackle, teams were forced to commit to the run or face certain failure. Stevens was often running free up the seam. If he had any kind of hands, he could have been a great receiver, but even in 2005 he was not anything close. I am not sure Seattle would have suffered too much if Stevens had been replaced with Ryan Hannam.

It was a mediocre group, truly. There was depth when Darrell Jackson was healthy, but Jackson was a No. 1 receiver in name only. It was a mediocre group that Hasselbeck breathed greatness into. All the struggles, the hard work, the failure and breaks, had turned him into a confident and adroit West Coast quarterback. He achieved greatness through his offense, if never independently of it. Eventually, even Holmgren began to trust him. Hasselbeck knew how to audible, and that made the Seahawks' offense even more deadly. He carried the team through the divisional round, when the run stalled and Alexander left with a concussion. He was his best in the NFC Championship. Hasselbeck was agile, decisive, and consistently, improbably accurate. If it wasn't greatness, if it wasn't immortality, it was the closest Matt Hasselbeck ever came.

15 The Improbable Legend

Dave Krieg broke from obscurity to hard-scrabble his way onto the Seahawks' roster and into starting. His college folded before he was named official starter. He went undrafted. That's the NFL's way of saying "you may be talented, you may be good, but you are not talented enough, and you could never hope to be great." Everything in his life resembled every snap Krieg ever took: an ordeal.

Krieg attended Milton. He was the seventh-string quarterback, which begs the question: what tiny college has the funding to keep seven quarterbacks? Apparently Milton was a prodigal bunch, because they closed down in 1982. Before they shuttered their doors, they gave the Seahawks one of their all-time great players.

He probably couldn't have been but a Seahawk or a Buccaneer. Milton was the kind of starting point that could obscure any talent, and the truth is, though he crafted himself into a good player, he was never that talented. Milton sent tape to Seattle, and the Seahawks were happy to improve upon backup quarterback "Stirring" Sam Adkins.

His career started out predictably: Krieg stepped into an August 14, 1981, preseason game against the Cardinals, threw two touchdowns to put Seattle up 21–20, and then, when the Seahawks fell behind again, fumbled a snap from center to just about end it. Krieg could throw, and Krieg could scramble, but as often as not, he only scrambled himself into peril. He'd had one regular-season appearance in 1980, and before he ever completed a pass, he took a sack.

Krieg gave Seattle their first quarterback controversy when he started in place of an injured Jim Zorn. It was a typical quarterback controversy. Zorn was better, but Seattle won in two of Krieg's three starts. Fans loved the competition, and the media made it a regular story, but between Jim and Dave, it was a lot of hot air. There were pointed quotes. Then the offensive coordinator made the diplomatic claim that Krieg could "do anything Jim Zorn could do," and you know that inspired a few heated barroom debates.

Krieg ended the season as the Seahawks' starter and did enough to fuel the controversy. Had I been alive at the time, I think I would have backed Zorn. He had accomplished more with less, and was still very much a young man. He had a meaningful advantage in adjusted net yards per attempt, and unlike Krieg and his small sample, did it against all opponents. Then again, Krieg did it against two top 10 defenses.

History would have proved me a fool, because the difference in ability would soon become glaring. The two would duke it out in the 1982 preseason, with Krieg winning. He started in Week 1 and Week 2 and took sacks like Rob Johnson in cement shoes. Fourteen sacks in 74 attempts would be enough to convince most coaches to call for the hook, but Krieg wasn't benched. He was injured. An injured thumb put Zorn back into the fight. He responded by trading sacks for picks, and barely completing over 50 percent of his passes.

Everything started anew when Chuck Knox took over. He appointed Zorn the official No. 1 and put the controversy to rest. But where the controversy might have been fabricated in the past, it was real and vital in 1983. Zorn was suffering "quick-decision symptoms," which manifested as an inability to throw an accurate pass. His completion percentage was the worst of his career, and he was matching touchdown for interception. Eventually, Zorn burned every excuse, and his 4-for-16 showing against Oakland and then 1-for-8 start the next week against Pittsburgh ended his day and ended his starting career, respectively. Krieg did that thing coaches need a player to do before they can trust them: he won. He won five of the next eight and then led Seattle to their improbable playoff run.

Dave Krieg, in action in a game against the L.A. Raiders in October 1984, beat out fan favorite Jim Zorn in 1982 and went on to pass for more than 26,000 yards and 195 touchdowns in his 12-year tenure with the Seahawks.

After that, the controversy was over, and Krieg became the Seahawks' starting quarterback for good. He fought a perennial battle of improvising and attempting too much, which led to him taking sacks and losing fumbles, and forcing throws he couldn't make and throwing interceptions. Fans like to cite Krieg's quarterback rating: he finished at 81.5, ahead of contemporary John Elway, but ignore that quarterback rating does not count fumbles or sacks. Of course, Elway had many of the same problems. Compare the two statistically, and only two things truly separate them, longevity and postseason success.

Was Dave Krieg a great quarterback? I watched enough archived footage to know he could be thrilling, precise, and tremendously effective, but also nerve-wracking. Seattle never surrounded him

I Just Can't Quit Sacking You

The inimitable Pro-Football-Reference.com Blog (www.pro-football-reference.com/blog) is a great source for historical analysis and trivia. They looked through their game logs and created a list of the great all-time sack pairings. No, this is not Montana to Rice, but more like Bruce Smith to Ken O'Brien. Smith sacked O'Brien 17 times in his career.

Notable to Seahawks fans are both the players that most victimized Dave Krieg and the Seahawks that victimized others. Derrick Thomas sacked Krieg 15 times. Second to Thomas was Leslie O'Neal, who took down Krieg 14 times. O'Neal was also the scourge of Rick Mirer, and sacked the Golden Boy 10 times.

The Seahawks did a little damage themselves. The greatest pairing was Jacob Green and John Elway. Green took down Elway 13 times. That has to satisfy.

with much offensive talent, though. In 1994, three years after leaving Seattle and then with Detroit, he took over for an injured Scott Mitchell and had the best season of his career. Players don't peak at 36. Not even Dave Krieg. So what happened? Well, he went from Ground Chuck to Barry Sanders and Herman Moore. He had Lomas Brown protecting his blind side, which helped him keep his happy feet in check. The Lions got hot, and Krieg guided them into the playoffs. There they would meet Mike Holmgren's Packers and lose a nail-biter.

It makes you wonder. If Krieg arrived on a wave of hype, if he had surrounding talent as Joe Montana had, or a system that allowed him to distribute the ball instead of hand off and chuck, would he have made it? Would he have a plaque in Canton? By statistical measures, he was not so far off, and he brought a level of competitiveness to Seattle never seen before, but he mostly went unrecognized. The sacks were a problem, and Krieg fed his blockers to the dogs far too often, but the sacks weren't definitive. I guess it will just go down as another what-if. For a guy who did so much with so little, who accomplished so much from such modest roots, who was so good and yet waited years to even be honored by his own team, I imagine a little missed recognition is all in a life's work.

16 The Golden Ratio

The Golden Ratio is described by the constant φ. We're getting ahead of ourselves.

Picture a football field. It is 53.3 yards wide. It is 120 yards long. The secondary mostly play in the space beyond the line of scrimmage. Sometimes a defensive back blitzes. Sometimes a defensive back streaks in to make a tackle for a loss on a run or screen pass. But this is exceptional, added value because what a secondary must do is defend against passes beyond the line of scrimmage. And much thought and theory goes into just how best to do that.

Before Pete Carroll even took over for the Seahawks, the defensive brain trust of Gus Bradley and Dan Quinn began dabbling in the idea of specialization. The Golden Ratio I describe below is a particular type of that specialization, so named for how it balances matched talent of different types to make a whole.

The Squat Rectangle

Here are the perplexities of the squat portion of the rectangle: a receiver has two distinct and discrete ranges. The first is his range of locomotion, where he can run. The constituents of his locomotion are quickness, speed, agility, route running, ability to beat the press, and the ability to beat quasi-legal stalling tactics of the defender. The passing game at its simplest, a go route against off coverage, is almost purely locomotive range. The receiver attempts

JOHN MORGAN

to outrun the defender. The quarterback attempts to throw the ball to where the receiver is running: behind the defender, maybe behind all defenders. Such, in part is why arm strength and foot speed are such definitive measures of talent for quarterbacks and receivers, respectively, though both talents are somewhat, shall we say, deprecated.

Kam Chancellor is not a loaf when it comes to this particular kind of range, but he's NFL-bad. Though Seattle sometimes employs him in deep cover, it's a surprise type of coverage, one that banks on his ability to handle himself through savvy and good enough tools while the expansive half of the rectangle flies around all HOF-splashy and compelling.

The second type of range is immediate range, the range of arms and leaping ability and body control and boxing out and coordination when the locomotion has stopped or slowed (but not always) and the ball is arriving to its destination. This range has become more and more important as the NFL has placed greater restrictions on and greater emphasis of restrictions against interfering with receivers. The recent rise to preeminence of receiving tight ends is a direct result of these rule changes. Tony Gonzalez was so deep in his decline he could see Matt Hasselbeck, but as his speed has steadily diminished and his agility with it, his large frame, sure hands, and exceptional knowledge of and control over those tools kept him vital. The former prototypical strong safety—which not too many teams even still employ, preferring instead symmetrical safeties—is outmatched. Linebackers suited for run stuffing and zone coverage are overmatched.

Chancellor has specialized against this new-breed of tight end. He is the doppelganger born to negate and destroy his double. Pit him against a Jimmy Graham or Vernon Davis and unlike more typical defensive backs, Chancellor will not be bullied, will not be screened out, will not be out-reached or out-contested for the ball. If you printed two copies of the same body and taught one only receiving and the other only viciousness and disruption, that second would be the boom of The Legion of Boom, the squat rectangle of Seattle's golden ratio of safeties, Kam Chancellor.

The Expansive Rectangle

By definition, the expansive rectangle should be 1.68 times the size of the squat rectangle. In reality, there's no way such a precise relation could be possible on the football field. But breaking down game film, the relationship between Thomas and Chancellor is pretty close. Chancellor typically plays about 10 to 15 yards downfield. And Thomas typically plays another 20 to 30 yards beyond that.

Earl Thomas rode an exceptional and never likely to occur again hype that maybe undermines the specialness of his achievement. Personality, commentator, failed professional safety, and draft analyst Mike Mayock singled Thomas out for praise, pinning his then sterling reputation on Thomas exceeding uber-prospect Eric Berry in potential. This was heady stuff for draftniks. Berry was a rare prospect. But Mayock swung a big bat. He had likewise singled out Matt Ryan for praise, and Ryan had done the then seemingly impossible and truly excelled as a rookie quarterback. People that follow or work in deeply unstable businesses develop habits like old gamblers at the horse track. Success imparts in the successful an almost mystical quality. Mayock wasn't good and lucky or even just lucky, he was Fiver, Sybil, a divining rod that dove earthward wherever great talent was buried. For a little while, anyway. And you couldn't help but get caught up in his enthusiasm for Thomas.

Turns out, dude was right.

Thomas is rangy, which compensates a bit for his shortness. His official Combine height was 5'10"—not too different from

Josh Wilson, actually. Though Thomas was only 20 at that time, and it's not too uncommon for men of that age to continue to grow. But whatever his height today, he's shorter than typical for a safety. The classic safety's always been a bit of a generalist, with only one real specific duty: let no offensive player get past you. Tall safeties are favored because they would seem to have an advantage or at least no disadvantage when competing for a deep jump ball, and many deep passes are jump balls because many deep receivers are tall and can jump three feet-plus and higher with a running start. But Thomas isn't too tall, and his listed vertical is 34. Also his listed 40 yard dash time was only 4.43.

Most passes travel less than 20 yards in the air. But long passes are exceptionally valuable. In many ways, they are the end product of a successful process. The quarterback is both not under immediate pressure and able to step into the pocket. This isn't always true, but it's mostly true. A receiver has gained some kind of advantage on a defender or the secondary overall. That receiver may be clear to the end zone. That receiver may be single-covered. That receiver may be double-covered but has the angle on both defenders and is slanting through a post route, clear to the end zone, etc.

All offenses seek to throw the ball deep, even so-called West Coast Offenses, and so all defenses must be able to defend the deep pass. Thomas specializes in defending the deep pass. On any given snap, some 10 to 15 yards in any direction fall under his jurisdiction.

Despite his posted Combine time, Thomas is known to be sensationally fast. What he is, really, isn't straight-line fast but alert and able to read and react to a play very quickly, quick in that he builds to top speed faster than most, and fast running at angles. This last ability is easily the most underappreciated "tool" in all of football. Rarely does a player have the luxury to run point A to point B. Typically a route is somewhat circuitous, both because of opposition, and because of an imperfect read.

The Golden Ratio

The Seahawks play two coverage schemes primarily. One is press-man. In this coverage, Chancellor plays foil to the opposing tight end often or drops deep as Thomas plays foil to the opposing slot receiver. The other, and increasingly throughout 2013 the more common type of coverage, is three-deep man. In this, both corners drop into deep zones, and along with Thomas, the three form a shell over the receivers. Each is assigned a receiver, but defenders break from their zone only when a receiver is clearly being targeted. When playing three deep, Chancellor plays like a linebacker, dropping into underneath coverage but ever vigilant to stop the run.

Life is such that much of what might be thought a talent or skill comes with some inseparable weakness. Were Thomas bigger, he would probably be less agile. Were Chancellor faster, he might be no better than Taylor Mays: a seemingly world-class talent who cannot control himself well enough to hold coverage. Completeness comes in matching complement to complement.

Thomas and Chancellor are able to do together what neither could do alone. If Chancellor is the master of immediate range but merely adequate at locomotive range, then Thomas is surely the master of locomotive range but still very good at immediate range. Together they are the best safety tandem in football, and, with Sherman, the heart of the best defense in the NFL.

XL 5: Final

Super Bowl XL. Ford Field, Detroit. Late Third quarter...

Seattle forces a three-and-out sometime between my breaths. Rocky Bernard is doubtful to return.

This stuff is important, but it's just flying by. The whole game is flying by. It's deep in the third, and I don't know whether I am anticipating or dreading the conclusion. I kind of want to close my eyes and look up and see Matt Hasselbeck hoisting the Lombardi.

Stevens drops another, and I'm done, just finished with Jerramy Stevens. It's his third drop of the game. Whatever it is that supposedly excited the Seahawks about Stevens, I am ready for it to excite another team. For all his potential, he's a sink, a cipher, an unfilled position on most plays.

The camera zooms on Alexander just in time for him to flinch violently, drawing the flag. Running back false start. That's keen. Hasselbeck overthrows Joe Jurevicius, and then Holmgren burns a play with a pass to Strong underneath. Punt.

John Madden says it's about time the Steelers run a gadget play, but they don't. Tato tips it away to put Pittsburgh in second-and-long. Roethlisberger scrambles, drops his throwing shoulder into D.D. Lewis, but is stopped short of the first down. Pressure, throw away, and then a punt. It's a tight game and a tight score, and every little play seems magnified because it is. No small error is okay. No missed opportunity, no broken concentration, no blown assignment is okay.

Peter Warrick does not field the punt, and it rolls deep, deep down to the Seahawks' 2.

Alexander powers up the middle for five. Matt runs play-action and then breaks free for the first. It's awesome. I love Matt Hasselbeck. It's stupendously, tremendously gutsy and smart and valuable because it gets Seattle out of jail.

Fresh downs on the 15. Hasselbeck rolls left and finds Hannam for three. Hannam for nine on the right. Alexander Duplo blocks, and James Farrior nearly fights right through him, but Hasselbeck is poised and precise and keeps the drive clicking. Then it's a perfectly timed pass to Engram that he curls, receives, and extends for 21. That should be the end of the quarter.

But it's not. Seattle attempts to squeeze in a play, and it looks lost from the start. Hasselbeck drops, lobs toward Jurevicius, and it floats incomplete as the clock expires. It never looks right. It looks panicked. The quarter ends.

Nose tackle Casey Hampton tracks down Alexander after five, and that just doesn't feel right. Third down. Seattle splits trips right, wide receiver left. Pittsburgh is in a 3-3 nickel. They blitz, but Mack Strong steps up and seals off the pressure. Hasselbeck looks left, center, left, and then finds Engram wide open on the right. He receives and sprints upfield for 17. Alexander runs for six. Alexander runs for five and the first. Sean Locklear is beat badly off the edge, but Hasselbeck steps forward and zings it to Stevens! Catch! Seahawks on the 1!

Penalty.

Flag, holding. It's not clear on the replay. Does he grab the pads? Does it matter? The penalty means everything. It's a 28-yard swing. From one to go for a touchdown to first-and-20 on the 29. My stomach is stirring, and a cinch is closing about my temples, and I'm cussing myself for caring so much, but cussing the NFL double. This isn't right. It's not even anger I feel now, but ganged up on, hated.

A play later, Hampton throws Robbie Tobeck down with one arm and sacks Hasselbeck. Mike Holmgren attempts to surprise with his never-surprising draw play, and Alexander puts Seattle in better position for a field goal.

Third down. Hasselbeck looks left, throws to where Ryan Hannam is supposed to be, isn't, but Ike Taylor is. Interception. Throws to where he thinks Hannam is supposed to be? Overthrows Jackson? Throws it directly at Ike Taylor for an easy interception. Hasselbeck runs left, throws a shoulder into Taylor, stopping the return, and it's flagged. Flagged—unjustifiably, incorrectly flagged.

Flagged…

…flagged.

What happens next? I don't know. Football.

* * *

...Roethlisberger pitches it to Haynes, Haynes hands it to Antwaan Randle El, and El zips it to Ward for the score.

* * *

...Hasselbeck scrambles, cuts in, fumbles! The ball is recovered by Pittsburgh. Of course, the ball is recovered by Pittsburgh. It's reviewed. We know which way this is going. Oh. Overturned. Golly, the semblance of fairness.

Drive falters, ends, dies, writhes, curses its God, and clutches it heart and extends its arms and legs and thrashes and then gets real stiff.

Steelers get the ball back and run a long, back-breaking, clock-control drive.

Punt.

Seattle needs to score to tie. Seattle needs a touchdown and a field goal. It's academic. Get in range, kick the field goal, and then pin your hopes on an onside kick. It's academic. Play the sidelines, control the clock, take your shots, and know you will probably lose, but that you can't beat yourself.

1:51 remaining—Hasselbeck finds Stevens over the middle for six. What the f—?

Between snaps, Darrell Jackson is nowhere, lost. Seattle sets, and Jackson runs long across the field, finally positions himself in the slot.

1:28—Hasselbeck finds Jurevicius dragging across the deep middle, he hits, bounces off Hope, twists, stumbles forward, and is tackled.

1:05—Throw away.

1:00—Hasselbeck scrambles left, stops before crossing the line of scrimmage, surveys, sees nothing, sees Mack Strong, tosses errant across his body. Strong looks bewildered. Strong looks unprepared. The ball falls incomplete.

:52—Hasselbeck throws it to…somebody. Seahawks are not finishing their routes. It's fourth down.

:47—Engram for 13. Run up, clock it.

:35—Spike.

:34—Hasselbeck throws into the right flat, and the bad decision is saved when Alexander characteristically cannot hang on.

:27—Hasselbeck finds Stevens in the right flat for three, and instead of diving to get out of bounds, Stevens attempts to break it upfield, before being wrapped and futilely laying out toward the sideline. The official swings his arm. The clock runs. Bill Cowher smiles.

:08—Hasselbeck targets Stevens just short of the goal line. Stevens drops the pass.

I find my girlfriend, look her in the eye, and swear to never watch football again.

Subtle Like a T-Rex

Here's a bit of smugness that's true in fact but lacking in spirit: chiefly what a high-definition TV, a good one, or a nice set of speakers, or a nice car or most any luxury really, most of what they accomplish is to ruin for you what was once totally okay but now *sucks hard*. Watching *X-Files* on DVD on the TV my wife fished out of the dumpster, that was fine back then. And those van speakers I was swindled into, I thought I heard arpeggios and stuff I'd never heard before. But that's a bitter, nostalgia-poisoned take on progress. It's a bit like saying my wife's cooking has done a number on my taste for Totino's pizzas rolled up like burritos. Have I really lost anything but ignorance and inurement? (Have I really lost anything but delicious red and white goo enveloped in a flaky, spongy pizza-dough shell?)

Now I've had good seats and I've had bad seats but I've never a seat that floats yards above the line of scrimmage, adjusted to an ideal angle, and which banks and zooms to follow relevant game action. Never have I had a scat which affords a replay of past action, from multiple angles and captured in such a way to slow the infinitely dense sequence of images to an intelligible crawl, so every subtle moment may be appreciated. This hyper-reality does not fictionalize, but in surpassing human senses, it creates reality beyond reality. The ability of technology to not fictionalize but instead capture the real as a person never could, and make that real in all its infinite complexity available. Or more available anyway.

There's this moment, seconds into the Beast Quake, when Marshawn Lynch is planting his foot for the cutback lane. You can see Lynch's torso, the way his right foot is tucking in to better distribute weight over his plant foot, and how his helmet seems to point to where the hole is materializing between Michael Robinson and John Carlson. It's frozen on my computer right now, in fact. And he looks like he could topple. He looks like he should career rightward and into this blockers, missing the hole. At best, it seems his angle will force him to stall his momentum, neutralizing the running start designed into the play. Instead, micro-seconds later, his torso upright and squared, his feet leftward so his body makes a flipped California, crouched, center of weight slightly before his feet, but moving, fast, and approaching the hole with impetus—a damn good chance of breaking the pivotal tackle, the defender in the hole, the last assigned line of defense before it's up to the free safety, corners, and maybe a lucky chase-down tackle to stop him. Ultimately this is what running in gridiron football is about: having the superior force vector hitting the hole. It's the culmination of coordination, explosiveness, balance, vision, anticipation, and fearlessness or at least fear sublimation. Right? And there, publicly available, captured in a way as if to survive for eternity, is Marshawn Lynch subtly displaying his greatness at the pivotal moment of the greatest run of his career.

Sport and reality television have seen a concurrent rise in popularity the past few years. Both benefit immensely from the subtlety caught by modern high-definition cameras. However tawdry the premise or trashy the people, there's no denying that people feeling the complexities of real emotion is compelling, and compelling in a way even the best acting never is. Subtlety is hard to fake.

Lynch is perhaps the most subtle and complex running back I've ever watched. When one thinks of great all-time backs, three names rise above all others: Jim Brown, Walter Peyton, and Barry Sanders. Each belonged so beautifully to their era, not just their era of football but their era of broadcasting. Brown's physical dominance was apparent even in black and white. Peyton's easy power, his incredible acrobatics began a movement toward a more nuanced appreciation of what made a great running back great. Sanders' incredible change of direction, his ability to embarrass defenders in the open field, was perfect for a time when TVs were becoming big enough and broadcasts of a high enough resolution that such athletic marvels weren't lost in a sea of hard to differentiate jerseys. Lynch has power and speed, a remarkable ability to escape from tackles, but it's the feints and shivers, the baby stiff-arms, the jukes, the incredible feats of balance, that are most awe inspiring. It's all very subtle, very complex, and fluid, apparent for a split-second and gone. Were the picture grainy or a telecast on and then gone forever, it would be impossible to properly appreciate. Luckily for us, all that brutal subtlety, down to the way his dreads double over in confusion when he makes a stutter-step cut, is captured, can be replayed, can be scrutinized, and re-appreciated and appreciated anew, forever.

19 Paul Allen

Team owners typically are not well known until they do something boneheaded or selfish. To bankroll the franchise but retain a certain anonymity is the job of a team owner. It is like a hyper advanced franchise mode in a video game but a toy available only to billionaires. Apart from a little accrued value, a little fun hanging out with the guys, pretending they know what they're talking about, throwing in their compulsively ignored two-cents, and some hiring and firing, some consulting and hair loss, some back door dealings and clandestine meetings with other owners, other billionaires, team owners are fans. Fans with excellent luxury box seats.

Smart owners understand how to collaborate, how to delegate, and their own limitations. Foolish owners earn a benign notoriety. Jerry Jones, the old oil tycoon, is known for being his team's de facto chief executive. The late Al Davis, especially toward the end of his life, was known for his quotable press conferences, decrepit appearance, and string of bad decisions. Jones is surely selfish, but his passion is sincere, and he wants the Cowboys to be good as much or more than any fan. Davis tried, and the Raiders had been good and great in his time. It's a lucky thing to get old. But it's sad how the great in their senescence become their own most cutting satirist. Still, Jones is a good owner, and Davis was a good owner. At their best, each were owners who loved football and their team and existed within the community instead of exploiting it.

Other owners, like Bud Adams and Robert Irsay, are sort of the opposite. Both squeezed their home cities, demanded civic support impossible for the depressed economies of Houston and Baltimore, respectively, and then, despite political concessions, moved their team anyway. For a sports fan, nothing burns like losing a franchise. No loss, no injury, not even the sulfurous smoke that surrounded XL, can possibly hurt like losing a franchise, because hope is the impulse that keeps a fan's heart beating, and no loss can kill hope, except loss of life. Men like Clay Bennett are killers. Like Elizabeth Bathory, they steal life from others thinking they can own it themselves.

Men like Paul Allen are not heroes but the compassionate common citizen—simple but given great means. They are more than philanthropists, because they do not simply give charity but breathe life into a city.

Allen was born in Seattle. That might not have seemed so important at the time, but it colored the rest of his life. He attended private school, befriended Bill Gates, and so forth. You can read about it almost anywhere. It's one of the great nerd-buddy romps of the latter 20th century. Kids meet, buy DOS, get wealthy, become despised, nevertheless become more wealthy, buy yachts, sports teams, museums, maybe pine for lost innocence, give money away, lose money, have others take pleasure in their steadily declining fortune, clutch snow globe on their deathbed, etc.

Allen stepped into the lives of Seahawks fans on the eve of the most important spring in team history. The Kingdome was crumbling, killing people, and though building a new stadium is never practical, fans knew it was new stadium or SoCal SeaBrahs. Seahawks owner Ken Behring was posturing. He had no connection to Seattle. He had moved Seahawks operations to Anaheim, California. He was big-game hunting and had an entire city in his sights.

The NFL forced Behring to move his operation back to Seattle and offer the team to a Seattle-area investor. In mid-April 1996 Allen bought an exclusive option to buy the Seahawks. The projected value of the team was $200 million, and a year later, Allen would pay just that to buy the team outright.

Never the overgrown kid playing football owner like Jones or Davis, Allen also hasn't settled into frustrated resignation. If there's a middle ground between the mad, Richard the III-like tyranny of an old team owner battling imminent death, and the stingy ministrations of a Ralph Wilson, it can be found in Paul Allen.

Allen is engaged and has the wherewithal (i.e. $$$) to take risks, as he did when the Seahawks traded up to draft Walter Jones. That same engagement and wherewithal motivated and allowed him to make two splashy and expensive coaching hires: Mike Holmgren and Pete Carroll. But where that engagement might inspire another owner to meddle and overreach his knowledge, Allen understands the value of expertise and delegation. It's a wise man that knows his limitations, but it's a smart man that, with the help of others, overcomes those limitations. As simple and sensible as it seems, few owners have the discipline to control and lead a franchise but avoid drowning in micromanagement.

Discipline requires sacrifice. Maybe Allen is a naturally phlegmatic guy, and maybe I'm reading into something that's not there. But when the Seahawks organization crowded round and scaled the podium Sunday February 2, 2014, to accept the Lombardi trophy, no person seemed less satisfied or happy than Paul Allen. Had he been Jerry Jones and his fingerprints were all over the team, perhaps he could have felt a sense of personal pride. Had he been Ralph Wilson, and the victory meant some kind of financial solvency, some momentary respite from the dilemma of a dying franchise, perhaps he could have felt relief and optimism. But Allen took the hard path. Everyone was grinning but him. He looked sad if anything, like a proud father at his youngest daughter's wedding.

When he spoke, he spoke ineloquently but elegantly, as one might expect a nervous engineer to speak whilst navigating foreign emotions but with something very specific to say. I'm not inclined to talk up the nobility of rich men and their expensive toys, but I don't doubt Allen's sincerity, either. "It's such an amazing feeling to be able to take the Lombardi Trophy back to…Seattle and the Northwest, and the 12th Man who supported us in such an amazing way all year," he said.

Allen is a fortunate man, and all that started with being born in Seattle. I think he knows that. He bought the Seahawks, so the city he loved may keep the team it loved. And when that team won it all, he knew he didn't own that championship. Super Bowl XLVIII was his gift to us.

20 Emerging from Still Watters: The Rise of Shaun Alexander

It was too easy. It always was. Too fluid. Effortless in the pejorative.

WTF, Shaun Alexander? You quittin' on us?

He jogged through the ACC, all grin and grace. Never looked muscular or pounding or even breakaway fast. He tested out of testing at the NFL Combine. His tape was that good. Some team would surely select him in the first round, and so though Alexander attended the annual sizing up of extraordinary young men, he ran no 40, never contorted his way through a three-cone drill. Alexander was Alabama fast? or Alabama strong? or just God-given good at running the football.

He came into camp and outclassed the aged Ricky Watters. Watters was still flitting about the league, clinging here and there when a wise coach could be seduced. Holmgren got it. Guys like Watters who could receive and rush created scheme versatility. A yard rushing was worth a yard receiving. Alexander split touches. Watters wringed his once abundant talent. He produced. Alexander amazed.

Shaun Alexander takes the ball and looks for a hole during a 28–24 victory over the Tennessee Titans at Nashville in December 2005. Alexander rushed for 1,880 yards and 27 TDs en route to an NFL MVP Award and Super Bowl XL.

How can a guy running so slow get down the field so fast? How can a guy who doesn't battle, bruise, or stiff-arm break so many arm tackles? How is a guy as gentle as Alexander ever going to intimidate a defense?

By excelling at the subtle art of reading his blockers.

Mike Holmgren teased us with him in 2000. Alexander excited in the snaps he got. A start and 11 carries against K.C.: 74 yards, quality runs none longer than 17, but a fumble. Back to single-digit carries, young man. Dropped a 50 burger second go round against the Chiefs, but fumbled again. Back to the bench. Maybe you can flash a little something in Week 17, it's been a long season: 8.4 yards per carry with none longer than 17, that's enough to warm Seahawks Stadium on a drizzly winter day. Or start it shivering.

Or shouting. Watters began the season as the Seahawks starting running back in 2001. The former promising rookie now presumed franchise tailback was waiting in the wings, and only Holmgren fully understood why. Holmgren's heart sank when Watters was diagnosed with a cracked right shoulder after Week 3. Watters was the steady vet who kept Seattle afloat, was seemingly what Holmgren thought. Yet Seattle was still sinking fast. Watters' injury was another terrible blow to a team that squeaked out a victory in Week 1 and then was blown out in the following two weeks. Football coaches often fail to see the forest for the trees. Holmgren envisioned his team as a delicate machine with each player as an irreplaceable part. In some peculiar way, at some particular assignment or executing some particular job, Watters was better than Alexander. Substituting a mismatched player, however superior, seemed disastrous. Another season would be getting away from him, Holmgren bemoaned, and how many more until fans started calling for his firing?

Holmgren should have been singing, but coaches are a stubborn lot. Alexander took his first start of the season and second start overall and rushed for 176 yards and two touchdowns. One

201 Yards in the Snow

One game that has always defied the neat picture of Shaun Alexander in decline is his 201-yard performance in Week 12 of 2006. It was a strange night in a lot of ways. It was the first time it ever snowed in Qwest Field. Alexander was returning from his foot injury, but he wasn't rested and ready. That would seem to be the knee-jerk thought: that maybe Alexander could play well as long as he could get an occasional break.

That seems dubious. He had rushed 17 times the week before and averaged 2.2 yards per rush. He should have been more rested then and, facing one of the league's worst run defenses, able to do whatever it is some thought he could do with fresh legs.

My guess is that the snow just slowed everyone down a little bit. He was still a better back in 2006 than he would become in 2007, and with a little slickness, a little loose footing, his vision and decision-making overcame his vanishing speed. It was not vintage Alexander. He needed 40 carries to top 200. And on a busted foot, I always thought it was reckless of Mike Holmgren to run Alexander so hard, but however I try to explain it, he really was good, and without that performance it is unlikely the Seahawks would have made the playoffs.

hundred seventy-six yards! *Seattle won! Boom!* One hundred forty-two in the next game. Win. Then a downer: 87, 60. Loss, loss.

If Watters could start, maybe he should. The kid had showed some magic, but teams were catching on.

266!

Yards!

And not just against some so-and-so, but against the play-off-bound Oakland Raiders. The second-to-last playoff-bound Oakland Raiders team before Al Davis's death. It was the then fourth-highest rushing total ever, only behind Corey Dillon (ahem), Walter Payton! and O.J. Simpson!

Alexander didn't have the bruising style of Sweetness or the slashing style of the Glove, but he did have that effortless grace, knack for cutback lanes, and blinding smile. He was his own rusher. The very first Shaun Alexander.

So, after all that, and even with some dwindling production and Watters' return to health, it took some kind of stones for Holmgren to start Watters in Week 14. We're told coaches are paid to make the hard decisions, but how often do they really just make the easy decisions hard to swallow? Seattle won easily against an inept Cowboys team, a team led by none other than Quincy Carter, but it certainly wasn't starting Watters that did it. Watters didn't somehow force Carter into completing 14 of 33 passes for 135 yards and a pick. He didn't shut down Emmitt Smith or sack Carter four times. No, he ran for 104 yards on 28 carries. Watters finished his day and his career with a broken ankle in the fourth.

Shaun Alexander became, finally and for too long, Holmgren's unquestioned starter.

Loyalty, we love it in friends and family, but hate it in our football coaches. We want that coach to separate person from athlete. Holmgren could befriend Alexander and motivate Alexander through that friendship. They could eat together, do charity work together, and stake their respective and shared dreams on each other, become close over the years. But when it comes time to do that rotten, hypocritical thing, and tell this person you've trusted, built-up, and depended on, that no matter what he thinks, no matter what he, the coach, had so recently said about still believing in him, that he's lost a step and must be benched or cut, fans demand all that humanity be stripped away. It seems sometimes Holmgren could not be a bad enough guy to be a good coach.

21 Curt Warner and the Vanishing Breed of Dominant Backs

Warner hails from a dying era of back. Backs who weren't zone-blocking backs, or scat backs, or even feature backs, but backs who were the physical embodiment of pounding the rock. Who took the ball and then, with whatever peculiar blend of freakish athleticism, strength, quickness, agility, and/or speed they had, humiliated the grown men around them. Vince Lombardi said "Football is first and foremost a running game. That will never change," and in Curt Warner's prime, this was only becoming false.

Warner did all sorts of things wrong—technically wrong. He carried the football like a mugger carries a recently snatched purse. He initiated contact without incentive of extra yards. That cost him. An ACL tear cost him his second season. He had an unusually short career, just five seasons as a feature back; short even for a short-lived position. And when he went out, his era of back sort of went out with him—guys like Payton, Campbell, and Brown. Men who could physically dominate their peers but still outrun them. Guys who could break a tackle by breaking the tackler. Warner could man-slap 32-year-old Woodrow Lowe without losing balance. Cut. Go.

Shaun Alexander has the numbers, but Warner was likely the best back in Seahawks history. The kind of back you build an offense on. The kind of back, when he's on, you hand the ball to and marvel at. The kind of back who makes Ground Chuck appetizing. Warner could best good run defenses and abuse bad ones.

In his rookie season, Seattle rode Warner right to the AFC Championship Game. In the divisional round, he dropped 99 on Denver in a blowout win over the Donkeys. Notched 113 against the Dolphins the next week and scored the game-winning touch-down. When Warner lost his mojo in the Black Hole, gaining only 26 on 11 carries, Seattle's offense followed. The Seahawks were down by 20 at halftime and were blown out by the eventual Super Bowl–champion L.A. Raiders. It didn't turn out to be the worst thing Tom Flores ever did to the Seahawks.

All that pounding added up, and Warner popped his ACL in the first week of the 1984 season. You can replace the tendon, but you can't ensure the player returns the same. Warner was so good, it can be easy to ignore what he lost. He did lose something though, a little agility maybe, a little glide. Something.

He returned and earned three more thousand-yard seasons. In another, he fell 15 yards short after missing three games. Good had replaced great. The numbers, yeah, the numbers were there. Warner could stumble into the numbers even at his most ground down and beat up. The production was gone, though. Warner was a shadow of himself by 1989 and lost from the league partway into 1990.

So it goes.

* * *

It may seem that Marshawn Lynch, with his sublime mix of lever-age, technique, and wanton violence, is every bit the back Warner was. And in some ways, Lynch is very much like Warner. Both are nominally power backs but with breakaway speed. Lynch, in terms of pure talent, may even best Warner, so much has the league gotten bigger, faster, and more athletic in the last 30 years. But even in Darrell Bevell and Tom Cable's run first and second offense, Lynch lacks the value of Warner. Though Warner played during the dawn and popularization of Bill Walsh's revolutionary pass-heavy offense, football in the 1980s was still primarily a running game. Strategic changes lag, in part because by nature personnel changes lag. Coaches and general managers cannot be finicky, cannot chase

Curt Warner tries to beat a defender to the corner during a 34–21 Seahawks victory over the L.A. Raiders at Memorial Coliseum in October 1983, Warner's sensational rookie season.

whatever trend pops up, and no one knew then that the NFL was forever (or maybe forever) changing to a pass-first league.

Though Lynch contributes an impossible to measure benefit to his team's passing game, through the opposing defense's personnel, spacing, and play calling, his value as a rusher simply cannot compare to Warner's. The reason is simple. In Warner's eight seasons, NFL teams averaged between 5.9 and 6.3 adjusted yards per pass play. In Lynch's seven seasons, that number has jumped to between 6.3 and 6.8. Completion percentages and correspondingly interception percentages were lower and much higher, respectively. So the run wasn't just safe, strategically necessary, or meant to set up the play-action pass. In the 1980s the run was valuable in and of itself. Nowadays, in raw contribution, the sum of all run plays by Lynch are often *negative in value*. Running backs are battling their own obsolescence. Lynch, as a pure rusher, is in many ways only valuable relative to other backs. And historically great offenses like the 2009 New Orleans Saints, 2007 New England Patriots, and 2013 Denver Broncos have all but excised the feature back from their team. They patch with placeholders to keep the opposing defense from squatting on the pass. And those placeholders, like Knowshon Moreno and Pierre Thomas, contribute more as receivers and pass blockers than as running backs.

In 1983, his rookie season, his greatest season, and what would become Chuck Knox's greatest season in Seattle, runs and receptions by Warner constituted 35 percent of the Seahawks total offense. In 2012 in what will most likely go down as Lynch's greatest season, runs and receptions by Lynch constituted 32 percent of the Seahawks total offense. Franchises by sheer coincidence develop legacies. The Seahawks have had great safeties, great fullbacks, great left tackles, and great running backs. After Lynch, after maybe Christine Michael, some great running back no one yet knows of will don the Blue. He will be fast. He will be powerful. He will make jaw dropping cuts, hurdle defenders, bust through tackles, and take it to the house. But it is likely he will never be as integral to the success of his teams as Curt Warner was to the success of the Chuck Knox Seattle Seahawks.

XL 6: Aftermath

Super Bowl XL. Final: Steelers 21, Seahawks 10.

I swore off football forever. My fandom flagged. A season of ecstasy punctuated by 15 exclamation points killed one penalty at a time. I held my head, wanted to yell. Probably did. Surely yelled. I stood, wanted to punch something, kick something, destroy something, looked about my future in-laws' house, sat back down, held my head. Outrage became heartburn became heavy legs became defeat. My hopes flagged.

Half of all Super Bowl teams lose. Perceptive little factoid there, huh? And when it's over, it's tempting to wish it never happened. Why feel so good only to feel so, so bad? There are blowouts and grinders, games that were closer than the score, comebacks, failed comebacks, and historic comebacks. A kid named Namath once promised the whole shebang. Got himself enshrined with that moxie (and little else).

Blow a team out and, however anticlimactic, there's something about it that sings to a man's soul. Any team can win a Super Bowl, but embarrassing your opponent is like cuckolding your boss. It's triumph with icing. Dust off that jersey and wear it out, because for a few months you're not just king, you're destroyer. You hate me, but you fear me more.

Getting blown out births perspective. Maybe it was just worth it to get there. Team never had a shot, anyway. Maybe it was all

Win Probability: 0

A minute and a half into the fourth quarter, a six-yard run by Shaun Alexander pushed Seattle's win probability in Super Bowl XL over 50 percent for the first time since the second quarter. They would maintain that slight advantage for about 30 seconds of game clock. Sean Locklear's hold knocked them down to 44 percent. Casey Hampton's sack pushed them down to 38 percent. It was the interception by Ike Taylor that really killed them.

It is not a surprise. Seattle was well within field-goal range and still had some small chance at scoring a touchdown. The interception cost them three points if we assume Brown would have been able to kick the field goal. It cost them field position, especially following the bogus low-block call on Matt Hasselbeck. It just about cost them the game. In barely more than two minutes of game clock, the Seahawks' chances of winning Super Bowl XL plunged from 55 to 14 percent.

just a dream awaiting interruption, but a sweet dream; a sweet few months of stolen bliss. Can't complain about achieving so much with so little, right, pal?

Grind it out and win the way your elders want. Maybe it's morbidly bad football, 11 minutes of action deactivated. All pile-ups and dropped passes and timely penalties and lucky breaks, but whichever way your team lands, it was manly football, unadulterated by flash, bang, whiz, touchdown! Touchdown! Touchdown!

Make a comeback and win without winning—or win! The Titans were thwarted at the 1, and however much that stung, and I'm sure it stung like Tabasco on a scratched cornea, the savor lasted long after the finish. That's a team that fought every damn down and nearly hustled their way past a better opponent. Builds character or some such nonsense. Rams won, but Titans earned respect.

Or you can watch your team stripped of glory, one yellow blur at a time. No one wants to complain here, no one wants to be sour, but, damn it, I was sour. I was complaining. I was pissed. I didn't want apologies; I wanted conspirators. I wasn't looking for explanations; I was looking for mortal rage, the kind that burns buildings and topples governments.

So that was XL, the aftermath, as known by one fan, but what about XL the game? Was it all ugly penalties and Steelers standing around the Lombardi Trophy? Was there never hope, never a thing worth watching, but dross, nothing but loss?

No. No. No, no, no, nononono—can't let my bitterness blind me. It was indeed sweet for a series, a quarter. Right? Maybe. Right? I needed to know, so I rewatched it, second by second, gut out of it, cognizant of the outcome, with new eyes maybe, right?

Right. It was not savory, but it was not fixed. Seattle did not win, and they were in fact beat. They fought hard, though. They very well may have been the better team. It was a great game, dramatic, and the Steelers did not pull away until the very end. It was better seeing the Seahawks lose again, but I could finally see the loss was bitter, but not the game. The game was epic.

23 AFC West

The Seahawks were born into the NFC, but grew up in the AFC. Older fans still harbor rivalry between the Seahawks and the existing AFC West, while many younger fans see the division as alien as the NFC North. I straddle the line somewhat. I know and loathe the NFC West, but I understand still-lingering enmity for the AFC West. It might not matter anymore, the way that Arrowhead rocked, or how it became dead quiet thanks to Marty Ball; Dan Fouts, Don Coryell, and the true West Coast Offense; the Black Hole; Elway, but it matters as history, as roots, as part of being a complete Seahawks fan.

The American Football Conference was comprised primarily of the remnants of the AFL. The history of the American Football League is complex and cool and better left to another writer, but noteworthy to Seahawks fans because the franchise's original rivals were all AFL originals. The Los Angeles Chargers became the San Diego Chargers. The Oakland Raiders emerged after the Minnesota Vikings joined the NFL. The Dallas Texans became the Kansas City Chiefs, the AFL's most successful franchise. Denver were Donkeys all the way back to their foal days.

The Seahawks began life in the NFC but switched in their second season. The NFL wanted the Seahawks and Buccaneers to play each other twice, and each of the other teams in the NFL once. So they did. As it turned out, the Bucs ended Seattle's losing streak at five. Tampa would lose its first 26 games.

Seattle faced its first division opponent in Week 3 of the 1977 season and lost 24–13 to the Broncos. Oakland smacked Seattle around in Week 8, and San Diego edged the Seahawks in Week 11. Seattle finally beat a division rival when they clipped the Chiefs at Arrowhead. Kansas City finished 2–12, but I am sure losing to the expansion Seahawks hurt extra.

It was a trend. From the time the Seahawks joined the NFL to the time Marty Schottenheimer took over in Kansas City, the Chiefs had two winning seasons and one playoff appearance. They were blown out by the Jets in the 1986 wild-card round. The Seahawks never developed a very strong rivalry with Kansas City. It was a token rivalry, but 13 years of bad football and losing took the piss out of it.

Oakland was different. The Raiders were good, very good. They were closer geographically, and years of winning had created pockets of Raiders fans in Seahawks country. Had Oakland and later L.A. smacked around and demolished Seattle, it wouldn't be a rivalry, but the oppressed meekly cursing the oppressor. It wasn't that, though. It was good football, meaningful football, and for years.

Oakland crushed Seattle in 1977. The Seahawks lost by 37 points. Seattle then won the next four games. Seattle finished 9–7 both seasons on the strength of those victories; and those losses kept Oakland out of the playoffs. The Raiders would win the next five, but three were within a touchdown. The losing is what mattered, and although it was exciting football, in the end it was just another loss. Seattle was fading, and Oakland was emerging, and the young rivalry seemed destined for obsolescence.

Then came Chuck Knox and 1983.

The Raiders had moved to Los Angeles prior to the 1982 season. Al Davis was turning heel. He had lobbied unsuccessfully for luxury boxes to be added to the Oakland Coliseum and responded by signing an agreement with the owners of the L.A. Coliseum. The move went to an NFL owners' vote, and needing three-quarters approval, Davis got none. The relocation was defeated 22–0. Davis filed an antitrust suit, spent eight days on the stand, had his character run through the media wringer, won the suit anyway, packed up, and moved the Raiders to L.A.

Seattle was suddenly not just fighting a division rival, but against the forces of evil. During the trial, the prosecution presented an interview with Davis in which he revealed his boyhood fascination with Adolf Hitler. It was later disallowed, but the damage to his character was done.

Knox put an end to rebuilding. He decided whatever had been built previously probably wasn't worth building again. Seattle started hot but fell to 3–3 after a close loss in San Diego. Being at .500 has a nervous feeling to it. You're one step away from Heaven or Hell. Sort of the opposite of purgatory, like Bart on the escalator to Heaven. Redemption is close, but the ride seems long, and you're one sin from eternal damnation.

Seattle next faced the 5–1 L.A. Raiders at the Kingdome. Jim Zorn was still starting. He had been underappreciated for his success on a piecemeal offense. He was falling apart at the seams.

Steve Largent was out with a knee injury. The Seahawks netted two passing yards. Two, on 16 attempts. Two, 13 yards forward, 11 back on a sack. Two—2—two yards passing, and only 153 total.

But won.

Seattle's defense scorched L.A. for eight sacks, six fumbles forced, five recovered, and three interceptions. Paul Johns returned a punt for a touchdown. Zorn scrambled for a score. Curt Warner rushed for a score and Dan Doornink another, and Seattle, improbably, impossibly, won, beating the Raiders 38–36. They beat the Raiders again two weeks later.

Seattle squeaked into the playoffs, made a surprise run, and met the Raiders in the AFC Championship Game. Los Angeles won in a blowout and went to the Super Bowl. The Seahawks' rivalry with the Broncos revolved around John Elway. Horseface deserves and gets his own essay.

I never detected strong rivalry between Seattle and San Diego. The two teams never managed to be good in the same season. The Seahawks were building a loser when Don Coryell turned the Chargers into the most exciting offense in the NFL. Seattle was respectable in the '80s, but the Chargers became mediocre—too good to laugh off, but never good enough to become a rival. Seattle was sifting through the rubble of rebuilding when the Chargers rebounded briefly under Bobby Ross, and once Ross was forced out and San Diego was back to seasonally hiring and firing coaches, Seattle was getting good again.

Seattle's two lasting AFC West rivals were Oakland and Denver. Oakland was the scheming, cutthroat spawn of overlord Al Davis. A good rival to any club, but especially the Seahawks. Denver was the pious sons of John, and equally repellant in their own way. Elway backers evangelized the West and suffered no heretic, so it was always kind of special seeing Denver be just good enough to get blown out in the Super Bowl. Rivalries, they lose currency over time, and nowadays most Seahawks fans think little about Davis or Elway or the drama of traveling to Mile High or the Black Hole, but they never lose importance, and for every Seahawks fan, there should be some vestigial bile somewhere deep inside that still burns for the Broncos and Raiders and Chiefs and Char—well, maybe not the Chargers.

Shaun Alexander, Middle Years

Alexander finally fought his way into starting. Wait, no, that's incorrect. Ricky Watters busted up his ankle and was placed on injured reserve. He happened to be an unrestricted free agent. Lucky us. I know it angers some when common sense is applied to the arcane decision-making of coaches—NFL coaches are next only to doctors and admirals in never having their decisions questioned no matter how foolish, but coaches should be questioned. Unchecked power is an evil without qualification.

Shaun angered some with his breezy running style, bad hands, and unwillingness to block. The middle years for Shaun Alexander were all about good stats, great running, and a lot of bad football between his touches. It wasn't very popular to question Seattle's young superstar. He was good-natured and sweet. He was active in the community and the team's only real face. Never mind he was the team's third-best player and fourth-most important. Never mind that his backup, Maurice Morris, and fullback, Mack Strong, bested him as a receiver and bested his yards per carry. He was Smilin' Shaun Alexander!

That is how the middle years go. The young stud had settled in, and as the prestige of youth and novelty wash off, familiarity-bred contempt settled in. His overall play annoyed some, his picky,

Hitting the Wall

The reason most could not tell that much had changed in Shaun Alexander is that the skill Alexander had lost is almost imperceptible to the human eye. As Chuck Knox recognized in 1984, it doesn't take much lost quickness before a running back is too slow to reach a hole. Franco Harris was constantly hitting a pile, and rather than fire the offensive line, the Seahawks decided to fire Franco.

That is exactly what plagued Alexander. He was never the fastest rusher, but he was quick and lived off his initial burst. He had lost enough by 2006 that he couldn't reach the hole before it was already closing around him. Or, too often when he could get himself into the hole, he would attempt to cut back as he always had, and his burst just wouldn't let him. He would be tackled in the pile.

Running backs can run 40 yards in under five seconds. They run the five yards it takes to get to a hole in less than a single second. Alex had lost literally fractions of a second, but those fractions were enough to take a man from the pinnacle of success to complete failure. He is far from alone, though. Every year another rusher hits that wall, and the vital speed/quickness that made them a professional abandons them.

high-leverage running style frustrated others, his personality could grate, and in that oh-so-modern way, his religiosity was just too much.

The thrown ball bemused him. Holmgren wanted a dual threat. What he got was a reluctant receiver who wasn't so much bad at receiving as disinclined to bother. He was targeted a ton but never did much with it, and by his third season starting, the targets started to vanish, too. Alexander never threw more than a perfunctory block. Football fans want blood, but Shaun was content to play.

That bled into his rushing style. Alexander was not a power rusher, and he didn't bust through blockers. At its heart, football is entertainment, and the polite-acquiescence out of bounds can never replace the *crack* of bodies smashing with the force of a car crash. Of course, football fans don't have to wake up Monday morning with that beat-by-a-tire-iron feeling, either.

Alexander was someone who would tell you about his humility. Or so it felt. Who wore his achievement and good deeds on his sleeve and made those achievements and good deeds reflect poorly on him, somehow.

He believed in predestination, and for good reason. Predestination tends to be controversial when applied to children born with HIV, but wears like an expensive suit on millionaire professional athletes. When his career began to sag, Alexander attempted to treat an untreatable broken bone in his foot with prayer and was convinced it would and did work. It didn't.

Of course, this reporting on the life and times of Shaun Alexander, from which the above list of facts is culled from, is nonsense—a portrait of a man through a media filter that changed as its audience changed. The bad brushed to the side when Alexander was contending for rushing titles and scoring touchdowns in bunches. We want to know the ins and outs of heroes until they're not heroes anymore. Without reason but prominence and exposure, Alexander was a role model. You too could be Shaun Alexander if you work hard, thank God, and win the genetic lottery.

Alexander did his best in the way he thought best and achieved more in his field than most ever will. He made three straight Pro Bowl appearances, was named All-Pro in 2005, won the league MVP that same year, and set the single-season record for rushing touchdowns (before LaDanian Tomlinson broke it the next year). Critiquing how he rushed is akin to chastising Pablo Picasso for abstraction. It was beautiful. It just was. It was a time of pride and glory for Seahawks fans, Mack Strong, Walter Jones, Steve Hutchinson, Robbie Tobeck, Chris Gray, Sean Locklear, and Mike Holmgren. We all fed a little bit off what Shaun could do. We all drank in his talent and pumped our fists when he scored and scored and scored.

It was the middle years, the glory years, the years Alexander was so great fans could take him for granted. It ended like fireworks: all fire and ash.

25 The Hidden Zorn

The history of a football team is the history of its players, and the Seattle Seahawks' quarterback history started slinging the ball wrongways 'round. The sixth Ring of Honor inductee in franchise history was a lefty; his chemistry with the first Ring of Honor inductee, Steve Largent, downright sinister.

Starting this book, pre-zygote during Zorn's peak seasons, Jim Zorn was lost to me in a fog of nostalgia. Seventies-era Seahawks fans might have missed Zorn's excellence. Modern fans see his stats and figure he was a placeholder. He was neither a loser nor a placeholder but arguably the third-best quarterback in team history—arguably, the second-best. He didn't have Dave Krieg's longevity, but he didn't fumble like fumbling scored points, either. He didn't have Matt Hasselbeck's success, but he didn't line up behind Walter Jones and Steve Hutchinson, either.

No, Zorn was thrown to the wolves. Expansion franchises chew up and spit out quarterbacks like they chew up and spit out head coaches. The two represent the face of the franchise, and when the franchise loses, fans want to punch that face in the face. Tampa started Steve Spurrier at quarterback in 1976. He retired after one season. Then they tried Gary Huff. Huff was a Chicago Bears quarterback, which translates to "marvelously bad." Carolina turned to rookie Kerry Collins. Collins turned to the bottle. Houston selected David Carr first overall. Carr left a few million neurons on the football field. Thank me for avoiding the Carr crash joke.

Zorn was like Mark Brunell. Brunell didn't have a great arm, wasn't prototypical, and didn't ride into Jacksonville on a wave of hype. He wasn't even supposed to be the starter. The Jaguars' first overall pick in the expansion draft, Steve Beuerlein, was supposed to take the fall. He was experienced at that. Cornelius Bennett once sacked Beuerlein so hard it was immortalized in a painting. Beuerlein was destined to be an expansion quarterback.

Brunell was built to succeed on an expansion team. He was smart and mobile and won in ways that chagrinned as much as defeated his opponents. He wasn't a pure pocket passer but wasn't a scrambler, either. Brunell was an opportunist.

Zorn was that, but better. His career, shorter, but his peak, higher. What is commonly misunderstood about Zorn is that his career began in one of the most hostile periods for passing in NFL history. Before the 1978 season, something commonly referred to as the "Mel Blount rule" was passed. Blount is a Hall of Fame cornerback who played for the (hated) Steelers. He was known for his extremely physical style. The rule commonly bearing his name banned defenders from contacting receivers after five yards past the line of scrimmage. It remade the league.

By efficiency, using the Hidden Game of Football standard, a statistic that includes net yards lost on sacks, rewards touchdowns, and debits interceptions, 1977 was the worst season in post-merger history for throwing the ball. Teams averaged only 4.7 adjusted yards per attempt. In other words, it was a league full of Rick Mirers. From there, efficiency rose dramatically, through the '80s, '90s, and on through the modern game. Teams now average roughly 6.8 adjusted yards per attempt. From his second year through his fourth, and again in his sixth, Zorn performed well above league average. And unlike Krieg or Hasselbeck, he did it despite little surrounding talent.

He did it with bootlegs and smart scrambles, and that essential expansion quarterback ability, toughness. He did it with trick plays and outlet passes, and a brotherly bond with Largent. He did it with resolve and canniness, abilities that made him a great quarterbacks coach two decades later. He did it ugly, but he did it, and left it all on the field. Zorn fought like 10 devils and had nothing

The Seahawks' first star, Jim Zorn, looks downfield during the franchise's first regular-season win, a 13–10 whuppin' of their expansion counterparts from the NFC, the hapless Buccaneers, on October 17, 1976, at Tampa Stadium.

to show for it but the victory. He had piloted Seattle to its first two winning seasons, but it aged him. He was fading fast by his late twenties. Zorn brought respectable football to Seattle, and when the Seahawks franchise was ready to catch up and make a run of its own, Zorn had to step aside because he had given all he could give. He didn't play like a franchise's first starting quarterback, but he suffered like it. His eventual benching ended a long, awkward, painful but hope-instilling first quarterback controversy. And much better football was eventually played. In 1976 two franchises—the Seahawks and the Buccaneers—were born, and those Bucs really did lose 26 straight. We can thank Zorn for his martyrdom. His starting career was short and almost entirely lacking in glory. But Jim Zorn gave a young franchise, built from one draft and the cast-offs of other teams, a little life and a little promise. All it cost him was his dream and his career.

Zero

Zero was not recognized as a number for most of human history. Early civilizations understood zero—"void" or "null"— as a place-holder, but not as a number. It was first recognized as a number by the Indian mathematician Brahmagupta. Before then, one would never count zero. How could one count to zero?

One *could* count down to zero. But what number to start with?

566: Walter Jones starts opposite rookie Will Smith. The first-round pick would eventually establish himself as one of the best players on the Saints' first Super Bowl–winning club, but on this day, he's just an overmatched kid. Jones slaps him around, locks him down, and blows him up. Matt Hasselbeck stands tall, but his Seahawks are shut down. 565, 564…

537: Jones faces off against one of the greatest defensive ends of his generation, Simeon Rice. Rice had 30.5 sacks over the past two seasons, appearing in the Pro Bowl both years. In Super

Bowl XXXVII he sacked Rich Gannon twice and helped harass him into five interceptions, en route to a blowout win for the Bucs. A surefire candidate for Canton, shut down by Walter Jones. Jones holds the edge and provides blind-side protection when no other protection can be found. Hasselbeck is sacked five times, but not once by Rice. Rice cannot even record a tackle.

506: The Seahawks return home against the collapsing 49ers. Jones smacks around Brandon Whiting. Two games later, Whiting plays his last game in the NFL. Ever wonder why 49ers fans hate Terrell Owens? Whiting and a fifth-round pick was their prize for trading one of the best wide receivers in football.

The Seahawks embark on a bye week. I envision Jones following around Hasselbeck, pancaking solicitors, drive-blocking WashPIRG members into nearby WashPIRG members and generally creeping out Sarah Hasselbeck and terrifying Mallory and Annabelle. The quest for nullification is an unyielding task.

473: Next came the hated Rams, Seattle's first NFC West rival. The Rams had been great but were fading. The Greatest Show had turf burn. Marshall Faulk was in his twilight. Marc Bulger had replaced Kurt Warner. It seemed like a shrewd move for a season, but time was testing that theory, and fast. Jones squared off against future Seahawks hired gun Bryce Fisher. Fisher was a low-profile guy but entering his prime. He would have 8.5 sacks that season and another nine for the 2005 Seahawks. He would get shut down that day. Jones would mirror his every movement and trade clubs with counterpunches. Seattle couldn't win that day but started out like a contender. The Seahawks led 27–10 in the fourth quarter, but a defensive collapse sent it into overtime. Seattle lost but won the division. They were beginning their run of dominance behind a tackle who could block out the sun.

437: To Foxboro and to face the reigning and future Super Bowl–champion Patriots. Jones faced a young Richard Seymour. Seymour was in his prime. His mix of size and athleticism was special, and Seymour was one of many irreplaceable parts in the Patriots dynasty. He could fight through two offensive linemen and still challenge plays in the backfield. Seymour was a star. Walter Jones more anonymous than known. The *Boston Globe* asked Seymour what separated Jones from other tackles, and he said with a smile, "Their contracts." Two tackles and zero sacks later, maybe he would revise that estimate. New England won, their 20th consecutive victory, but Seattle fought hard, fought against a 17-point deficit and within three by the fourth quarter, and scared the Patriots. Scared them, and as for Jones, gave their brash superstar something to remember.

384: Seattle had traveled to Patrician New England and fought hard against the Patriots but lost. They were 3–2 but had the mix of high highs and moderate lows of a developing contender. Two thousand four was a tease. The Seahawks were developing something special, but as quickly as they could excite, they would crush your spirit. The Arizona Cardinals were not good. They were bad, very bad, and without their best player, Anquan Boldin. Seattle should have exploded into Sun Devil Stadium and left only atomic shadows in their wake. Walter Jones did, batting around right defensive end Peppi Zellner as a lion would a shrew, and sending another veteran end to his premature retirement. Zellner never played another down after the 2004 season. But Seattle was awful. Matt Hasselbeck was gruesome. Maybe the recent signing of Jerry Rice gave him the yips. He completed 14 passes in 41 attempts and threw for four interceptions. Seattle lost, fell to 3–3, and everyone was just a little worried about Hasselbeck.

342: Seattle picked themselves up, traveled home, and talked themselves into bringing their best against the 1–5 Carolina

Panthers. The Panthers were "better than their record," a victim of the "Super Bowl losers' curse," who "had to be taken seriously" and "couldn't be underestimated." The Panthers were, eventually, a good team again. In late October they were still reeling from the loss of Steve Smith. Jones was matched against a fading Mike Rucker. Rucker had been a Pro Bowler in 2003, but at 29 was already losing a vital step. He peaked at 12 sacks in 2003, but had just a split sack to that point in 2004. Jones didn't dominate, and Rucker was able to stay active, but he did shut him down. Seattle won and again crawled over .500.

311: Seattle traveled to San Francisco. Jones had left his brand on Whiting and was instead matched against Tony Brown. Brown recorded half a sack, but not against Jones. He was a defensive tackle playing out of position. Jones had the power to pop and the quickness to do it twice before Brown blinked. Seattle dropped 42 on the 49ers and then traveled to St. Louis for a rematch.

280: Jones got his second go at Fisher and finished him off. I am sure the two had some kind words to exchange next season. Fisher: "I am honored to play on the same team as you, Walt." Jones: "Do I know you?" Jones did his job, but Hasselbeck completed only 15 passes in 36 attempts, and Seattle fell again to their division rival.

244: It was Trent Dilfer versus A.J. Feeley in an epic struggle for terrible. The Dolphins were 1–8 but took the fight to Seattle. Jones squared off against Jason Taylor, and Taylor squeezed out half a sack, but from the strong side. Jones polished up and pushed the Dilfer-Hawks through to victory. It was victory and continued pursuit of the NFC West or loss and shame, agony, and irrelevance.

213: Shame, agony, and irrelevance rode in on a train from Buffalo and broke open a can on Qwest Field. Hasselbeck threatened to forever humiliate anyone who ever supported him with another POS showing. Jones would not abide. He squared against another emerging talent, Aaron Schobel, and shut him down, allowing only a tackle assist. Drew Bledsoe reminded Seahawks fans that beating New England had brought them Rick Mirer, and the score was lopsided enough that J.P. Losman made an appearance. It was a shameful day for the Seahawks, but Jones quietly kept the streak alive.

173: Then it was hosting Dallas and dropping a bomb on Marcellus Wiley.

131: To Minnesota to drop another pile on Lance Johnstone.

94: At New York Jets, Bryan Thomas held without a stat.

58: Home and another clobbering of Bertrand Berry.

31: Seahawks battle the Falcons for their playoff lives and the NFC West title. It's a close game, and the two teams battle back and forth until Seattle takes a third-quarter lead that holds through the fourth and to victory.

0: Jones completes one of the most incredible runs in NFL history, shutting out pass rusher after pass rusher and helping lift Seattle to the playoffs. What is the number zero? In this case, testament to 566 snaps of doing everything right.

27 Visit Seahawks Stadium

I had a punched-in-the-kidneys feeling from living the high life late into the late night with some Bears-fans family of mine. I was standing beside Shrug. We were in Qwest. My back hurt and my blood felt full of broken glass and a headache was peaking over an ibuprofen wall.

You would never know I was deliriously happy.

My dad was a mechanic, and a nefarious pay system known as the flag system kept us in perennial poverty. He wasn't real good with people, either. So it was bad jobs and unemployment. We never had money to go to football games. We didn't have the money to go, much less attend.

Tickets are expensive. Parking is expensive. Food is expensive and bad. I started to feel faint, and so I bought some nachos. I was sort of packing it down to try and stay standing. The chips were chips, but the cheese sure wasn't cheese.

I walked back and nodded at Shrug. We continued to not say much. He had season tickets and knew the regulars, and there were some head nods and small talk, and I wasn't brooding but could have been mistaken for as much. Shrug was doing me a solid for writing on Field Gulls. It was my second game at Qwest and only the second football game I had ever attended.

Qwest is beside Safeco. You pay and park and get out, and all around there are Seahawks fans. I think that is the moment I first felt really happy to be there. I am a satellite fan. I live a few hundred miles from the team, and in Portland there is a mix of civic pride and neutrality that makes it no more a Seahawks city than Portland, Maine. I've looked for Seahawks bars, and you'll find some in Vancouver, but Portland is fiercely independent.

That kind of sucks, honestly. When the Blazers get going, it's the talk of the city. Not like local news, which I couldn't give a flip about, but on the tongues of the people. People care and know what's up, and it's vigorous and tangible. Portland is a Blazers town. Exclusive.

I feel very distant from Seahawks fans. There are some in the area—pockets—but there is never mania or crippling disappointment. The Portland area sports shows almost revel in the team's failures. They thumb their noses at Seattle. It's a Boston–New York vibe, but less abrasive, more passive-aggressive.

Grass: Safer Alternative or Gateway Turf?

The Seahawks pioneered FieldTurf in the NFL. Paul Allen paid to install it in Husky Stadium, and players were so impressed, he installed it in Qwest, too. Astroturf was famous for causing fluke injuries and shortening careers. FieldTurf was a welcome improvement. It still is nowhere near as safe as grass.

A study published March 11, 2010, indicated that one of the most severe injuries an athlete can endure, a complete tear of their anterior cruciate ligament (ACL), is 88 percent more likely on FieldTurf than on natural grass. On top of that, serious ankle sprains are 32 percent more likely.

Health is an essential part of winning football. Injured players perform worse, and when a player is lost, most teams lack the depth to adequately replace him. Allen introduced FieldTurf because it was better than the alternative, but if players are still endangering their health by playing at Qwest, it creates a significant disadvantage for the Seahawks. Not only are they more likely to lose their own players, but they are less likely to attract free agents.

So when you walk toward Qwest on game day and all around you there are jerseys and excitement and whole families schooled in Seahawks tradition, it's like nothing else. You can tell people are up for this, and they are locked in, and there's nowhere else they'd rather be and all that jazz. Maybe it's a cliché, but when it wraps around you and permeates your senses, the original thought is alive again. You don't feel so stupid for caring so much about something so abstract as a professional football team.

I can't remember exactly where our seats were. I have been near the field and I have been up high, and either has its charm. Something about the live experience, the speed, but also the authenticity, reconnects you with the sport itself. On TV, you are seeing football as television. There is running commentary and updated information and shifting camera angles, and after a while you do not even feel like you are watching a football game but a football show.

From the stands, it is up to you what you see. You surely do not see it all or well. The mystery feeds the excitement. Everyone around you bleeds Blue, so it's a partial crowd. A mob, really. You don't really think through if a penalty was right or not, only who it affected. There is a collective spirit, and it's partisan. Who will cast the first stone? Why, I'd be honored.

It was a great game. Seattle won. I will forever remember, late in the fourth, Seahawks up seven, Chicago ball, watching Patrick Kerney come free around right end. There was a bad feeling about that drive. Bernard Berrian had made a miracle one-handed catch, and big plays trigger panic in a crowd. Kerney came around right end and fought through a double team. Rex Grossman was holding the ball away from his body and absently plodding toward the left flat. Kerney closed, stripped, and Darryl Tapp recovered. Qwest erupted. That pretty much ended it.

I recorded the game and rewatched it and that play many times, but the memory that persists is the memory from the stands. The angle, the tininess of the players so far away, the stillness around me, and the way everything seemed to develop so slowly. I can still recall perfectly within my mind, but it's like a silent film, grainy, jumpy and short. Yet it sticks like nothing I have seen on TV ever has. Just a few seconds, but as important to me as XL or the NFC Championship.

28 Learn to Love a Rookie

Tim Ruskell had his guys. They needed to be virtuous, preferably soft-spoken, and God-fearing. They needed to be from a major conference, and if that conference was the SEC or PAC-10, ever the better. Mostly, they needed to scout well. A Ruskell guy could be too slow, too small, a workout blunder, but they had to shine on the field. They had to play football.

It was a surprisingly controversial approach to building a roster. Ruskell was always at odds with fans and media types who wanted bigger, stronger, and faster Seahawks, but circa April 2007 he was high on his horse and impervious to most criticism. Back then, his controversial stance of drafting good football players instead of good athletes was spoken of in the reverential tones afforded ahead-of-their-time thinkers and artists. How quickly that changed.

Brandon Mebane was too slow and too small and wouldn't survive the jump in competition. I was sure of it. Rest assured I was on the Internet within minutes, registering my disgust throughout the world. It was 2007, I was young and foolish and didn't know half as much about the NFL as I wanted to, or wanted people to think I did. My opinions were one part my own and two parts the garbled nonsense proclaimed on high by the great media megaphone.

Stupid as I was then, I didn't take my opinions for fact. There was no John Morgan brand to sell, no need to sell an overweening, helmet-headed public persona, no need to don the false pretense of expertise. And so, I wasn't fond of the Mebane pick, but I was open. Two years later, Brandon Mebane was my go-to jersey on game day.

It started in preseason 2007. If you don't watch the preseason, start. Watching kids battle their hearts out for a chance at Sunday football is compelling. Mebane was compelling. He smashed through a double team and forced Charlie Whitehurst to lob a panic throw toward the sideline. He drove Paul McQuistan into Dominic Rhodes and blazed the trail to a Darryl Tapp safety. Late in the fourth quarter, he bullied through a Packers double team and engulfed rusher Corey White.

Me! Bane! and the Art of Nicknaming

I have a real thing about nicknaming players. I end up typing the same names so much that eventually I just go nuts and start calling them something else. I think nicknaming is a kind of art. A good nickname should be concise, specific, and fresh, but also in some important way match the player himself.

I got to calling Brandon Mebane "Me! Bane!" because I would sit by myself watching tape, and Mebane would stir something inside me, and I would just shout it out like that. "*Me! Bane!*"

The worst thing that can be done is forcing a nickname. A website I respect, Kissing Suzy Kolber (kissingsuzykolber.uproxx.com), decided to nickname Chris Johnson during his record-setting 2009. They decided on Zulu Cthulhu. I cannot fully express how awful and stupid that is. Why would someone opt to say "Zulu Cthulhu" instead of Chris Johnson? It's long, it's forced, and the literary reference has no connection to the actual player. A nickname must be natural, but maybe most importantly, it must make sense to you. The only way it will ever stick is if you believe in it yourself and continue to use it no matter how stupid others find it.

Whitehurst, McQuistan, White—it wasn't an all-star cast of victims. It was the preseason, and most football fans would rather mow their lawn than suffer four quarters of jobber football. But it was the beginning of something special.

Mebane made the 53-man with ease but was buried deep on the depth chart behind Chartric Darby. Soon I was on a crusade. Darby was Old Man Football, a respected veteran, a seasoned pro, and about a thousand other vague clichés, but he wasn't Mebane's equal, and he didn't deserve to start over the kid. But football, however much we would like it to be, is not meritocratic. Starters have inertia. Darby was the starter for the Super Bowl–champion Tampa Bay Buccaneers. He started most of the season for the Super Bowl–bound Seattle Seahawks.

That prestige doesn't force double teams and it doesn't stuff rushers. It doesn't do much but populate a fan's memories and inform a coach's superstitions. In fewer snaps, Mebane was doing more. Through my love of Mebane and honest desire to see him entrusted with more, I was learning the game and learning to love it more. I could see what made a good defensive tackle through what Mebane did. His first step was lightning-quick. His power, lower center of gravity, and active hands kept the pile moving backward and stopped rushing lanes from forming. Opponents needed to double- and sometimes even triple-team him, and that freed other defenders to run to the ball carrier or attack the quarterback.

Brandon Mebane was doing special things, and I wanted to spread the word. I recorded games and watched snaps in slo-mo. *Me! Bane!* was born. I was a crusader who would rather die on my sword than leave my work unfinished. People needed to know about this kid, his power, his presence, his passion, and his deserved place as a starter.

As these stories often go, Mebane earned his spot not through eminent ability or my tireless prosthelytizing, but by chance. Darby was injured six games into the 2007 season and placed on injured reserve. Mebane was the next man up. He stepped in, and not coincidentally, the Seattle Seahawks' defense took off. The run defense became stifling, and the pass rush able to take over a game.

The winner wasn't Seattle or Ruskell or even Mebane. The winner was me. I developed a bond with a player through a common cause. From being an unknown to being a young stud, on the lips of head coach Mike Holmgren, announcers of all ilk, and eventually, even the local media. Brandon Mebane has yet to make a Pro Bowl and maybe never will. He's not a star; he's my favorite Seahawk ever. It just took some time, some work, and some devotion.

You'll never love a team until you're truly a part of it, and though I will never line up in the trenches, never grab the game-winning touchdown, break tackles to the end zone, strip-sack and recover for six, or jump a route and high step to pay dirt, I did my little part to become a part of Seahawks Nation. And after months of spreading the word, years of pumping his name, I know, once you've fallen in love with that player, seen him from obscure mid-round draftee to young star, you're hooked. You're a Seahawks fan forever.

The Student

Lofa Tatupu was more than a great middle linebacker. He was a star. (Sadly, I must revise that status to the past tense. I must move Tatupu down the list of 100. I must settle myself with his premature retirement.) Diehard football fans may care as much about their team's stars as they do their team's assigned parking spaces, caring only about winning and who helps the team win, but a star has value that transcends the gridiron. There are hard, cold truths: stars sell jerseys, and Tatupu sold his share. There are strategic considerations: Tatupu gave Seattle a national presence, and that makes Seattle more attractive to free agents. There is something else, though. Tatupu was a hero, an entry point for fans young and old, someone to care about beyond his football contributions, someone to admire.

Tatupu embodied what fans want. He is not the biggest or most athletic player, but he played with intensity and fire. He was not the most ostentatious player. Tatupu is the anti-Boz of Seahawks history, arriving not hyped but derided and proving his doubters wrong rather than right. Tatupu was a vocal leader, and people are attracted to leadership to a fault. Did Tatupu's manic gesticulations and booming commands put Seattle in a better position or make the Seahawks more aware? We may never know, but a defense needs a leader, if not to command them then to give purpose. Fans understand this instinctively. Humans understand this instinctively. It's an ugly shame sometimes, how even the basest leader can rise in a vacuum. So smart, dedicated leadership like Tatupu's was revered.

He transformed Seattle's defense his rookie season, or so it will forever be remembered. Tim Ruskell transformed Seattle's defense, patching holes at end, tackle, corner, and obviously linebacker, but Tatupu became the face of Ruskell's greatest achievement. As opinion of Ruskell soured, Tatupu continued strong, became independent of that first success, and if a complement to a good team in 2005, Tatupu became essential to the 2007 team that won because of its defense.

All that, the shine, the reputation, the beginnings of a legend, does not do Tatupu the player justice. He was more than just a figurehead; he was great and seemed destined to future greatness.

Tatupu was a connoisseur's tackler. No, he didn't always wrap. And yes, after bulking up, his arms retreated into his thickening torso. But unlike flavor-of-the-week middle linebackers who tally great tackle totals on struggling teams, Tatupu's contributions were constant, precious. At its heart, the tackle is both a good and misleading stat. It is good because it is concrete. A tackle is something we can fully understand and witness on a football field. Something more abstract, like pass defended, is up to the scorer's interpretation. Did the defender deflect a long completion to force a punt? Did the defender misread an errant pass and bat away what should have been an interception? Was the defender just nearby an uncatchable pass? Pass defended doesn't account for any of that, tells us nothing about why the pass targeted the receiver in the first place, or the quality of the coverage. It doesn't even inform us exactly what happened. So a tackle is a tackle—concrete—but a tackle is not of equal value to any other tackle, no.

Lofa tackled downhill, striking a rusher at the earliest point possible, taking efficient angles and if not always wrapping, almost always slowing, jarring, facilitating his team's collective gang tackle. Many linebackers produce huge tackle numbers by landing thrift tackles that do not help their team. Consider, a rusher runs left, behind left tackle. Tatupu attacks the gap between the tackle and the guard and attempts a difficult tackle behind the line of scrimmage. If he succeeds, the tackle not only stops the ball carrier, but stops him for a loss. Now consider another middle linebacker. He does not attack the gap, but takes a long angle to the left flat. Instead of attacking the ball carrier, he corrals the ball carrier, capping his run but not stopping the play from achieving success. Yes, he sinks the tackle, and if he always pursues like this, he will amass many tackles, but they are bad tackles that do not help his team.

Tatupu attacked. By storming through gaps and tackling downhill, he pushed the rusher toward the sideline, turning the sideline into a defender and moving the rusher in a direction no rusher ever wants to run: laterally. Tatupu attacked. He didn't always target the rusher at all, but worked in concert. Tatupu exceled at jamming the lead blocker into the hole and creating an uncontested path to the rusher. Tatupu and LeRoy Hill double-teamed backs like few linebacker duos in the league.

Tatupu was a smart and versatile pass defender. He dropped deep but adjusted quickly to plays underneath. His read and reaction time were so good that his field speed was excellent. He didn't blaze—Tatupu was not a burner—but he appeared in pass lanes and punished quarterbacks with poor vision. On one exceptional afternoon, Tatupu intercepted three passes from quarterback A.J. Feeley. The final came with the game in the balance. He intercepted a pass from Jake Delhomme in the NFC Championship Game. On each, Tatupu did the same thing: hid out in a zone, disappeared from the quarterback's read, then burst into the throwing lane, and undercut the route. That incredible anticipation not only feeds his field speed, but his return ability. For a guy who was considered too slow, his average interception return was remarkable.

Brian Urlacher shot up the boards when he ran a 4.59-second 40. Tatupu dropped after a 4.83. Yet Urlacher averaged only 14.7 yards per interception return, and Tatupu 23.2.

That is the essential Tatupu. He was not the greatest athlete, but he was good. He was not the hardest hitter, but he was jarring. He was not the fastest player, but he was quick. He was the most prescient defender I have ever witnessed. Tatupu took tired tropes about being a film junky, about being cerebral, and fulfilled them. He did not claim but play with undeniable, unimpeachable football intelligence.

And then, in the off-season of 2011, he was cut, and with good cause. NFL football, like all professional sports, puts incredible demands on its players. Unlike most sports though, football players rarely enjoy a protracted phase as has-been and sinecure. The sheer strangeness of some sports lends them an opaqueness. How many outs must a batter make before it is clear he is not in a slump but washed up? Football is primarily a sport of athletic ability, freed of some of the more witch-crafty elements of basketball and baseball. Tatupu, it seemed, could no longer string out wide to stop runs to the outside. He had seemed to be a player that played above his talents. In fact he was a player that had maxed out, playing exactly to his capacity like so very few ever do. When injuries sapped him of that vital edge that separates professional from talented wannabe, it showed fast and definitively. I can only imagine those dreary final practices. His mind screaming his body to do what it just couldn't anymore.

Ah Tatupu! Ah humanity!

30 2005 NFC Championship Game

Matt Hasselbeck was quick, evasive, and could make accurate throws on the move. I barely remember the 2005 NFC Championship Game. It was such a thrill, and Seattle was up so much so early, the whole day became a merry blur in my memory. I remember being unbelievably happy. I remember Seattle shutting down Steve Smith. I don't remember much else, and I wanted to. So I sat down with my notebook and started rewatching every play, frame by frame. What was it that Seattle did that Carolina couldn't stop? Was it just Smith? Surely not.

Seattle did lock down Smith. The Seahawks bumped him off the line and doubled him over the top. It was not a novel strategy, though. New England had attempted the same method in Super Bowl XXXVIII, but Smith was still able to receive for 80 yards and a touchdown. Moreover, Jake Delhomme passed for 323 yards and three touchdowns. New England assigned multiple players to slow Smith, succeeded somewhat, but could not succeed in slowing the Panthers' passing attack.

Seattle grounded the Panthers' attack by controlling the middle. Rocky Bernard had the best game of his career. He consistently tore through the Panthers' interior, shut down passing lanes, and pressured Delhomme. Delhomme tried to slide outside the pocket and, in doing so, opened himself to exterior pressure. Bernard had two sacks and another discounted when Seattle accepted a holding penalty. Delhomme couldn't step into his passes. He doesn't have the kind of quick release or cannon arm to overcome interior pressure, and pressure was on him every time Bernard was in.

Alexander was at his drunken-boxing best. People underestimate just how quick, agile, and, yes, powerful Alexander was. He

Mr. January Goes Cold

The Carolina Panthers' Jake Delhomme had the highest postseason quarterback rating in NFL history when he took Qwest Field on January 22, 2006. In 2003 he was clutch against the Cowboys, sensational in St. Louis, solid at Philadelphia, and hung 323 on the New England Patriots in a three-point Super Bowl XXXVIII loss. He then blazed into the 2005 playoffs, cutting up the Giants and dropping 319 on the Bears in compiling an overall passer rating of 108.4. Midway through the third quarter of his NFC Championship Game against the Seahawks, his rating stood at 1.6. He eventually boosted it with some garbage-time stats, but finished with an embarrassing 34.9.

Maybe the Seahawks broke his brain. Mr. January struggled from then on, playing in only one more postseason game, another blowout loss against Arizona, in which Delhomme threw five interceptions and finished with a 39.1 rating.

never looked like he was working hard, but that is because he's a natural. Alexander would weave and cut three times to make one yard. There was better blocking and better holes, but Alexander was at his absolute peak. He was nothing like the back that would return next season. It must have been frustrating for opposing defenses. The lines he would take were outrageous. I started charting his path, and he wasn't north-south, he wasn't east-west, he wasn't one cut and go, Alexander was running a squiggly line. He broke arm tackles because defenders would get seasick tracking his progress. It was all ankle-breaking, floating, and effortless-looking, but awesome.

The greatest story of the NFC Championship Game was Hasselbeck. Maybe it's the baldness, the perennially worried face, the modern dodderer some confuse his former self with, but I forgot how athletic and graceful Hasselbeck once was. He wore out Julius Peppers. He stepped through pressure, could pass from any position, could begin a rollout, sense an end coming free, abort, and throw with zip. Hasselbeck was once an athletic and intelligent scrambler. He had great footwork and made honest-to-God open-field moves. He was confident in his reads and could throw all over the field, just supremely in the moment as only the greatest can be. Hasselbeck had the perfect mix of touch and zip, and his passes appeared in windows he'd never think to attempt anymore. He was a different man. A younger man. Decline denial only seems more odorous after watching just how great he once was.

Mike Holmgren frowned and frowned and frowned until Craig Terrill hit Smith from behind and forced the game-ending fumble. That was Mike, and that was the attitude he fostered in the entire team. Seattle ran away with the game, but to see their scowls, to see their intensity, their frustration with every minor failure, you would think they were being beat. Holmgren motivated by making players believe perfection is possible. In its pursuit, something so close was attained.

This game is like candy for a Seahawks fan. It didn't have the in-the-moment intensity of XL. Tom Rouen made it interesting, too interesting, when he punted a line drive to Smith and created an easy touchdown return. That was short-lived. The defense was on it. Lofa Tatupu was quick and limber and could as easily shoot a gap and drop Nick Goings for a loss as jump a route and pick a pass. He did both before Goings led with his helmet, knocked Tatupu woozy, and knocked himself out of the game. Lofa continued, but there was a kind of before and after.

It was the greatest moment in the history of Qwest. The greatest triumph in Seahawks history. It was easy like an Alexander run. It squiggled and sawed its way past defenders and led to paydirt. The season ended with a lot of heartbreak and disappointment. It ended with maybe more frustration and outrage. Before all that, there was a moment when every Seahawks player was at their very best, and the plan came together like never before and perhaps never again.

31 Mike Holmgren, General Manager

On balance, he succeeded almost as well an any Seahawks fan could hope. He lost battles but, with a little help, won the war. Mike Holmgren ended as Seattle's all-time leader in wins with 86, led Seattle to the playoffs in six seasons and five straight, and to its first Super Bowl appearance.

It took a little while.

Holmgren replaced much disrespected head coach Dennis Erickson. Erickson was actually building something of a contender. His 1998 Seahawks had a better point differential than any of Holmgren's first four iterations. It had a talented defense that Holmgren dismantled. Erickson added Walter Jones and Shawn Springs. Holmgren added Lamar King. General manager Mike Holmgren was the first employee Seattle had to fire to become a contender again, but it took a lot of blunders to determine that.

As I mentioned, Holmgren headlined his first draft with Saginaw Valley State defensive end Lamar King. King was a big man. Draft experts projected him as a strong-side defensive end. Against a right-handed quarterback, typically the strong-side end is the lesser end. Pass rush is traded for presence. That is not an absolute. Reggie White spent most of his career attacking from the strong side. But it's typical, and White was atypical in almost every way.

King was never quite the bust he was made out to be. Exaggerated expectations and the onus of replacing a legend lost King and Holmgren the PR battle, but he had a not-terrible career for a 22nd overall pick. King started his second season but battled injuries. Those injuries never stopped and, like Brian Bosworth,

Sawed-Off Shotgun

Mike Holmgren was always a very conservative coach. He did not like trick plays and rarely implemented them into the playbook. When Pittsburgh ran a reverse to Antwaan Randle El that ended in a touchdown pass, the play was a staple in their playbook and well-known enough that color commentator John Madden hinted at it the drive earlier. Seattle seemed unprepared, and they probably were, because their own passing game never practiced it against them.

Perhaps more telling was his reluctance to implement the shotgun in Seattle's offense even as the formation became an essential part of the modern offense. In his final season in Seattle, Holmgren began dabbling in the semi-modern formation. As if to prove his reluctance, the Seahawks mostly snapped out of what is called the "pistol," a sort of half-shotgun, half-dropback.

eventually cost King his career. He left the league a young man. Holmgren had little to show for his first ever pick. It became a trend. If King was only a modest failure, the rest of Holmgren's draft made up the difference. The closest it came to producing a regular starter was Antonio Cochran, and Cochran was a fringe starter. His next draft was similarly thin. It produced two very good players, Shaun Alexander and Darrell Jackson, but no other starting-caliber talent.

Holmgren found some success, suffered some bad luck, made some blunders, and never was able to fill out a roster, but the problem wasn't that Holmgren was outstandingly incompetent, but that under Holmgren, the Seahawks' power structure was monolithic.

Consider Ahman Green. Green was selected by Erickson the season before Seattle hired Holmgren. Holmgren didn't like him. He had the stink of ex-coach on him. In 26 attempts in 1999, Green fumbled twice. As a head coach, Holmgren couldn't tolerate that. As a general manager, Holmgren should have been able to see through his own frustration. It was 26 attempts, so small a sample it's hardly a sample at all. Holmgren couldn't see through it. He made snap judgments like a coach. That's bad business.

Holmgren was fed up with Green and wanted to cut the talented young back. He was talked into trading him for pennies on the dollar. When all was said and done, Holmgren traded away an All-Pro rusher for a second-string and soon-retired corner. He had too much power and too much responsibility; the power made him irrational, and the responsibility made him sloppy.

Could he have been an effective general manager if he was just a general manager? Maybe. His three years in Cleveland serving as Browns president would suggest no, maybe not. But Paul Allen wanted head coach Mike Holmgren, and general manager Mike Holmgren was a compromise and an experiment. It was a failure.

Seattle fell to 7–9 in 2002, and pressure mounted for general manager Mike Holmgren to step down or head coach Mike Holmgren to be fired. He assented to a demotion, begrudgingly. Holmgren was never very happy with his replacement, Bob Whitsitt. Goodwill born through Super Bowl XL was quickly burned through, and his relationship with Whitsitt's replacement, Tim Ruskell, was adversarial. Perhaps if he had a John Schneider, someone that was his organizational inferior and who ultimately bowed to Holmgren's decisions, but who could lessen his burden, temper his often pigheaded decisiveness, and broaden the overall perspective of the front office, Mike Holmgren, GM, would have succeeded. We'll never know. Which is too bad, because if general manager Mike Holmgren was a failure, head coach Mike Holmgren was a smashing success.

32 The New Prototype: Legs and Arms

Quarterbacks used to be arms, and then arms and brains, and now arms and legs and brains.

On Arms

When describing a quarterback and apart from those descriptions that are near universal (height and weight, specifically), you start by describing the quarterback's arm. And "arm" means that particular composition of muscle, bone, tendon, and ligament that allows some strange men to throw a leather oblong spheroid at high speeds and with amazing accuracy. So vital is the notion of arm strength and accuracy to the evaluation of a quarterback, few but the strongest armed quarterbacks are considered by the NFL.

When Matthew Stafford was only 17, scouting firm Rivals ranked him as the best overall pro-style quarterback prospect. On that same list were: Josh Freeman, Sam Bradford, Christian Ponder, Andy Dalton, Colin Kaepernick, and someone who didn't turn out to be a quarterback, but might matter to Seahawks fans: (Kam)eron Chancellor.

Mel Kiper Jr., well-branded NFL celebrity and recipient of more scorn and revilement than Pol Pot, famously predicted Stafford would be selected first overall. And he was in 2009, and perhaps more importantly, he's actually succeeded, or mostly anyway. Stafford's reasonably mobile and reasonably smart it seems, but his arm strength sets him apart.

There's a first order common sense to this. To wit: if the ball is mostly invulnerable between being thrown and being caught because it is thrown too high to interfere with, and the catching receiver receives full credit for whatever yardage is achieved through the air, and most of the defense is crowded up along the line of scrimmage, near the quarterback, and far away from the receiver, why not throw it as far as possible? This maximizes potential yards gained and minimizes potential defenders to beat. Which common sense is why, to this day, teams still love the deep pass, and why many vertical pass offenses, like New Orleans Air-Coryell derived attack designed by Sean Payton, are still very popular.

But there are subtler reasons arm strength is so valued and also a subtler kind of arm strength to be considered.

On Legs

Legs, that is, scrambling, called runs and now the read-option has been a work in progress. Many legs quarterbacks have been rumored to break open the NFL, establish a new standard for greatness in quarterback play, but none have really succeeded.

A quarterback that can scramble effectively creates a schematic bind for the defense. Defenses want to, as best as possible, anticipate what kind of play the offense will run, run or pass, and counteract it. A scrambling quarterback can turn a pass into a run. Deep into a pass play with pass rushers well behind the line of scrimmage, no gaps contained, and linebackers and defensive backs scattered in coverage, a sudden surprise run can be almost unstoppable. Kaepernick proved as much against the Seahawks in the 2013 NFC Championship Game. He averaged 11.8 yards a run on 11 carries.

A running quarterback also helps the running game even when he isn't running. The ability to decoy with the quarterback overtaxes the defense. Defenders attempting to stop both back and quarterback can be drawn away from their gap by this decoy. Marshawn Lynch's sensational 2012 season should in part be credited to Russell Wilson's ability to scramble.

Most successful NFL quarterbacks are strong armed quarterbacks. And many of the legs quarterbacks have had strong arms.

But until now, those two attributes were largely discrete. Some players could switch between them, but no player could use them simultaneously. We had the strong armed quarterbacks like Drew Bledsoe that couldn't move or escape pressure but could kill you deep. And on the other end of the spectrum, we had the mobile quarterbacks, some that could also kill you deep, but all who could escape a deteriorating pocket and potentially dash through a disorganized secondary for a big gain.

The New Prototype

What sets apart Wilson from Randall Cunningham and Michael Vick is the ability to turn pass to run to pass. This fluidity creates something like a built-in play action, and one that isn't part of the play design, but one that can be called on in an instant.

Football is essentially a game of running and passing—those two things. Every play, an offense must choose one of the two, and the defense must attempt to respond. Some defensive play calls are neutral. Defenses like the Tampa 2 attempt to be universal in scope and not vulnerable to either. But all defenses exist as planned and as executed. And once the ball is snapped, only as executed.

When a quarterback with breakaway speed and game-breaking agility like Wilson begins to test the edges of his pocket and threaten scramble, a defense must begin to close around him. This crashing toward the ball carrier is exactly what a play fake accomplishes. So a running quarterback doesn't need those defenders to close within 10 yards or anything. He only needs their attention to be split, their spacing to become disorganized, or their focus to lag.

Most scrambling quarterbacks before Wilson could pass when they were asked to pass, and begin to run when they thought they needed to run, but not exist within a between state that could become run or pass in a moment. It is, needless to say, an exceptionally difficult thing to do. It is hard enough to throw accurately on the run. What Russell Wilson does, and with some regularity, is take the snap, make his reads, sense pressure and where that pressure is coming from, begin to scramble away from pressure, make his *new* reads. (Once a quarterback's broken contain, most notions of route are out the window, and receivers are charged with the duty of just scrambling free.) He can decide whether a receiver is now open enough that a possibly awkward and somewhat inaccurate pass is advisable and then near instantaneously decide to tuck it and run or stride into a pass and zip it to an open man. It's maddeningly hard to defend and not a gimmick but a fundamental evolution in how the game is played.

Irrational Exuberance

Similes of a sort plague professional sports. These similes have a lifespan. Never have I read an NFL Draft hopeful compared to Sammy Baugh or Frank Nesser. So these similes can be harmless nostalgia. Some Sunday, some *Sunday Night Football* broadcast, not long ago and immaterial to the point, Dan Patrick compared LeSean McCoy to Gale Sayers, placing Barry Sanders as a kind of midpoint. Patrick framed this comparison by saying he does not compare anyone to Sayers lightly. The restraint seemed sincere. Patrick was an adolescent during Sayers' brief prime.

What Patrick meant was not so much that McCoy and Sayers are equivalent or even similar players, but that the effect McCoy and Sayers produced in defenders are equivalent. That's okay. That's a fan being a fan. But similar similes rear their ugly heads come NFL Draft time, and unlike Patrick's warm comparison of a former great to a present great, these similes attempt to be definitive, and so doing, are wildly inaccurate.

The secret's out about Russell Wilson. He is now a championship-winning quarterback, and the drive to find the next Wilson, the next Kaepernick, or Cam Newton, will only intensify. It makes quarterbacks little but their constituent parts, arms and legs, height and weight, stats and stereotypes and manages to lose the very essence of the player. I can say this with some confidence because Wilson is very, very special, very, very rare, and though the NFL misevaluated him, put too much emphasis on his height, that doesn't mean players of Wilson's talent are just lying around.

In all likelihood, another Wilson will never appear again in my lifetime. Some players of similar value but different particulars will play like Wilson, sure. Wilson, in fact, plays a lot like some other successful quarterbacks that preceded him. Aaron Rodgers is a valuable if by no means game-breaking scrambler, and his ability to break contain, draw in the defense, and throw on the run has been invaluable to the Packers. Andrew Luck is somewhat similar. Ben Roethlisberger, whose name pains me even to type, accomplishes a similar disorganization of opposing defenses by being so damn hard to tackle. But even among accomplished quarterbacks of a similar athletic profile, like Newton and Kaepernick, Wilson is unique. Those two can scramble and throw, sometimes. It's within their arsenal. But Wilson is preternaturally natural within that crazed few seconds and is able to initiate this run-throw potential many times a game. Yet rarely gets hit hard and rarely turns the ball over through fumble or interception.

His arm, remarkably strong and accurate; his legs, remarkably quick and agile; are governed by a brain that coordinates those tools. And it's his brain and its ability to switch so quickly and so seamlessly between seemingly contrary impulses, that makes Wilson a once-in-a-generation player.

33 Ronin

Kenny Easley sued the Seahawks for ending his career and endangering his life. The case was settled out of court. He suffered kidney failure and charged that an overdose of Advil administered by the team trainer and team doctors was the cause. Even the great cannot control their ending. Still, Easley's ending was particularly ugly. He wasn't injured but ill, and wasn't hurt in battle, but poisoned trying to recover.

Easley was great, everything a fourth overall pick is supposed to be and, despite the brevity of his career, one of the greatest Seahawks of all time. He was plug and play, good from his rookie season and astounding through his prime. He tackled like a demon, possessed good ball skills, and had rare interception return ability. His coverage wasn't always pure, and as his injuries mounted, his performance could be inconsistent, but it's petty to take something so amazing, clean, and beautiful and find faults.

He was an international star before breaking through as a pro. In the annual Japan Bowl, Easley set Yokohama Stadium ablaze with two interceptions and a fumble recovery. The Japan Bowl was a college all-star game, but cool. And Easley was a star among stars. He looked into Indiana quarterback Tim Clifford's eyes and said, "Stop. Stop crying. It's pathetic." But Clifford continued to sob. "I hate pathetic people. I'll have to kill you."

It was while still in Japan that Easley learned of the Seattle Seahawks. I guess he probably knew the team existed, the way some contemporary NFL fans are aware of the Cleveland Browns. (I thought they moved?) But it wasn't until this particular moment that he learned the team had substance, an identity. Thanksgiving

Kenny Easley looks to lateral one of his two interceptions against the Raiders during a 35–13 win in October 1987 at Los Angeles Memorial Coliseum.

of 1980, a USO station broadcast Seahawks at Cowboys. Easley happened upon the game in progress. The Seahawks were down trailing a mere 51–0. Easley joined the Seahawks in a bleak period between Patera's antics and Knox's success. He proved his vigilance right away, recovering four fumbles. Easley was an intimidator. He tackled with passion and power, and more than that, need. Easley had to make every tackle. He needed to be everywhere. It was his goal to intercept every pass. He excelled in coverage, and long into his retirement insisted he should have played free rather than strong safety.

He could cover a tight end in man cover or patrol the deep zone. At 6'3", 210, he was huge for his time. That made him not just an intimidating tackler, but an intimidating presence deep. Joining a terrible team he didn't want to be a part of, he finished the 1981 season by promising Kingdome fans a better future. The Seahawks clobbered the Cleveland Browns in Week 17, and Easley intercepted two passes, returning one for a touchdown.

His 1982 was a bit like Ken Griffey Jr.'s 1994. Easley had four picks and two sacks in just eight games. He was peaking. The Seahawks' defense was coming together. Seattle finished 4–5 in the strike-shortened season. They just missed the NFL's postseason tournament. There was promise, the feeling of something great dawning.

Like Griffey, Easley's health couldn't honor his talent. He did not miss many games, but he was constantly banged up. He had muscle spasms in his back and rib cage. He hurt his knee. He hurt his ankle and double-downed on the Advil.

If a man can make a career out of a single season, Easley was Hall of Fame bound after 1984. He had 10 interceptions, two returned for touchdowns. He returned punts. Easley emerged as the best defender in the NFL. The Seahawks had the best pass defense in football, and despite losing Curt Warner in Week 1, despite enduring Franco Harris, surged to 12–4. It was their best record ever up to that point. It was the best season of Seahawks football before 2005, and Easley was the team's best player.

As early as 1985, Easley wasn't the same. Things were breaking down. He suffered the ankle injury that would end his career. His interceptions diminished with his quickness.

In 1986 he hurt his knee, compensating for his ever-injured ankle. In 1987 he hurt his shoulder. Following the strike, he suffered irreparable damage to his ties to Seattle. Easley was the Seahawks' player representative. After the strike, fans booed Easley and the returning players. Easley was hardcore. He held nothing back when he heard Jim Zorn say he would cross picket lines. Zorn was out of the league, out of the union, but Easley did not care. Zorn only threatened that unforgivable act; Steve Largent actually played. The team's offensive leader and the true face of the franchise not only disrespected the union, but disrespected Kenny Easley.

Easley forced a trade to the Phoenix Cardinals. Seattle got Kelly Stouffer in return. During a routine physical the Cardinals discovered severe kidney damage. If you watch game tape, you can see his failing health hanging on him like a monkey. The man who was cover-quick, agile, and explosive into his tackles was getting beat. I won't elaborate, though. It's a rotten thing to elaborate the ugly of something so beautiful.

Ronin refers to a samurai without a master, a samurai that refuses to take his own life after his master dies or dismisses him. This life maybe seems romantic to a modern reader. But in feudal Japan, *ronin* were mostly thieves and mercenaries. Rather than be independent of a master, *ronin*—prohibited from legal work—were subjugated by all of society. Easley claims he took 15 to 20 Advils a day to treat an ankle injury, and for three months. A teammate of Easley's claimed that Advil were kept in large dispensers, and players self-administered with little supervision. Easley sued the Seahawks organization and the case was settled out of court. In 1990 he received a transplant kidney. According to Easley, no former teammate and no member of the Seahawks organization called to offer sympathy or congratulations after the surgery. For a very long time and because of mutual bitterness and resentment, Easley was shut out of the Ring of Honor. He was a great player, that only ever played for one team, and during his time he was beloved by fans and fellow players. But team owner Ken Behring and Behring's cronies throughout the Seahawks front office resented the uppity Easley. For a very long time, he slipped into the shadow of retirement. But in 2002, 15 years after a life-threatening ailment ended his career, Easley was enshrined in the Seahawks Ring of Honor. The great warrior had returned, not to his master, but to his home.

34 Greatest 3-4 End to Ever Play?

Jacob Green is among the greatest players in Seahawks history, but one who somehow is neither appreciated by the mainstream media nor Seahawks fans. A few things work against Green. Most notably, he started his career on a bad team and without much talent around him. His original position was at left defensive end in a 4-3. In 1980 that was as much a run-stopping position as a pass-rushing position. Tackle stats were not recorded at any point in his career, and so we can only guess how "active" Green was. Sacks were not recorded until his third season. Seattle never received a lot of attention, and very good players like Green didn't register with the national conscious. What really hurt Green most was that he played end in a 3-4, and 3-4 ends have always struggled for recognition.

Green was selected 10th overall in the 1980 draft. It was a good class, headlined by Hall of Fame offensive tackle Anthony Muñoz. Green was a stud at Texas A&M. He had a staggering 20 sacks and 134 tackles in 1979. Maybe if he had been drafted by the Cowboys or 49ers he would have been inducted into the Hall of Fame. Instead, Green became a great player for an often lousy franchise.

He didn't start with great surrounding talent. To his right, there was defensive tackle Robert Hardy. Hardy played just four seasons and was off the Seahawks and out of the league upon the arrival of Chuck Knox. To Hardy's right was Manu Tuiasosopo. Manu was a solid and versatile player who stuck with Seattle for a little while before moving onto greener pastures in San Francisco. Tui is best known for his progeny: Marques, Zach, and Matt. Green's first bookend partner was Bill Gregory, but Gregory lasted only a season alongside Green in Seattle before retiring. Manu moved over in 1981, and then some other players substituted in at tackle, but it wasn't until 1982 that the Seahawks achieved any kind of consistency. That year, they added Jeff Bryant, and Bryant would be Green's partner in crime for the rest of Green's career.

Seattle lost a lot his first three seasons, and losing tends to take sacks away from pass rushers. Teams can run more, and run more in pass situations. They can run shorter pass patterns and shorter drops for their quarterbacks, and that shortens the time the pass rusher has to close in and tackle. In blowout wins, especially, an opponent stops taking risks entirely, and a pass rusher plays most of the game with little chance to do more than pressure the opposing quarterback. Why risk a fumble? Check down. In Green's first three seasons, Seattle lost by two touchdowns or more 12 times. Unofficially, he tallied 18.5 sacks in his first two seasons. That's good for any 23- or 24-year-old, much less on a weak defensive line, much less on a bad team.

When the team became good, Green suffered a different setback to his recognition. Chuck Knox ran a 3-4, and ends in a 3-4 arrest tackles rather than rush passers. The all-time sacks list is populated by two specific types of players: ends in a 4-3 and linebackers in a 3-4. Whether you're Rickey Jackson or Reggie White or Lawrence Taylor or Bruce Smith, you either played end in a 4-3 or a linebacker in a 3-4. Of the 24 players that rank ahead of Green on the all-time sacks list, only Neil Smith played most of his career as a 3-4 end. If we include Green's unofficial sacks from '80 and '81, he is the all-time sacks leader among 3-4 ends. With that designation, it's arguable that Green was the greatest 3-4 end to ever play in the NFL. Maybe Howie Long was better, but it's debatable.

What really separates Green from Long is image. Long played for the Raiders, won a Super Bowl, and retired into broadcasting and movies. He was the big white guy with the flattop and the smile and the stage presence. Green was quiet everywhere but on the field. When you run a 3-4, you are supposed to have a linebacker who functions as your primary pass rusher, your Derrick Thomas, DeMarcus Ware, or Lawrence Taylor. They say Taylor changed the game forever—that he was so fast, every team had to protect the blind side like never before. Seattle never had that player. Knox never found a true pass-rushing complement to his line. Fredd Young had a couple good seasons, but that was it. Tony Wood was supposed to provide speed around the edge, but he was just average. No, it was Green, Nash, and Bryant, and those three were the heart of the Seahawks' defense.

Seattle often rushed three, and Green was constantly fighting through double teams. He would smash through the right tackle and right guard and tight end if they dared, and break through and punish the ball carrier. Fans didn't always know about Green, but opposing coaches did. He was athletic and indefatigable. You don't see too many ends who can make plays sideline to sideline like Green did. He was powerful and had great technique and could fight through blockers with terrifying ease. Green had to be game-planned around. He was that kind of disruptive force on every snap.

Seattle could win without Warner and it could win without Easley, but Green was irreplaceable. Luckily, he never got hurt. He missed two games his rookie season with a leg bruise and then not another game until Week 10 of 1989. That would be the final game he ever missed for the Seahawks, but also among the final games of his career.

There is no sure way to determine how great Green really was. Was he the best 3-4 end ever? Green deserves mention if not outright recognition. Was he the greatest defensive lineman in Seahawks history? Him or Tez; him or Tez. Was he the most indispensable player for Chuck Knox? Green, Krieg, or Largent, yeah. Green was incredible. And if you get your hands on some old game footage, he is worth watching the entire game through. He probably isn't famous enough to be inducted into the Hall of Fame, but were it the Hall of Game, there would be a Jacob Green bust where a Joe Namath bust now stands. It's all right if others don't get it, but if you're a Seahawks fan, you know Green or you don't know jack.

35 The New Prototype: Brains!

When we respect someone or at least respect their accomplishments, we want to know who that person is. Now I don't mean what type of chip that person eats, or what music they listen to, or what primetime television they enjoy. If that's all there is to a person, then Facebook has truly won. No, we want to know how they think. What motivates them? What is it like inside their brains?

Russell Wilson's legs and arms make it possible for him to become an NFL quarterback, but it is his brain that makes him great.

By certain standards, Wilson is a smart young man.

By the standards of athletic competition, he's brilliant. When Wilson is snapped the ball and drop backs and works through his progressions, he is not calculating the speed of the opposing cornerback and how quickly he may make up the distance between him and the receiver. He is not counting pass rushers, determining whether his blockers are winning or losing their matchup, interpreting the stress points on the line, and determining where it may fail, where he may scramble to. He is not knowingly calculating an equation beyond the scope of a super computer. He is instead comparing moment to moment his precise impressions of what's going on and comparing those impressions to thousands upon thousands of similar experiences and feeling what he can't know. The comparison is unconscious, but the feeling is conscious.

We, of course, all have this ability. There's no possible way to anticipate every possible outcome of traffic speeding, swerving, changing lanes, taking exits, and on-ramps off and onto the 405. No one determines the force vector of a semi versus a compact. We don't account for wind resistance, the exact stopping power of our brakes, our personal reaction time given our less than restful five hours sleep, or how quickly our foot may jam on the brake pedal. Over years and years, we accrue a library of similar experiences, and intuitively act. We pick up subtle swerves and know maybe that driver is impaired or distracted. Sometimes I know someone is about to change lanes or take an exit and I can't confidently explain why, but I know and most times I am dead on.

Achieving dead on decision making while driving is a routine part of American life. There are good drivers and bad drivers but not too many incompetent drivers. Sadly, bad drivers are often just competent drivers that have become arrogant in their competence. It's hard and maybe not helpful to remember every second behind the wheel, that this is unnatural. This is the most potentially deadly thing I will do all day. And so bad drivers are often just Brett Favre-ing it: having fun out there, taking their immense responsibility a bit too lightly, sometimes to tragic effect.

Football, by contrast, is always welcome to remind its young quarterbacks just how crazy dangerous and difficult what they're doing really is. A single hard sack is enough to remember for a lifetime. Hundreds and hundreds are enough to forget a lifetime.

Wilson's juicy, chess-club brain is above average at executing what we think of as brainy stuff. That's neat. I derive some tiny satisfaction from Russell Wilson being a nice, smart young man and so wholesome. But where Wilson's brain excels is at doing brawny things.

What we call his coordination—that's his brain. His poise under pressure—brain, too. Take that brain, put it into the body of Wilson, and incredible plays are possible.

In the second quarter of the 2013 NFC Championship Game, 8:07 on the clock and Seahawks down 10–0, Seattle took the field in a spread formation. Wilson was in shotgun. Zach Miller played right tight end, and Marshawn Lynch was aligned as the left tight end. Both stay in to block. This backfires.

Snap.

8:06—The 49ers send five pass rushers. Seattle's three receivers run toward six defenders.

8:05—Sensing the futility of the play call, Wilson begins to loop toward his right. He looks downfield. He looks ahead to see three 49ers pass rushers matched up against three Seahawks blockers. He may have to run, but for now pressure is still safely far away.

8:04—Miller is losing his matchup with Ahmad Brooks. Linebackers Dan Skuta and Patrick Willis are in an underneath zone, but as the play extends, it's obvious both have committed to containing Wilson. This means seven 49ers are within five yards of the line of scrimmage.

8:03—Wilson lowers his body into a sort of crouch, as if he's about to scramble, but seeing something break down in the 49ers secondary draws the ball back up and resumes buying time for his receivers, looking to pass. To his blind side, nose tackle Glenn Dorsey has slow played James Carpenter and Max Unger. Unger and Carpenter have counted him out and are standing around as if the play is dead. Dorsey creeps slowly past Carpenter until he has the angle and begins sprinting toward Wilson.

8:02—Wilson sees him and waits for the lumbering defensive tackle to over-commit.

8:00—Once Dorsey is within a yard or two, Wilson doubles back, taking a looping path toward where his pocket, now totally disintegrated, once was. Brooks is now free from Miller and charging hard toward Wilson.

7:58—Wilson has only just ended his looping motion and has less than a second to read his receivers before Brooks fires into him, knocking him hard to the turf. It's enough.

7:55—Baldwin is behind the deep coverage tandem of Eric Reid and Donte Whitner. He stands 56 yards from where Wilson throws. Brooks has run some 15 yards and is charging at Wilson with the kind of force rarely achieved by a pass rusher. But Wilson zips a pinpoint spiral straight to Baldwin and he receives, barely able to pivot and turn upfield before Reid and Whitner have closed the gap and mobbed him for the tackle.

Brooks slams into Wilson. He rolls with the hit and bounces up almost immediately to see if the pass has found its mark.

The play results in a 51-yard completion. With one play Wilson and Baldwin have improved their team's chances of playing in the Super Bowl by 28 percent.

We tend to think of this as a series of incredible physical accomplishments, but Wilson wins this play with his mind. In 10 seconds he has sensed the futility of Darrell Bevell's play call and improvised. He has judged the quality of his protection and determined where pass rush might come from. He has stopped the 49ers underneath defenders from sagging deep and created potential holes between the deep and short zones. He has lured Dorsey into being overaggressive and used Dorsey's own immense inertia to evade him. He has tacitly communicated to Baldwin to scramble open. And in that final split second, he reads Baldwin as open, whips through a long, low throwing motion to deliver a beautiful deep pass and whatever microseconds remain, braces himself for a massive hit by Brooks.

Many a quarterback before Wilson could run. And many a quarterback before Wilson could throw on the run. But what makes Wilson a generational talent is the incredible brain power he possesses that allows him to quickly switch between run and pass, cognizant of all the crazy variables so involved and do so with startling accuracy. It's not book smart. It's battle smart.

36 Be Irrational

It's good to be rational, right? I mean, licking a light bulb and expecting candy is no way to go through life. Feeding oneself when hungry, defecating when it's called for and in the designated place, trusting in gravity, these are good things, I think. Rational, rational is good. It helps glue the days together, it keeps one gainfully employed and out of straight-jackets, it ensures life and a certain quality of life. But too much rationality is boring, ludicrous.

Humans stay in a kind of perennial adolescence. We stay curious. We learn, forever, or as much as forever grants us. We never lose our appetite for fun or play. We turn 50 and rock out in our convertible. We believe youth is an eternal good and God-given right.

When I say, "Be irrational," I do not mean punch your neighbor in the face and place your porkpie under his mouth, awaiting a torrent of Skittles. I do not mean eat dirt and drink ball bearings. I do not mean, even, buy lottery tickets. That's dumb. I mean, never let reality stomp on your hopes.

When Seattle's down two scores in the third quarter, yeah, we get it, they're probably going to lose, but don't be that guy, don't be the self-important dude dying to declare time of death. Believe. Believe, goddamnit. Because believing in the face of certain failure is virtuous, is essential. Believe and believe, and if you're in the stands, scream your lungs out. And about that...

Don't be civil in the stands. Be a lunatic. Believe you cheer your team on to victory. Despise that rival fan arrogant enough to show up in your stadium in his colors. Revile him. Cast stones—figurative stones. Well...yeah, probably shouldn't cast real stones.

Cheer every first down until the last. Go berserk on big plays: chest-bumping, voice-killing, last-day-on-Earth berserk.

Love every member of the team, and like a wayward brother, have a heart-to-heart with the struggling ones. I loved you, Brian Russell. I loved your stupid face. And you sucked. Oh—oh! Did you suck. But until your very last, I wanted better for you. I wanted my every criticism to blow up in a wave of forced fumbles and pick-sixes and form tackles and good angles and *grit.* Grittygritgritgrit.

Leave it all on Sunday and take the loss to heart and let go and care again on Monday. Know every name on the roster and know, just *know* that Bruce Irvin is about to turn the corner and become beastly. Sweat the little things. Sweat the assignments and the blocking and the coverage and not just the great reception, great run, great pass.

Waste a bunch of money and buy a jersey and wear it around like a little boy, and instead of feeling shame, buy another. Own shirts and sweatshirts and vintage caps emblazoned with the Seahawks logo, the old logo, the embarrassingly outdated logo. Join a fansite, join Field Gulls, tell me I'm an idiot, and then engage in a purely rational discussion about the merits of the outside linebacker versus the stand-up end.

Don't be a dilettante. Don't be a box-score skimmer. Know the names, know the spellings, know the hype and refute it. Have a player you like too much and whose every mistake you both ignore and suffer; and have a player or two you root to get it right, one day, finally, get it right, and know they never will, but never know. Don't check in during the playoffs and be that guy during the off-season with a brain full of bad ideas and misconceptions.

We're fans. We never signed up for rational thought. We agreed to heartbreak and bad breaks and broken promises, and we did so willingly, because it speaks to our crazy soul and our crazy need to belong and be part of something big, that's unpredictable like the weather and can kill you like lightning or rain down sunshine.

So be irrational. Believe in the face of doom. Shudder in the face of victory. Love something cold and indifferent that doesn't know your name and can never love you back. Soar with the wins and swallow hard with the losses, and see someone in a 49ers jersey and hate them. Start every season with dreams of the Super Bowl and end every season with dreams of next season. Start every game with dreams of victory and end every game with dreams of next week's victory. Start every play with dreams of long receptions and sacks and broken tackles and forced fumbles and end every play with confidence in the next.

1976

Critics, art critics, rock critics, critics of all kind are prone to the chronology trap. Elemental, seminal—pick your bad adjective—it may be essential, but that does not make it paramount. Sometimes, what comes first is almost arbitrary. More often than not, what comes first is a matter of definition. Try asking a punk rocker who originated punk music. Ask a metal head who coined the expression "heavy metal music." Many credit William S. Burroughs. Burroughs' father made the family fortune reinventing Blaise Pascal's adding machine. Or he didn't. Because nothing done can be redone, and every new thing is some kind of first. In the words of Heraclitus, "The sun is new each day." And so, yes, 1976 was the first season of the Seattle Seahawks. But little but a name and some few longtime fans connect those Seahawks to the present day Seahawks.

Before 1983, before 2005, before the team became Super Bowl champions, there was 1976, and good God, 1976 was thorns and thistles. Seattle molded their cellar-dweller from the discard pile. It was dust to dust, indeed.

I decided to honor the Seahawks' origin not with a sequentially significant placement within the book, but an essay befitting its actual value. None of the following is an accurate presentation of the events that preceded or took place within 1976, but an extended metaphor for the season itself.

In 1972 the city of Seattle conceived a thing, a thing without head or heart, constructed from the bodies of the deceased, all arms and legs. This thing was not meant for practical purposes, but sport, and would be pitted against others of its kind. They conjured and schemed and assembled but could not bring it to life. They tried fire, but fire was anathema to the creature. They tried persuasion, but it would not listen. Finally, they brought their creature to the gnarled and hoary wizard named Rozelle and pled, "Give it life! Give it purpose! Give it pigskin and painted lines!" Rozelle twirled his long, tangled brows and decreed, "Your creature feeds on money. Feed it and feed it, and it shall rise."

And so it was in 1972, the city first began this boondoggle we would one day call "Seahawk." It constructed an arena for its brutal games, and as millions were poured into the Kingdome, and as the concrete monstrosity took shape, the creature began to stir. The location for the Kingdome was selected, a mudflat stolen from the sea, and concrete was poured, millions of gallons, and a distant heartbeat was heard. Lloyd W. Nordstrom dedicated his riches, hired John Thompson and Jack Patera to tend to it, teach it, and give it purpose.

Seahawk took the field on August 1, 1976, to face the warped and neglected thing known as 49er. It was a troubled period for 49er. A post-Nolan period for 49er. Seahawk and 49er slugged it out, threw brutal haymakers and crushing jabs. It was exhibition football, but neither team wanted to lose. 49er feared the embarrassment of losing to a rookie team. Seahawk feared if it started losing, it might never stop.

Seahawk lost. It lost and lost, battered and splattered by more seasoned creatures, and away from battle it retired to dejected meditation. What brought its miserable self into existence? Why did others look at it and look away? It felt low. It felt ugly, and it was. It was sloppy and deficient. Parts were old, and others too young. But some things were standing out, shaping into something better. It had a left arm that could throw and two hands that could catch. Patera gave it inspiration, and what it lacked in grace and coordination, it overcame with guile.

It trudged across country and ended in Tampa. The beast known as Buccaneer was every bit its equal in ugliness, loss, squalor, and desperation. The two saw each other, saw themselves in the other, and hated what they saw. The two stepped into Tampa Stadium desperate to destroy the other and whatever they shared. It was a grueling, miserable affair. Buccaneer struck first and last, but Seahawk prevailed.

It won, and three weeks later, it won again. Not by a little, but handily, mercilessly brutalizing Falcon at home. And the Kingdome shook. And the fans poured praise and affection on Seahawk. And it stood straight up. And the action created fissures across its scaly body. And through those sores the city of Seattle could see something beautiful beneath.

38 Touchdown Alexander

We save our praise for the funeral. Shaun Alexander was broken. His foot was broken. His career was ending. Shaun Alexander was plodding toward his ending. He didn't know it, maybe Mike Holmgren didn't know it, some fans refused to know it, but it was written in every approach, every plant, every panic spin to the turf. It had been too easy, and when it left, well, that was excruciating.

Many braced themselves with denial. His performance had changed so suddenly, though his style looked so much the same that it was common for people to blame not Alexander but the offensive line. The 2006 line was in rough shape, but could it account for how far he had fallen and how fast? Seattle plugged in Porkchop Womack at left guard, then center Chris Spencer, and when Robbie Tobeck went down, moved Spencer to center and played Rob Sims at guard. Sims took the brunt of the fans and Holmgren's abuse. His major sin was not being Steve Hutchinson.

Alexander broke a bone in his foot, and doctors determined nothing they could do or his body could do would make it heal. It was not enough to keep him out very long, but it eroded his already depleting ability. For so long, Alexander had excelled on a knife's edge. Every dangerous cutback, every run bounced outside, every weaving, wending, and unsteady run was beautiful but fragile and, when broken, bad.

All the bad habits he had developed and obscured with his talent came to haunt him. It was no longer acceptable that he couldn't receive. His hesitant, spotty pass-blocking became a liability his rushing could not compensate for. From MVP in 2005, Alexander became one of the least valuable players in football in 2006.

For the first time in his career, he averaged less than four yards per attempt. He had nearly as many fumbles as touchdowns. That was probably the greatest insult for a player who had always prided himself on his ability to score.

Denial took on another form in 2007. Alexander was only getting worse, and suddenly Seahawks fans of all stripes insisted he was never very good. It wasn't Alexander, but the offensive line that blocked for him. And true, Walter Jones and Hutchinson formed an unparalleled pair, but Alexander was the essential complement that revealed their ability. Jones and Hutch excelled at blocking in space, and Alexander's cutback ability and vision maximized their pull-blocking.

The real shame of the 2007 season was that Holmgren fiercely denied Alexander's decline. The 2007 Seahawks were the last gasp of a great run and were held back by not being able to run at all. It wasn't like the team lacked an alternative, either. Maurice Morris averaged 4.5 yards per carry. He couldn't block any better than Alexander, but he could receive. Morris allowed Seattle to start a full 11 on passing plays. Alexander offered so little as a receiver and blocker, for hundreds of downs the Seahawks were playing a man down.

He was cut in the off-season, given a charity run with Jim Zorn's Washington Redskins, cut after 11 rushing attempts, and then excluded from the league. Occasionally, a story would percolate about how Alexander still wanted to play. It was just sad. He wanted to play, but no team would offer him a contract. He had hit that wall that eventually all rushers hit, and because it had been so natural for him for so long, and because he got away with bad habits blocking and receiving, and because he had always been a gifted rusher, losing his wheels hit Alexander extra hard. He was great, and then he was gone.

Fidelity

Benjamin Franklin said "Time is money," and if only the reverse were so. How much would the 40-year old man spend to be 18 again? No, time is most precious. Having nothing we can spend it on of sufficient value, we squander it. Or so it seems.

One day, maybe soon, the Seahawks will win, maybe even win it all. Win the Super Bowl! And on that day, you will not catch a pass, you will not throw into a tiny window, or jack up a DB to spring a jailbreak screen. You will not run or jump or tackle. And as a bunch of young men—Seahawks by circumstance—are celebrating and the blue and green confetti rains down littering the field, you will not be with them. No one will call you world champion.

The win will matter in proportion to the time you wagered: the losses, the heartache, the triumph, the trust and determination and resolve and love you invested. This win, it could be cheap. You could run outside your home and bang pots and pans down through the neighborhood and know 10 weeks ago you didn't know the name of the starting free safety. Or maybe not know the way a cheating man forever knows of his infidelity and may say "I love her fully now," but never say "I've loved her with my all for all our years." There is shame and there is incompleteness. And maybe there is no deep shame in straying from a team when that team is particularly bad. Finding ways to keep one's love for football alive when cheering for Seattle is but a dreary obligation. You don't need to remember Frank Gore rushing for 212 yards to enjoy the Beast Quake. One doesn't need perfection to escape disloyalty and damnation. But as what we call "realization" arcs neuron to neuron, lighting up your brain with that new unique sense of ultimate victory—Super Bowl victory!—it will go where it has been, it will connect memory and memory, and that convergence, that pinnacle moment of being a fan, will be fed by years of hopes dashed, hopes fulfilled, players loved, players lost, seasons lost, and seasons you died inside hoping to save.

Satisfaction, however brief, ecstasy, however passing, rich laughter and high-fives and loud music and good beer, all the cheapest thrills, and the realization a week, two weeks, two months, 10 years from now that the Seahawks have won, after all that hope and frustration and above all time, time, time—that is the reward of being a loyal fan. Along the way it would have been easy to short-cut the dream for something practical and hitch a ride on this or that bandwagon. It is said anything worth doing is hard, but maybe it is the difficulty which makes something worth doing. Because when you're done, if you're ever done, that doing has become a part of you. All that time spent, all the setbacks and hardships and moments of screwing up your courage and sticking out the fourth quarter of a blowout, it is all redeemed. Fidelity is not external of us. Love is not external. Passion is not external. Years of being a Seahawks fan are wrought onto our brain, our very self, and never a second squandered, no matter how long it took for our time to be redeemed.

40 The Pick Man

Dave Brown was good, right? He was the best player Seattle selected in the expansion draft, was taken in the first round by the Steel Curtain Steelers in 1975 and was available because that team had secondary talent to burn. Pittsburgh literally had a Pro Bowler at every starting secondary position in 1976. Getting a Dave Brown was almost like a loophole in the expansion draft. He wasn't a reject, but overabundance.

Brown arrived in Seattle, started right away, and continued starting for the next 11 years. He started for Jack Patera and then started for Chuck Knox. When Brown left for Green Bay, he started first for Forest Gregg and then Lindy Infante. In fact, after leaving Pittsburgh, Brown never played in a game he didn't start.

Sure as he started, he did something magic. In 14 years in Seattle and Green Bay, Brown snagged 62 interceptions and at least one every year. He ranks eighth all-time. Among players who played in the post–Mel Blount–rule NFL, he ranks fourth, behind only Rod Woodson, Darren Sharper, and Ronnie Lott.

It sounds like a fairy tale—Brown, a hidden talent, obtained for nothing. Brown, a core player on a building team. Brown, something to watch before there was anything to watch. So what gnaws at me?

Watching a football game, it's pretty easy to see the front seven. We can see the blockers block and the pass rushers pass and linebackers tackle and runners evade. We understand receivers and quarterbacks because they produce robust stats, but also because they initiate action. For a receiver to receive, he must first flash open, and getting open is the primary job of a receiver. So yards reflect ability. Receptions reflect ability.

That hardest riddle to crack in football analysis is how to evaluate a secondary. A standard TV angle obscures the majority of their actions. In fact, we mostly see corners and safeties when they've made a mistake. We know they've made a mistake, because their receiver is being targeted. We know they've made a mistake precisely because we see them at all.

Interceptions can be had because of great coverage or lousy but lucky coverage. Some players fixate on interceptions and abandon coverage attempting a pick. Season to season, interception rates vary wildly. We can scout ball skills, but we can't anticipate the exact situation that allows for an interception. Over a career, a player like Brown surely proved his ability to snag picks, but at what cost?

Brown started for 14 seasons, and yet, he rarely ever started for a good pass defense. If we use adjusted net yards per attempt as our standard, a stat that factors in sacks and interceptions, he played for two elite defenses. The 1982 Seahawks ranked third, but in a strike-shortened season. The 1984 Seahawks ranked first. No one expected Brown alone to make Seattle elite, but apart from those seasons, the Seahawks were rarely even good. In 14 seasons, teams Brown played for ranked 17th on average. Seventeenth out of 28. It wasn't just because Brown's late '70s Seahawks are dragging down the average, either. He played in just four above-average units his entire career.

It wasn't like Brown was a lone talent among jobbers and scrubs, either. Jacob Green joined in 1980 and Kenny Easley in 1981. The line was considered the strength of Seattle's defense, and so I don't assume Brown was suffering because lack of a pass rush. But maybe he was. Even if I could find sack totals from before sacks were recorded, and even if I adjusted them for passing attempts and game situations, sacks still only vaguely represent overall pass rush.

For almost any argument there is a counterargument of equal merit. He only played in one Pro Bowl. The Pro Bowl is often a lousy indicator of ability. Brown played on lousy pass defenses. We can't be sure that was because of Brown. He started for 14 years. Maybe he was just better than the alternative. It isn't like Seattle was content with Brown. It drafted Terry Taylor in the first round of 1984, and Patrick Hunter in the third round of 1986. Of course, a team always needs defensive backs, and how do we know the Seahawks were replacing Brown instead of another corner?

We don't.

Dave Brown's career ended in Seattle when Chuck Knox traded him to Green Bay for an 11th-round pick. The modern NFL Draft doesn't even have 11 rounds. Of course, Brown was the oldest starting corner in the NFL by 1987, so it's not like Seattle was selling high. He started in Green Bay for three seasons and had 12 more picks. Three years after he retired, he was the second player ever inducted into the Seahawks Ring of Honor. The city and team appreciated Brown, and that counts. But I can't tell you if he was a great player or overvalued for his interceptions. I can't tell you if he was good in coverage. I found an article saying Stanley Morgan lit Brown up for 161 yards receiving. The author, Michael Vega, says Brown "had just been reduced to toast." Reduced to toast, how often? Reduced to toast, rhetorical flourish? I don't know.

So is Dave Brown an underappreciated star who was hidden in Seattle? Was he the 1980s version of Dante Hall? Would he have been better on another team, or was he hurting the team he was on? I don't know.

41 Pete Carroll and the Power of Failure

Pete Carroll is the second oldest head coach in the NFL. The one coach older than him, Tom Coughlin, does not look so much older as considerably more weathered, stressed, and tortoise-like. Coaching is an unpleasant profession, combining some of the worst qualities of management with the worst qualities of celebrity. The coach cannot hide. The coach must be available to the media. The coach is recognizable, and unlike an actor, cannot hide from his screwups. Flipping through Netflix's random picks section, you will not stumble upon a blowout loss to the Vikings you didn't know Carroll coached. And when Carroll in 2009 led USC to a 55–21 loss to Stanford, his accountability didn't end with his bosses and underlings. Millions of USC fans blamed him, too.

But Carroll's ability to control the outcome of that game was limited. He could help pick the personnel, and coach those players and scheme and play call, but down-by-down, second-by-second, it was up to the individual Trojans players to know and win their matchups. Carroll could only watch. Could you imagine Van Gogh dictating brush strokes on *Starry Night*? Coaches are often accused of being control freaks. The job in fact requires a suspension of control. A suspension of control but an acceptance of near-total responsibility. The drive to control is a drive to reclaim control. Curfews, draconian discipline, inspiration poster-like mottos, most are symbolic gestures. A hyper-compensation for the fact that come game time, the left tackle wins his matchup or the quarterback gets hit, the corner reads the double move or gets burned deep, the tipped pass tumbles harmlessly to the turf or it doesn't. When breaking a bronco, a tight grip is necessary.

In this way football coaches are like old generals.

Men think highly of those who rise rapidly in the world; whereas nothing rises quicker than dust, straw, and feathers.
—Augustus William Hare

Athletes represent a certain kind of rigid, unforgiving path to greatness. Gymnasts are washed up by their early 20s. Most track athletes by their mid-20s. And few athletes of any sport survive even into their mid-30s. But those paths that emphasize skill above talent favor those who persevere, and to persevere, by nature, is to fail again and again. There's a rather popular Samuel Beckett quote hot on the public consciousness about "failing better," which has always sounded a bit too much like "if at once you don't succeed, try, try again," for my tastes. I prefer this:

The purpose of life is to be defeated by greater and greater things.
—Rainer Marie Rielke

Always exuberant, always competitive, Seahawks head coach Pete Carroll celebrates during his team's Super Bowl XLVIII victory.

Not to win, but to lose. The winning is implied by the losing to "greater and greater things," but it is the losing that reminds us, the battle is never truly won.

But is that failure merely a coincidence, a hard to avoid toll that comes from constantly striving, from dreaming big dreams? Or is it essential?

It is almost necessary to cherry-pick in matters of anecdote. There is no absolute way to determine how best to mold a man's character. But it's not hard to find examples in which a little failure might have served the successful well. M. Night Shyamalan's first movie was a roaring success, but he's tacked downward ever since. Never being proven, as in tested through great trials, Shyamalan maybe never truly knew what it was he did well, nor what it was he did exceedingly poorly. Early success often creates a sense of invulnerability or of genius. Once someone is sure they are a genius, there is no hope for them. A genius may justify almost anything, any crap, any bad idea, or slipshod construction for they are a genius. And geniuses, like the God of the Middle Ages, are mysterious in their workings and not to be questioned. Perhaps he was warped by early success, too.

Carroll took a traditional path to head coaching success in the NFL. He's an older guy. He's worked as an assistant and a coordinator. He has been fired numerous times. The Seahawks' success in 2012 finally pushed his record as an NFL coach above .500.

He has failed over and over again.

The Always-Competing-est Guy You'll Ever Know

People who seek success in a field often look to those who have succeeded for shortcuts. One day, some years ago, I happened upon a list of tips compiled by *The Guardian* newspaper from writers for writers. It was called the 10 rules of writing or something, and it was stuffed with oddball peccadilloes like don't use adverbs (that's Elmore Leonard's thing, IIRC), and don't suck up to Vladimir Nabokov, and something about only bad writers think they are good writers.

But wouldn't a better suggestion be: don't go to some accomplished writer, commercially or critically accomplished, and seek some formula for success but write, write, write, and know success is always unlikely and a damned fool's reason for writing? I write because writing makes me something more vital than happy or successful. Writing makes me well, or, better said, not writing makes me nuts.

I figure this is how Pete Carroll feels about coaching football and competing. And that's why I love him. The End.

P.S. Part of the loving of doing rather than accomplishing something is a lack of interest in shortcuts. Why shorten a journey you love?

In Mike Sager's piece for *Esquire*, Carroll described himself this way: "I'm a competitor. That's my whole life since I was three, four years old. I tried to beat my big brother in every game we played. All of his friends would just laugh at how hard I'd try. I'd be fighting and scratching and crying and whatever it took, from the time I was a little kid."

Like Walter Jones and Stephen Colbert, Cortez Kennedy and Aaron Rodgers, Carroll went to junior college. You either understand what that means or you don't, I suppose. All men but Jones and Tez can and have been accused of arrogance. Yet all men are accomplished, and all men seemingly sense the fragility of that accomplishment because not one ever took their status for granted. Not one sat on their laurels.

Sir John Pete Carroll French

People do not typically reach their professional peak in their 50s. Carroll is now 62, and his peak has, well, peaked higher. Most people I have known reach their late 20s and, to quote Homer Simpson, "remember when they believed in things." For most, that is simply because they get sick of failing. It seems noble and just from the outside, but stories like, say, the band Guided by Voices, who were a band for nine years but couldn't even hold down a bar band gig, and put every aspiration on hold for this seemingly doomed dream, only seem noble and just in the retelling. The living is hard, discouraging, tough to justify to others, and difficult to sustain.

Carroll probably could have made it as a television analyst. He's handsome, personable, and engaging in front of a camera. But he loved the guys, throwing spirals with the guys, eating McMuffins and shouting obscenities, and the way sport's mercilessness to the old is also its kindness to the young. Pete Carroll loves competing and winning. No matter how he may say otherwise, he, too, must then love losing. Steady jobs like spittin' clichés for Fox Sports are damnably steady, and no one ever wins because no one ever loses. It's a paycheck and go home life, like most lives.

Forty-nine and unemployed, still figuring out who he is, who he wants to be, because he hadn't let his prejudices and preferences and routines ossify inside him, Carroll took another in a countless series of losses, this time losing his job, and with that fire, that passion, became one of the greatest head coaches in football history. He didn't have to. He was blessed with a whole range of steady, high-paying job opportunities devoid of risk. But damn would've he missed the losing. Damn he would've missed the strength, conviction, will, and urgency only found in utter defeat.

42 The Super Bowl XL Conspiracy Conspiracy

Conspiracies: some are innately prone to belief, and some find ourselves prone because we're righteously angry and need a goddamn explanation.

My gut reaction to Seattle losing Super Bowl XL was that the game was rigged. When two teams of sufficiently equal ability square off in a winner-take-all match, it does not require much manipulation of the rules for an interested party to determine the winner. A game like Super Bowl XL would then not be a rare instance of game fixing, but one in which the preferred outcome was sufficiently difficult enough to orchestrate that the fixing became evident. Right? This game, football, so dependent on multiple judgment calls every snap—what constitutes holding by the offensive or defensive lines, what constitutes pass interference, what is roughing, etc.—is ever susceptible to judgment, and judgment susceptible to bias and worse: fixing. That somewhere deep within NFL headquarters, some team of analysts decided it would be better for the NFL brand if the Steelers were to win and so issued the "All-Star" crew of Super Bowl officials, a short list of ploys by which important plays were reversed through penalty, and certain penalties were ignored, is only far-fetched to the truly naïve. This stuff happens. History is littered with darting eyes and close quarters; people allied through scheme, secrecy, and bad intentions. And I believed, well…

My wife sometimes still reminds me of my words that Sunday: "I will never watch another football game."

And I meant it.

But I've thought a lot since then.

Victim Seeking Assailant

A team that loses the Super Bowl is a dead team, no matter how far and gloriously they marched. Initially, I think, most what I wanted was for the Seahawks to have not lost, to have won. If I felt spittin' pissed, it is because I thought the game had been stolen from Seattle by biased and perhaps crooked officiating. This was the 2005 Seahawks. This was prime Hasselbeck, prime Tatupu, the most graceful and unstoppable run game I had ever witnessed, and I wanted this group of players to be alive again, alive always as Super Bowl-winning teams are. My only thoughts were of survival.

Later I wanted more of an Alamo loss: sure defeat but a kind of valorous nobility in the guttiness and struggle of that defeat. But there is no Alamo loss to be found in the XL.

I watched the game over and over following the defeat. Then I didn't watch it for some time. I watched the game over and over when writing four essays for the previous edition of this book. And then I didn't watch it all for four years. Some few weeks ago, I watched it again in its brutal entirety and swore and paced and all but punched a hole in the wall.

Three may keep a secret, if two of them are dead.

—Benjamin Franklin

A good conspiracy theory must be plausible. It must depend on some difficult or impossible to prove or disprove set of facts. The target audience must want to believe it is true. From *JFK* to *The X-Files* and everything in between, the '90s very much loved conspiracy theories. This skepticism is very Gen-X, as is the supposed joyful participation in the suffering of the world. And I grew up in the '90s, was a child through the '90s and beyond, and had a taste for the Big Elaborate Con.

Given extremely entrenched and polarized opinions about such topics as vaccination, fluoridation, and the Second Amendment, this young millennium has seen a corresponding rise of intolerance of or an almost blind belief in conspiracies. One cannot fault skepticism. Yet chronic disbelief inevitably ends in a kind of madness, that condition Ray Bradbury explored in his short story "No Particular Night or Morning." Each year we are asked to believe a little more, trust a little more in ideas and science and technology we do not understand and that cannot easily be made understood. Our whole lives are ever more subject to ever more esoteric yet ever more powerful forces. Sometimes how can anyone help but wonder, as Bradbury's Joseph Hitchcock wonders, if anything but *this* moment is real?

It is not enough to call something a "conspiracy" and thus deem it debunked. History is rife with legitimate conspiracies. For instance, consider this historical factoid I stumbled upon while watching the BBC's *World War I – The Great War.* Sir John French, commander of the British Expeditionary Force, leaked to retired colonel and war correspondent Charles Repington that a defeat at Neuve Chappelle had been caused in part by a shortage of explosive artillery shells. The lack of explosive shells had been an ongoing problem, but Secretary of State of War Lord Kitchener and the Liberal Party government had sought to minimize and hide this fact—even at the cost of Allied lives, even at the endangerment of an entire theater of war.

But that conspiracy was exposed (and by a counter-conspiracy!) And we're talking life, death, war, the fall of the Liberal government, the fall from power of the beloved Kitchener of Khartoum, and, eventually, even the reassignment of French himself.

And though leaking this shell shortage may have been an act of heroism (you decide), French was not a heroic man. He was a man of mixed legacy that through skill, ambition, and fortune attained great power. His motivations were both noble—French is known to have (and perhaps too strongly) identified with the field soldiers—and petty. (French resented being under the command of French War Minister Alexandre Millerand, whom he called "a d-----d socialist little cad.")

Though it may take many years, the anonymity of conspirators rarely survive. Conspiracies happen, some achieve what they conspire to achieve, but gagging every credible source with knowledge of the conspiracy, or even the conspirators themselves, proves almost impossible. Sometimes people are communal. Sometimes people are nationalistic. But often people are self-serving. We live in a world in which Jose Canseco can become a multi-million dollar athlete through steroid abuse and become a multi-million dollar author and personality by fingering those he alleges abused steroids. We do not require character or credibility. The more sullied someone, often the more we believe their lurid tales. Silencing everyone who knew anything about a Super Bowl XL conspiracy would require coordination and influence undreamed of outside the minds of paranoiacs.

Yet...

It is impossible to prove no party conspired to fix Super Bowl XL. But, then, it is impossible to prove (for me at least) Super Bowl XL ever happened. It was merely something that appeared on my in-law's television.

It is improbable the NFL would feel motivated to fix the Super Bowl. I do not think a sound argument could be made that the league profited more from an existing dynasty winning a fifth Super Bowl than a team—not long ago rumored to be moving to Los Angeles—with a passionate, loyal, and comparatively rich fan base, winning their first.

It is perhaps yet to happen, but it is also unlikely that a story as potentially profitable as proof that the NFL (or for that matter *anyone*) fixed the Super Bowl would remain unearthed. Like Sir French, it is not necessary for someone of sterling virtue and fearless accordance and morality to break the story. It only takes someone who knows and someone who believes the benefit of leaking the story outweighs the cost. (French, it should be noted, died of bladder cancer in 1922 but not before resigning, being re-assigned to a much less prestigious post, and later being scandalized for blunders and inhumanities committed while at that post.) So there is neither clear motive nor probability of successful execution; meanwhile, the risk to a sports league of fixing its premier event is hard to overestimate.

So what do we have? The 2005 Seahawks, at the time of this writing, the second greatest team in Seahawks history but deemed failures because they lost Super Bowl XL. XL turned on penalties, turnovers, and one trick play. That was a great team, but it was beaten, and it would seem close enough to fairly beaten to not begrudge the loss. After all, official discretion is part of the game. So long as there is no provable bias, that discretion, the mistakes it can make, and how those mistakes affect the outcome of a game, are more analogous to the wild bounces of a fumble than a conspiracy. It happens. It is not fair. But if it costs one side the game, the game is still lost.

I cannot prove to you Super Bowl XL was fair or that the outcome was not conceived and executed through conspiracy. I cannot even prove to you that I am real. But that's madness. And it doesn't just rob the joy of XL, it makes life too cruel and isolating to live. After all, even conspiracy theorists seek confidence in others to share and substantiate their suspicions.

It's been more than eight years. Much has happened since. The Super Bowl-winning 2013 Seahawks' win over the 49ers in the NFC Championship Game involved a lot of good luck official discretion. One categorically botched call, Gene Steratore's decision to call running into the kicker when because Chris Maragos hit Andy Lee's plant leg, the proper call was roughing the kicker, benefited Seattle some 10 percent win probability. (Fifty percent cumulative win probability = a win.) It happens. We want sport to be this pristine island in a sea of corruption, where merit, hard work, and talent rule. But it has its pocks, its deficiencies.

One day in the late winter of 2006, Mike Holmgren's Seattle Seahawks took Ford Field as NFC champions. They were an underdog. The Steelers team they faced wasn't—over the course of the season and the playoffs to that point—better than the Seahawks, but they won. In part because of execution and talent and in part because breaks that could go either way predominately went theirs. The Steelers were crowned Super Bowl champions again.

Some Seahawks fans have conspired to deny this fact, and with that denial has come a forced forgetting of the wonder that was 2005. Personally I want my damn season back, XL and all. Because 2005 is too much for me to sacrifice so I may plumb the inky depths of high paranoia.

43 The New Prototype: Away from the Gridiron

People ignore advertising, or at least discount its effect on them. But consider the rather telling admission by respected rich guy and partial owner of GEICO insurance, Warren Buffett, that he would double GEICO's reported $1 billion advertising budget if he could. Or this quote from respected smart guy, Marshall McLuhan: "Advertising is the greatest art form of the 20th century."

Image matters, even in the NFL—that supposed last bastion of merit and determination.

This gauntlet of selling, make of it what you will, I have nothing political to say about it, but it gets the defenses up. As KRS-One once said, "you've got to be an educated consumer," which is pretty much true word one to word seven: you've got to consume—there's no other way to live in modern America. The move to brand and promote and control the image of…well, anything and everything, has overrun the corporate world and begun to permeate our culture. Through Facebook, through Twitter, Tumblr, Pinterest, etc. it is increasingly important to represent yourself and your interests with all the restraint and beady-eyed loyalty of a Jared for Subway.

This spokesperson-ing for brand, team brand, league brand, and individual brand, is an essential part of being a franchise quarterback. When Russell Wilson seems bland or robotic in an interview, it is not because he lacks personality or even that he is uncomplicated, narrow, put-on-this-Earth-to-play-football-and-only-that, though he may seem that way. It is because the far and away most successful model for what a good quarterback does with the media is be confident, be on point, be handsome, and talk much without saying anything. Wilson conducts interviews as one would expect a person that is dedicated to be the best at whatever he does would conduct interviews. He is not colorful, he never gives the other team billboard material, he is unflinchingly pro-teammate, pro-Seahawk, and pro-football; he is humble but not in a wheedling, forced, or self-effacing way. And in a way that almost calls back the age of royalty and the divine right of kings, he makes you feel good to just be in his presence.

Sometime soon Seattle is going to have to incur the cap damage and re-sign Wilson to a much larger contract, but for now he's making $390,000, something not far north of the league minimum. It's a number with too many zeroes to inspire actual pity for Wilson, but one that in his world is an exceptionally gross underpay. His profession is not a long-lived one, no matter how he may seem the exception in all ways. Even special players able to think and move amongst huge men running pell-mell and colliding at forces reminiscent a destruction derby, away from some of the meanest, fastest, most ferocious, most athletically gifted men on Earth with a rapidity and confidence that allows him to avoid most big hits. Even Wilson can suffer a career-ending injury on almost any play. Which is to say, brother's gotta get paid while the sun's shining, and that means commercials.

There's the American Family Insurance commercial that's dull but carried by the smile Wilson puts in his voice. There's the one that tells the (imagined) lifelong rivalry between him and Colin Kaepernick, in which Wilson kisses his own bicep. That's okay. For some reason Wilson speaks for a local car dealership. Ugh. And my mind all but blocks out his fine and charming turn in Levi's otherwise patronizing, pretentious, and almost hectoring "Go Forth" campaign. And this near overexposure has been built on hype, handsomeness, and promise. Imagine after he wins his first MVP? Imagine now that he's a Super Bowl champion?

There's probably a decade more of this to come. So rapidly do I roll my eyes, sometimes, I could badly sprain my superior rectus muscle enduring one of Wilson's interviews. But I don't have to watch, and Russell Wilson was not put on this Earth for my satisfaction. As refreshing as it may briefly seem when a prominent media personality is strange, outlandish, brash, quotable, crazed but penetratingly honest in a "I'm mad as hell and I'm not gonna take it anymore" way, it's inevitably exhausting and a distraction. It gets old. We may be tempted to think of it as authentic because it is not overly media savvy, but often it is little more than ignorant display given media attention. (And often, too, it is phoniness, a clumsy grasp at buzzword-ed ideas like "authenticity" and "genuine.") However, Wilson, for all his squareness, his orthodoxy, and corny beliefs, has never given any indication that he's insincere.

Wilson sincerely thinks himself to be blessed, and maybe there's a bit of modesty hiding in that boast. Wilson sincerely believes in God, team, and football. He works hard, he achieves, and whatever impossible to measure benefit the Seahawks derive from good press and goodwill, Wilson bolsters. He has never embroiled the team in scandal, even of the most trivial and media-created sort. In some ways the old prototype bleeds into the new. A strong arm will always be better than a weak arm. And it never hurts to be media-friendly because you are genuinely nice and well-meaning. Russell Wilson is a man that grandmas into perpetuity can be proud of, and that's okay.

44 Lease the Rights to the 12ᵗʰ Man

Texas A&M sued the Seahawks for use of the phrase "the 12ᵗʰ Man." Sometimes sports can be very stupid. Seattle settled out of court. The Seahawks must now pay a license fee and acknowledge the Aggies' ownership of the phrase. Pat Riley did something similar with the term "threepeat." Sometimes sports can be very, very stupid.

The 12ᵗʰ Man became part of Seahawks lore when Chuck Knox applied the phrase to the rowdy Kingdome crowds of 1984. It was a jubilant ejaculation, but he meant it. He more than respected fans, he could actually empathize with them. That same year, the Seahawks organization retired the number.

In some ways, it's just a marketing gimmick. Every team enjoys a home-field advantage, and the exact reasons why are well researched but not fully known. Some theorize home teams get preferential treatment from officials. In some sports the field conditions themselves change. The strongest argument is simply that players are more skilled at home because they are more thoroughly comfortable with their surroundings.

In the wake of Seattle winning a Super Bowl, 12 pandering has reached an all-time high. From most, this flattery has all the sincerity of a sleazy night club comedian saying "thanks. Thanks, you're a great crowd." What's the alternative? And though I won't go Neil Hamburger on you, I also do not wish to flatter the 12ᵗʰ Man. Nope.

I will not bring a decibel meter to the stadium to measure the crowd noise. Why? Because it's irrelevant. Seattle set a record for crowd noise September 15, 2013, but the Chiefs crowd broke that record not five weeks later. Seattle eventually regained the scare "title" scare quotes, but in the push to expand the relevance of the Guinness brand, the essential point of crowd noise was lost. It really doesn't matter how loud a crowd can get when competing for a stupid record. What matters is the ability to be loud and sustain it. I watched the game in which Chiefs fans broke Seattle's record. They were very loud for the little man waving his device, and sputtered out when the game started. The 12th Man creates a 112-decibel cheer that not only forces false starts but disorients and disorganizes an offense. Since 2005, Seattle has forced false starts at the highest rate in the NFL at home. But though those five yards can be crucial, it's the adjustments, the ear plugs, the piped-in crowd noise during practice, and the intimidation that truly affect opponents. The 12 is not to be patted on the head and told "nice job." The 12 is to be feared. Tens of thousands of angry voices crying for blood in unison target the opponent's basal ganglia and send waves of impulses to their frontal cortex: "Run! Hide! Wild men are after you! Wild men seeking blood have surrounded you! It's only a matter of time before they close in and tear you hulking Orpheuses limb from limb!"

The 12 are nasty, dream destroying. Ask Jake Delhomme. During the 2005 NFC Championship Game, Delhomme had to turn his in-helmet headset so loud, it produced feedback. He was lost, just another poor forlorn soul in the clutches of the 12. So disoriented, so bullied by sound, Delhomme couldn't make even minor adjustments at the line of scrimmage. The Seahawks' strategy of pressing Steve Smith and keeping a defensive back over top never failed. It should have been easy to pick apart. The Patriots attempted the same thing in Super Bowl XXXVIII, but unlike there, on neutral ground, Qwest was so loud that calling an audible was a near impossibility. Delhomme went from the highest-rated quarterback in NFL postseason history to a crippling liability, and Smith was shut down.

Because the 12 is brutal. The 12 is merciless. The 12 scares opponents into shudders and starts, cowardly retreats from conflict, and utter lawlessness. Any act is permissible, however pointless or cowardly, if only to flee the next wave of screaming, the next round of blood curdling shouts and wails, the next chorus of damned souls groaning for blood, sowing scandal and schism, shrinking the hearts of once brave men.

No, I will not praise you, 12. Because we are one. Just a bunch of fools that love our team too damn much and can't ever get enough.

We 12, We Seahawks

Sports is to warfare as porn is to sex.
—Professor John Wyatt

The headline read "Stabbing in Broncos Parking Lot" or something like that. It seems some people were mad after the Broncos lost at home to the Chargers, and something, something, stabbings. Two weeks earlier, a distraught Alabama Crimson Tide fan shot another Tide fan because the latter fan was not sad enough about Alabama's loss to Auburn. She shot her dead, and the two were all but strangers, the friend of a friend invited to fill out a football party because we like strange company and the unpredictability of strange people. We'd rather they not shoot us, though. If they are to shoot us, please not to death. And if they are to shoot us to death, please not because we're not sufficiently bummed about our team losing, please. It's rotten enough to die. As a minor character in someone else's bid to shred whatever fragile but remaining faith in humanity the American public may have, that's shitty.

This is a particularly malignant strain of the "we" fan. As in, we're gonna stomp the 49ers, we're gonna beat 'em by three touchdowns, we're gonna sack the stupid silent "e" out of the first syllable of Colin Kaepernick's last name. I've seen this fan ridiculed and I've seen people rush to this fan's defense. For whatever reason, the "we" fan is often not the brightest or at least not the most well-spoken. It could be, to be blunt, that the less one has in their own life to be proud of, the more that person depends on their sports team for pride. And the more a person depends on their sports team for pride, the more that person identifies with the team and the worse it hurts when the team loses. Maybe. Or maybe people just say "we" because it's conventional, and it's never occurred to them some jagoff would need to "pfft" and "Really?" their simple, unpretentious way of expressing that fandom.

I assume the latter because I assume we're all "we" fans, whatever our chosen pronoun.

Now not to bore or pontificate, and keep in mind there's a lot of interpreting going on and what's to follow could look real dated real soon, but research into what's called "mirror neurons" suggests when someone watches a sport, their brain activates a very similar pattern of neurons as the person playing the sport. That is to say, ostensibly it seems we are empathizing with the athlete: making that catch, sacking that quarterback, hitting that 20-foot jumper as time expires.

Which may explain why sport is more than entertaining. A drinking bird is entertaining. Sport is compelling, gut-wrenching, heart-stopping, brutal—you know these clichés. I know these clichés. Yet they have become cliché because they work. Those words, those phrases communicate what it means to hang on every down, the outcome of every play, and just how exhausting and exhilarating sport can be. Think of the chorus of hopeful "ahs" as a long putt rolls, rolls, rolls across a green and toward the cup. The cheer of it going in. The audible frustration of it rimming out. It's not our putt, our tournament, our life's dream (maybe), our millions in tournament winnings and sponsorships, but as ball ricochets off club, pass leaves quarterback's hand, baseball cracks off slugger's bat, basketball glides off shooter's fingertips, it might as well be. Because like the athlete, we're hopeful and powerless. And like the athlete, we watch this projectile, its journey fragile, its destination impossibly far away, and hope, hope, hope.

Yes! YES! WE DID IT! WE WON!

So, yeah, we're all "we" fans. Science sez so, (maybe). The 12 especially—you think we're screaming ourselves hoarse because we just really, really want a bunch of strangers, Seahawks by circumstance, to win a game? Get real. We want to win. *We want to win.*

And Seahawks fans far and wide, brothers and sisters, teammates, we did. We did. We did.

46 Brian Blades

I couldn't see the athlete in the old man. Brian Blades lived the tragedy of the historically good. By the time I truly understood football, Blades wasn't even that. It's difficult for me to be sure he ever was good, honestly. Most Seahawks fans probably know his name but not his game. Who was Brian Blades?

He was a Hurricane and before that a Bengal, a Piper High Bengal. He was a Hurricane during Miami's notorious but wildly successful "the U" period. Blades attended with his younger brother, Bennie, lined across from Michael Irvin, received for Bernie Kosar, then Vinny Testaverde, and was coached by Jimmy

Johnson. He saw Flutie's Hail Mary, won a national title in 1987, and probably did some other things we'd rather not know about.

Seattle selected Blades 49ᵗʰ overall, their first selection in the 1988 draft after burning their first-round pick on Brian Bosworth in the 1987 supplemental draft. He was Steve Largent's successor, in a way, and better fit Chuck Knox's attitude about the passing game. Knox considered him a first-round talent. Was he? Well, Blades was fast.

This is where the story careens off the rails. I was five when Seattle selected Blades. I didn't tape record games that weren't broadcast in my area, and I didn't pore over footage in my Hypercolor shirt. Actually, we couldn't afford Hypercolor. My shirt probably had a foam spider on it. I was rad.

So I can tell you that Blades was not well known for his hands—his catch percentage was typically low, at or below 60 percent—and because of that, Blades was not a very valuable receiver. If Largent was the new prototype, Blades was the throwback, the play-action burner who could get behind a defense but couldn't sustain a drive, the all-or-nothing receiver who could fill out a highlight reel but never carry an offense, the Joe Namath in the era of Steve Young.

He wasn't bad, but he wasn't great, and though he had four 1,000-yard seasons, that often means nothing more than being the best of a bad bunch. It was a bad bunch. A bad bunch of receivers, linemen, and quarterbacks who could never field an even average offense. But then, maybe Blades overcame such a desultory supporting cast and emerged as a star despite it. However you want to spin it. We may never know.

Blades spent his entire career as a Seahawk. Scandal and injury ended his career early at 33. He had some superficial highs, some very real lows, was great, just not great among the great, only good. And for an outsider like me, who can never hope to be good at anything like Blades was great at football, quickly forgotten.

Brian Blades gets congratulated by Dave Krieg for one of his two touchdown receptions in a 43–37 win over the Raiders that secured the AFC West title on December 18, 1988, at Los Angeles Memorial Coliseum.

Toward the end, before the allegations but after his prime, Blades had his best statistical season. Seattle selected Joey Galloway eighth overall in the 1995 draft. Galloway was a younger, faster Brian Blades, but was less skilled and less trusted. Blades won Week 1, with eight receptions and 107 yards. The two went back and forth, challenging each other, complementing each, and neither ever truly surpassing the other. By almost any measure, the two were equals. Galloway finished with 1,039 yards receiving, Blades, 1,001. Blades had 10 more receptions, but Galloway three more touchdown receptions. Pro-Football-Reference.com gives the edge to Galloway, assigning him 12 points to Blades' 10. Football Outsiders considers it a dead heat, assigning Galloway 1,084 equalized yards to Blades' 1,081.

Galloway was a rookie with promise, and Blades a 30-year-old veteran. Statistics struggle to assign individual credit, and some of Blades' seeming rebound was improved surrounding talent and improved coaching. It was the first time since Largent retired that Blades had a partner. But it came much too late.

So who was Brian Blades? Well, he was one of the greatest receivers in Seahawks history, but never much more than good. He was a first-round talent according to Chuck Knox, but Knox was losing his grasp on the game. He played for some miserable teams, and his career suffered because of it. He was a one-in-a-million talent at wide receiver, and yet somehow still only good.

47 "We Want the Ball..."

If you're not crazy young, if you're any kind of Seahawks fan, and if you're not prone to blacking out moments of extreme

More Hell in Lambeau

One of the more heartbreaking losses in franchise history came in the 2007 playoffs. After squeaking in on the leg of Josh Brown in 2006, the 2007 Seahawks were a legitimate, if not favored, contender. They hosted the Redskins and turned a close game through the third quarter into a lopsided victory after interceptions returned for touchdowns by Marcus Trufant and Jordan Babineaux.

They then traveled to Green Bay to face the 13–3 Packers. Things started out amazingly well, as two quick turnovers allowed Seattle to build a 14–0 lead. With 8:43 left in the first, the Seahawks had already pushed their win probability to 88 percent.

Then like the ash of Vesuvius, the snow fell on Lambeau Field.

What followed was a massacre. The Packers had pushed their win probability to 70 percent before the quarter was over. When the dust settled, Seattle was blown out 42–20.

embarrassment, you know Matt Hasselbeck's infamous proclamation after winning the coin flip in overtime of the 2003 NFC Divisional Round Game against the Packers.

Among Seahawks fans, this is sort of a taboo subject. It annoys, as much as anything, because as with complaints about Seattle's weather, it's overexposed, been run into the ground, and is more or less true. There's just no getting around how truly funny and embarrassing that series of events was.

Here's some very special episode type advice.

The Seahawks are too good to care about that anymore. Hasselbeck is no longer with the team, and no longer is the team's greatest quarterback, or even it's most accomplished. Being so defensive about that heartbreaking and darkly comedic reversal serves no purpose anymore, and the more it seems to bother, the more enticing it is to bullies and trolls to mention it. So let's own it.

Young Hasselbeck, in his first ever playoff game, and against his former team and the quarterback that would forever overshadow him, Brett Favre, played an okay game, which ended regulation as a tie. Beck had led the comeback, orchestrating an absolutely thrilling two-minute drill in the fourth quarter. That pass to Engram…

Hasselbeck was always sort of a dork. He overcompensated for his apparent lack of confidence. And when the Seahawks won the coin toss, he said those terrible, terrible words. "We want the ball and we're gonna score" reverberated over the Lambeau PA. Not five minutes later, it seemed, he threw a game-losing pick six to Al Harris.

48 Pete Carroll as Good Boss or Evil Genius

With 14:44–14:26 left in the fourth quarter of the 2013 NFC Championship Game, Seattle down by four, and the Seahawks drive stalled in that narrow no-man's land between punting and kicking a field goal with confidence, Pete Carroll did what orthodox football would deem prudent. He called on kicker Steven Hauschka to attempt a 53-yard field goal. Now, in the abstract, simplified world of statistics, kicking a field goal in this situation is a bad idea. The field goal even if converted would not give Seattle the lead. Seattle would then be kicking off to San Francisco and still trailing by one. But as *The New York Times* 4th Down Bot noted, it's close: "Interesting call coming up here for the Seahawks. In general, it's close, but I say go for it in this situation."

Seattle's defense had played very well all game, ending two second-half drives after nine total plays and 11 total yards gained, nearly ending a third drive with a strip sack that fortuitously (for the bad guys) bounced to center Jonathan Goodwin who then ran for six yards. Kaepernick found Anquan Boldin for a 26-yard touchdown pass on the next play. Closing to within one would allow Seattle to go ahead on a field goal. San Francisco's red zone defense that day and through the season were so good that scoring a field goal was much more likely than scoring a touchdown. And should the worst happen, and the 49ers score a touchdown, Seattle was within a touchdown and a two-point conversion of tying the game.

But that cataloging of real world considerations is a bit cherry-picked and blinkered. Seattle would still be down one and with no guarantee of another scoring drive. The field goal mostly becomes valuable in the above selected subset of scenarios. What if, for instance, San Francisco immediately scored on the ensuing drive? And Seattle's subsequent drive stalled? San Francisco would have the ball with no goal but to burn time. Seattle would be battling the clock, forced into a more predictable and less practiced pass-first game plan, and with only a chance to tie—conditional on both scoring a touchdown and converting a compulsory two-point conversion.

And, of course, the above assumes Hauschka converted the long field goal—which would be one yard short of his career long.

It was thrilling. It was stressful. It was an awful lot of emotions for a three-hour block of television programming.

This is what we home viewers heard and saw: (Carroll talking to special teams coach Brian Schneider, Hauschka walking out to the huddle, 13 seconds left on the play clock.)

Joe Buck: Hauschka's late gettin' out there…They reset the play clock. Hauschka had to be told a couple of times by Pete Carroll to get out there.

Buck: 53—

Troy Aikman: heh—

Buck: -yard try.

Aikman: That's usually not a good sign (derision in his voice).

Buck: No (laugh)

Buck: …aaand they maaay have to use a timeout.

(Camera zooms on Hauschka looking meek/nervous)

Buck: And they will…Shake of the head by Pete Carroll—that was odd.

What followed was either the culmination of the most subtle trick play ever conceived or an incredible display of good management by Carroll.

After the timeout, Seattle sent its offense back onto the field. Fourth and 6 is not that unlikely to be converted, and if the prudent decision before was to kick the field goal and "trust" your defense, the prudent decision now would be to call a play designed to convert the first. Every offensive coordinator has a whole stable of play calls designed for nothing else. There's a saying among football coaches: every play is designed to score a touchdown. Which isn't 100 percent true (consider the quarterback sneak), but it is rule-of-thumb true. The idea being, whatever the ancillary goals, the first goal of every play is to give the ultimate ball carrier his best chance to score by maximizing space and acceleration and minimizing defenders between the ball carrier and the end zone. Every play, from the ancient student body left to a jailbreak screen out of spread formation, strives to maximize ultimate ball carrier velocity and minimize defenders between him and the end zone.

On fourth and 7 from the 49ers 35 and against one of the best defenses in the NFL, that higher goal would typically be somewhat subsumed in favor of just keeping the drive alive. Think: stop route, out route, curl, china route, etc. Short. Finite. Practical.

Seattle did nothing of the sort.

Instead the Seahawks ran three verticals out of shotgun. Heath Miller stayed in as a sixth blocker, and Marshawn Lynch ran a stop edging toward the left flat. This was an ultra high-risk/high-reward play call, and surely a surprise. But either because they were incredibly lucky or because they were incredibly brilliant, the play call had a built-in fail-safe. Russell Wilson is very good at the hard count, but like so many talents of his, he picks his spots when to use it. This was when. He fooled Aldon Smith into jumping offside, which meant the play was "free" or without possible negative consequence.

Now maybe the above happened exactly as described. Serendipity is rarely far from the football field. But the whole five or so minutes had a disorientating, theatrical feel like one of Carroll's famous pranks. If you've ever watched a *Candid Camera*-style show, you may have seen an incredulous look cross the victim's face before the prank was revealed. A narrowing of the eyes or a pronounced flattening of the mouth that communicates an unease, a suspicion, but one that is difficult to act on. Who ever really thinks their friends and family have conspired to ensnare them in an elaborate trick? When does that happen outside of television? I saw this look cross Jim Harbaugh's face. I saw him mouth to someone off screen, "What's going on?"

The path from light paranoia to full blown space madness is a short and precipitous one, and NFL players, above all else, must forever be poised. But when Seattle's offense retook the field and San Francisco's defense responded in kind, and Seattle aligned in a formation they had not expected and a formation equally adept at screen or deep passes, I would argue the 49ers defense was kind of spooked, uncomfortable, and not sure what had just happened. I was. The commentators were. So the hard count, a much simpler act of deception, maybe was made that much more effective. Given the all-or-nothing nature of Seattle's play call, winning the hard count was an essential step in the scheme. A "free" play is hugely valuable. It allowed Seattle to take its shot without risk. And Seattle did. And Seattle pulled ahead for the first time all game. And Seattle never relinquished that lead.

So, Pete Carroll: Good Boss or Evil Genius?

This is how Hauschka related the series of events to Tom Rock of *Newsday*: "I didn't really want to kick it, to tell you the truth…It was into the wind…I didn't think it was the right decision and I let coach Carroll know that."

Hauschka said he'd never before passed up an opportunity to attempt a field goal. "You have to be honest with yourself," he said. "It was the wind at that moment. Sometimes you can make that, but I felt the wind at that moment was into the face enough to not want to try that kick. I grabbed him on the sideline as I ran out because I could see the flags [on top of the uprights] and I told him: 'We shouldn't kick this.'"

One day it may be revealed, who knows? But though there's something admirable and humanizing about an NFL coach willing to accept his kicker's show of weakness, that kicker admitting his limitations and doubts, and instead of excoriating the kicker, or questioning his manhood, or scheduling a punitive cut, or just forcing the kicker to do it anyway instead, really, as anyone that's played or watched football would assume, of Hauschka never even considering voicing his practical but "unmanly" reservations, and attempting the ill-advised kick and probably missing and trotting head down toward the sideline, all kicked-dog sadness. Angry men averting their eyes from him, Carroll staring toward no where in particular; though there is something dear and cool about the Seahawks of all teams bucking macho stereotypes, and Carroll respecting his kicker's opinion and changing the call, I think it's even cooler, and perhaps more plausible, that every moment, from Hauschka's timid and forlorn look, to the strange timeout taken, to the formation and play call, to the hard count—every moment was planned and goddamn beautifully so.

49 Share With the Less Fortunate

In everyone's life there will be a moment when one faces someone better than themselves. Not someone smarter necessarily or of better character or kinder or more clever or more determined, but better, better at that one thing you are both competing at. This person may be obnoxious, arrogant, foolish, and classless in victory. But this person will beat you. This person will beat you again and again until he simply tires of the competition and denies you another chance. Or you'll quit. And so your defeat will last into perpetuity. His victory will last only so long as he remembers it, which, given the almost shameful ease with which he beat you, might not survive the day. So he will own a little piece of you, this rotten jerk, your better.

Jim Schwartz, former head coach of the Detroit Lions, is a tough guy of sorts, of mixed achievement as a coach but a pretty good reputation (since tarnished). He took the traditional path to his position. Schwartz played linebacker at Georgetown. He didn't have a flea's chance of becoming a pro. But loving the game, presumably, and after graduating with a degree in economics in 1988, Schwartz became a graduate assistant at Maryland in 1989, a graduate assistant at Minnesota in 1990, and so forth. He is big and tough and intimidating-seeming relative to a regular man. And following a 25–19 loss to the 49ers in 2011, he was given a big brother bullying attaboy slap on the back by Jim Harbaugh that was kind of emasculating before it became downright sissifying. Schwartz followed Harbaugh toward the visitor's locker room, chirping at him, looking heated but in a fussy way, looking bullied by a bigger, badder, better head coach and man. This isn't the proper interpretation of two ships passing in the night going opposite directions, but you get me.

Harbaugh didn't take the traditional path to becoming the 49ers head coach. He was the 26th overall pick in the 1987 draft, had a respected and respectable if by no means glorious 14-year career as a quarterback, and took an abbreviated path to becoming a head coach. He is noticeably bigger and more athletic looking than your typical head coach. He is younger, stronger, and exudes that sense of casual cruelty that may be the true mark of Cain (and big brothers everywhere).

It's difficult to explain now and out of context, but this seemed a very important game at the time. Detroit was 5–0, and the 49ers were 4–1. Both coaches were relatively new and relatively young. Both were playing well on defense, and both had defensive stars. Both had young or forever young seeming quarterbacks, and both of those quarterbacks were former first overall picks (and one was even good!) Alex Smith's status as always developing, never really a bust nor a franchise quarterback, has done a number on more factual considerations: he was 27 at the time of this matchup; his career ANY/A+ was 86 percent of league average, his Expected Points Added was a cumulative -168.3, or comparable to David Carr, and his teams were 23–32 in the games he had started. Unlike Carr, though, Smith retained a sheen of promise. Coaches quarantine and bury busts like nuclear reactor runoff, but coach after coach, offensive coordinator after offensive coordinator, staked their career on Smith. And so, it was as if the league itself were telling the 49ers "Smith is good. It is those others that have failed."

A year later, Week 11 of the 2012 NFL season, Harbaugh benched Smith and started Colin Kaepernick in his place. It was one of the single boldest, bravest, and truly smartest moves an NFL coach has ever made. Kaeparnick led his team to a Super Bowl loss, which Seahawks fans can attest hurts but's also not nothing.

Seattle has outscored San Francisco 117–65 in their last five matchups. Seattle beat San Francisco in the 2013 NFC Championship Game and thus likely cost the 49ers a Super Bowl title. I am offering our rivals the dearest kind of disrespect, the kindest cut: flattery.

You're a very, very good team and city, San Francisco 49ers. And what a legacy! How nice it must be to remember all those decades-old championship teams. Like dear youth long departed.

R.I.P. NFC Worst

One of the essays in the previous edition of this book was entitled "NFC Worst." The fall that book came out, Seattle became the first team in league history to win its division and thus make the playoffs with a losing record. Those 7–9 Seahawks, Beast Quake Game notwithstanding, were the culmination of one of the truly worst four-year runs by a division in NFL history. From 2006 to 2010, NFC West teams were outscored by opponents by 1,388 points. The estimated Pythagorean record of those 20 teams would be about 6–10.

So truly desperate was it for Seahawks fans in 2008 that the thesis of that essay was "it's embarrassing to play in such a historically bad division but so long as it helps Seattle secure an easy berth to the postseason, who cares?" "The soft bigotry of lowered expectations," a speechwriter once wrote.

It wasn't that I was in favor of obscurantism. If the NFC West could progress, the Seahawks at the fore no doubt, I would have favored that. It's only that it seemed hopeless then. Bad football can create inertia, and despite the NFL's attempts to level competition, to create parity, those attempts are often inadequate and sometimes backfire. Busts like Smith, Matt Leinart, and maybe soon, Sam Bradford, anchor teams to false hope and onerous salaries. (Further, we're still not sure whether a quarterback busts because of innate deficiencies or if he's maybe ruined by the typically very bad team that drafts him. It's often not clear whether the quarterback is the canary in the coal mine or the noxious gas that killed it. Does throwing to Calvin Johnson make Matthew Stafford good? Did throwing behind Ray Willis, Sean Locklear, and Mansfield Wrotto make Matt Hasselbeck bad?) Midway through the first decade of the new millennium, all four of the NFC West teams began a death spiral that seemed inexorable. These were bad collections of talent, collected by incompetent management, and developed by incompetent coaches. But how quickly things change.

I'll kill him though…In all his greatness and glory.
—The Old Man and the Sea

By adding a couple of venerable old coaches and two young hotshots, turning over the roster (or in the case of San Francisco and Arizona, not squandering immense talent), and cleaning house at the executive level, the NFC West transformed itself. In 2013, it was the best division in football, and by quite a margin.

Which, now that all are good, all are reasonably compensated, all and sundry are respected in tangible ways and not dismissively flattered, we can do what we do when we respect and fear rather than snicker and console: kill, kill, kill.

Escaped NASCAR driver Jeff Fisher is the newest and perhaps bestest of a long line of organizational soldiers, company men, really, that are smart enough, can motivate and develop talent well enough, and know their particular discipline deeply enough (defense, in Fisher's case), to get their teams tantalizingly close to winning it all, before massive heartbreak, a few years of squandered excellence, and ultimate ruin.

He's already been gifted that butterwort nectar he so typically has to seek: a rotten quarterback never likely to be salvaged but with the pedigree of a champion, and the sustained mediocrity of a career backup. There's value in men like Charlie Whitehurst and Charlie Frye. They don't string you along. It's a quick smile and pill in the drink instead of years of footsie and ever delayed promises. Slow clap for the rotten bastards that hit you and get you on with your life; a thousand jeers for the promising seeming and "faithful" that give you the slow clap.

Good luck with Sam Bradford and Jimmie Dale Fishhardt in L.A., Rams fans.

Bill Walsh raised up a then very sad 49ers franchise and established in it a legacy of excellence. His successor, George Seifert, continued this, but a little reduced, a little worse. After Seifert, San Francisco became a proving ground for the Peter Principle: Good offensive coordinators (Mooch), good defensive coordinators (Mike Nolan), adequate college coaches (Dennis Erickson), and angry motivational speakers (Singletary) each took their turn failing. San Francisco was returning to a state of pre-Walsh awfulness.

Harbaugh, he's a good coach. Really good like surely better than at least 15 other head coaches. I would never compare Harbaugh to Dennis Allen or Doug Marrone or that ginger in Dallas. Now the man with a mouth like a wind sock has almost no chance of becoming a legendary coach, but football needs its Dan Reeves, its Marty Schottenheimers, its Marv Levys.

And like Harbaugh is good, Kaepernick is talented. And like Harbaugh is a Super Bowl champion, Kaepernick is skilled at playing quarterback. And since the leggy signal caller of the 49ers is so often seen looking blank, and threatening cyclopia when (often) furrowing his brow, you must really marvel at Harbaugh's ability to manage him, to keep the offense simple and run-centric, to measure the playbook in grams rather than ounces, and to sand the corners off any sharp objects.

As for the Arizona Cardinals, well...my interest in your team is about as tenuous as Carson Palmer's ulnar collateral ligament.

As I understand your franchise's management philosophy, it goes: a rebuilding season is necessary in any season not directly preceded by a rebuilding season.

Good luck with that.

I say such nice things because I totally and utterly respect you Rams, 49ers, and Cardinals. It is so nice to beat you and in so many fun and interesting ways. It will be fun watching you battle it out for second through fourth place these next five seasons.

50 Cable's Thug Cabal

It's better to build a tight chicken coop than a shoddy courthouse.
—William Faulkner, *As I Lay Dying*

There's little in the world less pretentious than line play in gridiron football. Right off, you're either big enough or you're not. Because of the short distances traveled by defensive and offensive linemen, the instantaneous velocity of the fastest and slowest are not that different, which means most of the force is derived from mass. A quick perusal of Pro Football Reference proves this: Two of 160-plus starting offensive linemen are listed as below 290 pounds: Texans center Chris Myers, who is 286 pounds, and Redskins guard Kory Lichtensteiger, who is 284 pounds. So you're preternaturally big, now slamming pads with this other preternaturally big dude—but, young lineman, the rules of football stipulate that he can do all sorts of stuff you can't. You cannot hook or encircle your opponent. Your hands must either stay within the body of the defender or work back to within the body of the defender as fast as possible and do not even heartily pat your opponent on the back or butt. That's a foul. But be happy. Some decades ago, pass-blocking offensive linemen were limited to folding their arms like coat hangers and bodily ramming defenders. It wasn't until 1976 that college football allowed offensive linemen to extend their arms halfway.

Not even Tom Cable remembers those cruel and silly days. He's old school like Run DMC is old school—i.e. from the '80s. His is very much the typical story of college great → failed pro → coach. But to know Cable truly is to know his men, that expression of his ideas, ethic, and tenaciousness: the Seahawks offensive line 2011–2014. Many are more talented. Many are more skilled. Maybe many are even tougher, though that's a tough one to pin down. But none are more punishing. No offensive line so reverses roles like Cable's thugs do. No offensive line so hammers defenders, keeps them on their heels, and attacks snap through whistle like Cable's Seahawks.

Thug...yes, perhaps because it is so easily rhymed with, "thug" was adopted by the hip-hop community and is now wielded against hip-hop, black culture, etc. because it bears racial connotation yet retains plausible deniability against accusations of racism. But that stupidity has no place here, and the word "thug" has a really, really cool origin.

The *thuggee*, Hindi for thief, were a gang of Indian assassins, originating before 1356 A.D. Here's how Mark Twain described his boyhood wonder for these strange, brutal men: "Fifty years ago, when I was a boy in the then remote and sparsely peopled Mississippi valley, vague tales and rumors of a mysterious body of professional murderers came wandering in from a country which was constructively as far from us as the constellations blinking in space—India; vague tales and rumors of a sect called Thugs, who waylaid travelers in lonely places and killed them for the contentment of a god whom they worshiped."

So (obviously, obviously, obviously) I am using it figuratively. I do not think Tom Cable or any member of Seattle's offensive line is a 19th-century Indian engaged in organized crime. Nor, naturally, am I implying anything racial. But it's such a compact and muscular word and so perfect for the unrefined, murderous yet thick-as-thieves character of Cable and his against-all-odds very good offensive line. And in Cable and his men, we find something like a refuge from the phony-sophisticated and unmanly, the dispirited husk of masculinity forced-upon or adopted by so many men of my generation.

That isn't to say I approve of Cable allegedly breaking the jaw of Raiders assistant coach Randy Hanson, but only to say I understand. What do I understand? I understand that big, bruising, and perhaps more violent than average, and more prone to violence than is acceptable, men have a place in this world. They are not subhuman. And when one beats up another, no animals go extinct, no wars are blundered into, and no rivers are poisoned. People get into fights. It's almost never necessary or worth it. That two people got into a fight, and those two people are also famous does not make it more bad or of national interest. Cable's a bad man, let's face it. But I'll let you decide which definition of "bad" I intend.

But he's a good offensive line coach, a hell of a good offensive line coach, and Seattle went to some lengths to hire him. The Seahawks organization is rich in convoluted and non-traditional power structures. The team's head coach is the superior of the team's general manager. The team's former defensive line coach, Dan Quinn, always seemingly ranked above or at least equal to the team's former defensive coordinator, Gus Bradley. When Quinn replaced Bradley as defensive coordinator after Bradley was demoted to head coach of the Jacksonville Jaguars, it was as if nothing happened.

Cable is the Seahawks offensive line coach, a position that inherently ranks below offensive coordinator, but Cable is also assistant head coach, which makes him part of offensive coordinator Darrell Bevell's staff and also Bevell's superior. I could speculate all day about exactly how that works, but I think it's all rather simple. Cable has head coaching experience; Bevell does not. Cable's expertise is coaching up offensive linemen, which is a facet of coordinating an offense, but one Carroll thought vital. Seattle wanted Cable. Awarding him the title of assistant head coach sweetened the pot.

The Seahawks first offensive line coach under Carroll was Alex Gibbs—who is easily the most famous and well-respected offensive line coach in league history. But Gibbs retired suddenly and without warning before the beginning of the 2010 season, and that left the Seahawks in a fix. Transplanted USC line coach Golden Pat Ruel played fill-in, but you don't hire Gibbs, get stuck with Ruel instead, and settle. Carroll doesn't settle. He retained Ruel and hired Cable in 2011 after Cable was fired by the Oakland Raiders.

What Cable did is not that interesting, really. He took a mishmash of good and so-so talents and created a very good, if never great offensive line. *How* he did that is very interesting.

Cable played well over a dozen combinations of tackles, guards, and centers through the 2013 season and postseason. Some of this shifting and substitution was done out of necessity. Every member of the starting five missed time with injury, and the three relative stalwarts, left tackle Russell Okung, center Max Unger, and right tackle Breno Giacomini missed eight, three, and seven games, respectively. But some of this shifting and substitution, especially at left guard, was done to battle fatigue and for purposes of specialization.

A popular notion among sportswriters is the value of offensive line continuity. De-jargonized, offensive line continuity is just a measure of a team's ability to avoid injury or a need to bench an offensive lineman. It's a plausible idea. Offensive lines work in concert, and players that are able to play alongside each other for longer presumably develop trust, communication—and other relationship buzzwords. And I cannot say for sure that an offensive line doesn't benefit from continuity, but it seems to me that the supposed surplus value of starting the same five linemen functions under the same logic as believing a shot duck dies because it falls from such a great height. That is, it's confusing the outcome for the cause. An offensive line is not worse because it is less continuous. An offensive line that must regularly substitute because of injury or under-performance is worse than a line that does not, but it is not the substitution that is the problem. In fact...

Fire up your copy of the 2013 NFC Championship Game—you should have one—and watch the Seahawks offensive line closely. Alvin Bailey, James Carpenter, and Paul McQuistan all took snaps at left guard. This kept them fresh, perhaps, but it also allowed Cable to play each to their strength. McQuistan is the most assignment correct of the lot, and the best able to identify and put a body between a free defender and Wilson. Very Chris Gray. Bailey and Carpenter are both big and bruising—Bailey a little better in space, Carpenter the more powerful of the two. Carpenter's never fully shook the injury bug and needs to be spelled just to stay active at all. Perhaps it would be better if one of the three was so good to simply win the spot and end such rotation. But all teams face their own particular resource pinches. Victory is won through the high and the low by emphasizing strength and negotiating weakness. Yet, in capable enough hands, even a perceived weakness may become a kind of strength. This is what Cable and the Seahawks offense were able to accomplish.

The Seahawks offense is predicated off the zone run. The brilliance of the zone-run game is in its simplicity. Offensive linemen are assigned a zone, a space on the football field, and block that zone and whichever defender happens into it. Unlike Mike Holmgren's elaborate series of pulls and traps, zone blocking requires little complex memorization, finesse, or coordination. It's: block left, block right, block strait ahead. That's oversimplifying a bit, and there's variation, there's nuance, and room to work in a wind back block, a full back counter block, etc, but primarily it is know your space, your place, and win your matchup.

That means maximum repetition through minimization of play variation, which means confident players beyond the so-called "thinking" phase. That means easy substitution, as the next man up is much more likely to be able to successfully "block left" than pull off tackle, pin the play-side end, and slide off and search for a free defender. And that means more attacking run blocking and less defensive pass blocking. The play-action bootleg, a staple of the Seahawks offense, typically begins with a stretch run play fake, followed by a boot motion to the opposite side. While the play fake is being orchestrated, the offensive linemen can attack, attack, attack like they're clearing run lanes. Offensive linemen like that, the attack. Cable's offensive linemen, especially like that, the attack.

The Seahawks offensive line personnel were certainly not among the most talented in the league. Their execution as pass blockers could be poor and could be made to look worse because of Russell Wilson's scrambling (and could be made to look better because of his elusiveness). Most people will tell you the 2013 Seahawks offensive line simply wasn't good. This is not at all true. What they were was crude and intermittent. Those imperfections were magnified by playing Arizona, St. Louis, and San Francisco twice, each a top 10 defense. But what the Seahawks offense line was, too, was punishing and effective. Zone blocking kept it simple. Cable coached up the kind of born-hard MFers he loves, and who match his personality. But they failed at appearing good, of wearing good line play like a laurel, and took much criticism. They failed at refinement and settled for cruel thuggery. They failed the eye test and the smell test. They failed to hold blocks, failed to stay healthy, and failed to ever earn a coronating nickname to impress the casual fans. All they won, it seems, is everything…and forever.

51 Elway

You, your dad, by the fireplace, Sunday; you played catch; he remembered your name; Sunday with the boy. Dad's so busy these days. Dad and I don't see eye to eye 'bout too many things. But you could share some things, football, the Seahawks. And perhaps, perhaps, one Sunday evening, Mom filling the house with smells of cookies, that disgusting stroganoff thing we eventually give to the dog, Dad leaned close and said, "My boy, that's Elway on the television screen. John Elway, m'boy. Some say he is the most talented quarterback that ever lived. I say I wouldn't drag his children from a burning orphanage."

Hating Elway is a proud tradition among Seahawks fans. He was hype incarnate, playing in our own division, both a rival and an enemy, the very horse face of evil. Elway was everything the common man learned to despise. He was good-looking, in an equine kind of way, easily athletic, confident, sublime. What you would fight all your life for, Elway could pick up and do. That girl you've done everything to impress, Elway could pick up and date. He was the übermensch, an American Adonis, may he die a slow death.

Elway was supposed to be a Baltimore Colt. The Colts drafted him first overall in 1983, but Elway refused the honor. He decided Baltimore would not allow him to succeed as he was destined to and told Baltimore owner Robert Irsay that, if the Colts would not trade him, he, Elway, would simply choose baseball over football. Oh yeah, Elway was also a New York Yankee. I shiver writing the word.

Irsay was over a barrel. Baltimore was forced to trade the greatest asset a downtrodden team can be given, a franchise quarterback.

Not a mediocre one, but a Cam Newton with horse teeth. Elway's ploy worked, but despite his Machiavellian intentions, he could not destroy the Colts. Not singlehandedly. Baltimore received Denver's fourth overall pick, left guard Chris Hinton, along with backup quarterback Mark Herrmann and the Broncos' first-round pick in 1984 in exchange for Elway. It was Irsay who destroyed the Colts, moving them from Baltimore to Indianapolis a year later.

Elway quickly became the most hyped player in the NFL. I can only imagine how disgusting that was. Wait. Wait. Oh, yeah. Like a golem born of vomit. Horse vomit.

He was one of the first great villains in Seahawks history. Elway had a necromancer-like control over fair-weather fans, and his hordes roved Seattle. Denver was the established franchise. It had been godawful for most of its history, but had a modest run of success from 1976 to 1981.

Before the Seahawks were established, the Broncos and 49ers made inroads with Seattle football fans, and when the Seahawks were suffering the embarrassing travails of an expansion franchise, the Broncos were taking off. Then, as surely as the Broncos sagged a bit, the 49ers became the team of the decade. San Francisco and Denver had the two most famous quarterbacks in football, Joe Montana and John Elway. Montana was good-natured and humble—hard to dislike. Elway was brash, and for many years, his performance didn't match his reputation—easy to hate.

He earned a special place in Seahawks fans' hearts: the right ventricle. What cardiologists refer to as the "hate ventricle." The cool thing was that for a few years, Elway sucked. Hard. And the Seahawks owned him.

As a rookie, Elway escaped the bench just in time for the Seahawks to plant a couple sacks on him and limit him to 134 yards passing. He didn't play two weeks later, but Seattle won nevertheless. In the wild-card round, the Seahawks stomped Denver 31–7 to start their miracle playoff run.

Old Horseface, John Elway, coughs up the ball after being hit by the Seahawks' Rufus Porter in the fourth quarter of a 42–14 Seattle win over the Broncos in December 1988 at the Kingdome. Porter also recovered the fumble on the play.

The next season, Seattle beat the Broncos, but Elway put together a good game. Then the Broncos stomped Seattle in Week 16, but Elway threw four picks. A loss but a toothsome loss.

For years, hype would ride high on the horse named Elway, and for a few years the Seahawks bucked the rider and put down his charge. It didn't last very long. Seattle finished the '80s 7–7 against the Elway Broncos. Elway kept getting better, and the Seahawks became gnarled and inept. In the '90s Elway was 13–4 against the Seahawks. Then there were the two Super Bowl wins and the "For John" crap, and Seattle wasn't even noteworthy as a rival, but hating him never went away, never got old, never gets old, even if Elway got the final neigh.

* * *

My, how the days run away like wild horses over the hills. It's true, Elway retired in 1999 after his second Super Bowl victory. The sight of him bounding and whirling, wither and croup, gaskin and hock, ending his eight-yard gallop for a first down, is now stamped into football lore. But Super Bowl XLVIII is the neigh that got away, I guess. Because after retiring from football, Elway joined the Broncos organization and eventually rose to the rank of general manager—surely on merit alone. He helped assemble the team's exceptional offensive talent, and whinnied and playfully bucked and batted his long wiry eyelashes at Peyton Manning. And Manning, formerly a Colt, became a Bronco.

Which afforded Peyton Manning the rare treat of witnessing total domination by the Seahawks defense of Peyton Manning. Two decades of vengeance and only 60 minutes of football to exact it in. So if the game seemed a bit lopsided, Pete Carroll a bit ruthless…but, of course, that essay's a horse of a different color, to be penned and put down somewhere else in this little book.

 **Rebuilding**

Rebuilding. It's the dirtiest word in sports. It's a concession of defeat. Rebuilding. May you not wish it on your worst enemy.

Seattle has spent most of its history rebuilding. Not building, no, rebuilding like what one does to a collapsed church or devastated city. Before the rebuild comes the collapse, and the collapse stings more, but that pain's almost savory compared to the rebuild. One can derive a masochistic thrill from the team collapsing. Rebuilding is like a Kafka parable.

(A franchise failed. It went to a rich man named Behring for help. Behring said I will help, but you must wait here until I am ready. The franchise waited and waited, until its hands showed the yellowed and diaphanous wrinkled skin of old age. It slowly propped itself up on wobbly knees and approached the rich man. "Behring, I am very old, and have accomplished so little. What more must I wait for?" The rich man laughed and put a consoling hand on the franchise's shoulder and said, "You were dead the whole time!"

(Maybe I'm confusing Kafka for Shyamalan.)

Ahem. The Seahawks were legitimately rebuilding before building much of anything. In their third year, Seattle had crawled from the primordial ooze, had a character, a core, a leader with some name value, even a little prestige. Jack Patera led Seattle to its first winning season and did so in the most fan-friendly manner: through a litany of gadget plays. Yes, the Seahawks were freewheeling, fun, breezy West Coast, but with a blue collar, timber-and-dock charm.

By the fifth year, they were rebuilding again. Oh boy. There were all the signs. A rookie quarterback with a little buzz, Dave Krieg. A defense that couldn't stop a ladybug with a quart of Raid and an atom bomb. The death spiral. Oh, the death spiral. Seattle started a promising 3–2 and then 4–3 and then lost nine straight. In a particularly pungent performance against Dallas in Texas Stadium, the Seahawks fell behind 51–0 before Zorn connected with tackle Ron Essink for a two-yard score. Seattle's little sandcastle had been kicked in by the big kids. Pity us.

Patera became a victim of the labor crisis and was shuffled out after only two games in 1982. He was replaced by Mike McCormack, whom we need not dedicate any more words to. Firing the head coach is the flare shot into the night, indicating both help needed and warning, avoid.

Then something kind of remarkable happened. Seattle eschewed rebuilding and instead decided to try and win. Not later, not at some indefinite future date, but now. Right now.

Ralph Wilson did his part. Wilson was a bit of a despised man in the contemporary NFL. He had the city of Buffalo over a barrel. This might sound quaint if this book is dusted off at some future date, but the Bills have become a rest home for failed head coaches and a minor league for other NFL teams. Within the constraints of the salary cap, Wilson spent as little as possible. Wilson's Bills were once a model organization, and Wilson a model owner: competitive, involved, and generous. There's no bad guy here, just a changing economic landscape. Western New York no longer sports a robust economy. They are, how do you say, rebuilding.

Wilson wouldn't pony up to retain the services of Chuck Knox, and so Knox and his brand of smashmouth football were recruited to Seattle. He became the Seahawks' head coach in 1983. Seattle canned rebuilding, started its best quarterback, and not simply its most accomplished, traded up for a rusher named Curt, and took their shot at immortality. What a concept.

Seattle charged to its first playoff berth and then made some noise before bowing out in the AFC Championship Game. They stayed competitive the next season, finishing 12–4. But enough about winning, let's get back to losing! I mean, reblosing—rebuilding (a loser).

The Sea-Scabs enervated the Seahawks' drive to win, and though Seattle would scrape out two more winning seasons before Knox's departure, rebuilding was looming. Seattle traded Kenny Easley for quarterback Kelly Stouffer. Lean Cuisine was supposed to be something special, and he proved as much by sitting out his entire rookie season. Special gets paid special money, screw football. Easley discovered his kidneys were shot and was forced to retire. A win for all involved. And an epic triumph for the forces of rebuilding.

The rebuild was finally consummated when Knox used a buyout clause in his contract and left Seattle to join the St. Louis Rams. General manager Tom Flores made the hard decision to hire himself as the next head coach of the Seattle Seahawks. He knew right away what he had to do: rebuild. Much had been destroyed under the incompetent management of general manager Flores, and only the brave, forward-thinking of head coach Flores could take that rubble, the broken concrete, and twisted rebar of a once great structure and huck it at the fans.

Rebuilding is full of fancy buzzwords like "Raiderizing" and half-smart tactics like running-back go routes. It usually features at least one failed quarterback prospect and the forced departure of a successful quarterback. Stouffer wasn't the big success he promised, and he couldn't ever overtake Dave Krieg. Krieg was facing the ravages of age and injury and couldn't keep himself on the field. Even the great Steve Largent faded in the late '80s and retired in 1989.

Seattle upped the rebuilding by cycling through not one, not two, but three failed quarterback prospects. Apparently, franchise death rides an ambulance because Stouffer and Dan McGwire exited the crypt-like confines of the Kingdome on a stretcher.

Mired in rebuilding and looking for a way out, Seattle rolled the dice on another can't-miss prospect, the Bill Walsh–approved next Joe Montana (though Joe Montana was not the next Joe Montana), Rick "Golden Boy" Mirer. Mirer was named the AFC Rookie of the Year. Could he end the cycle of rebuilding? Oh, God no. But after Mirer Seattle took a long break from rebuilding. Even our very own Playoffs Jr. had the fool idea his team would compete. When the 2008 Seahawks didn't, Jim Mora was fired because Mora and the Seahawks organization lacked the excuse of a rebuild, which maybe proves rebuilding isn't an action but a mentality. Teams in a rebuild are teams pre-excusing themselves of future failure. And ever since Paul Allen took over ownership of the Seahawks, failure has been tolerated, but announcing your advanced intentions of failing has not been.

53 The Next Joe Montana

Rick Mirer was the next Joe Montana. So said Bill Walsh. And when Walsh says something, people foolishly believe it better accords to the truth than say, when Fritz Schlitz of Climax, Colorado, says something. Walsh knew a lot about Montana, but he didn't know squat about Mirer. Remember, Joe Montana was not Joe Montana before he became Joe Montana. Montana was a third-round pick and the fourth quarterback taken in 1979. He was Schmo Montana. And he stayed Schmo Montana until halfway into his second season.

No, Mirer was always Jack Thompson, the Washington State Cougars quarterback selected first among all quarterbacks and third overall in the 1979 NFL Draft. Thompson finished his college career the all-time leader in passing yards. Mirer wasn't quite so accomplished a passer, but he did have another title: winner. Mirer was 29–7–1 as a starter and led Notre Dame to three bowl games. Think of other recent winners: McCoy, Tebow, Keenum…Vince Young, Matt Leinart…Slingin' in a Sling, Sam Bradford. Winners.

Mirer was Seattle's prize for finishing 2–14. In 1992 Seattle couldn't even lose right. Apart from cratering in a season in which the NFL was threatening to abolish the draft, the Seahawks won the tiebreaker by defeating New England and thus lost the first overall selection. That meant Seattle missed out on another Cougars legend: Drew Bledsoe.

It was preposterous to compare Mirer to Montana. Montana completed a higher percentage of passes as a pro than Mirer could in college. Not by a small amount, either. Mirer completed 54.4 percent of his passes at Notre Dame. Montana completed 63.2 percent of his passes over his pro career. Montana was much better

Once the "next Joe Montana," Rick Mirer drops back to pass with a look of panic mixed with confusion. Despite mediocre (at best) numbers and a losing record (6–10) in 1993, Mirer was named the AFC Rookie of the Year.

against much better competition at the fundamental quarterback skill: completing passes.

But compare Bill did, and his words moved mountains. Seattle signed Mirer to a five-year, $15 million contract. For a while, everyone was happy. Bledsoe brought his artillery cannon to New England, and the Patriots crawled over the Colts to move out of the AFC East cellar. Seattle stayed in last place but bested New England six wins to five. Mirer started 16 games and set rookie records for completions and passing yards.

One accomplishment created another. Mirer was never good; he just slung a lot of pigskins. It took 486 attempts to set the completions and yards record. After factoring in his league worst 47 sacks, Mirer averaged just 4.9 yards per attempt. The sacks dried up a bit after his rookie season, and he threw for the lowest interception rate of any quarterback, but those were hollow achievements. Mirer avoided interceptions and sacks at the expense of a functioning passing offense. His completion percentage dropped to 51.2 percent, and despite fewer sacks, he still only averaged 4.9 yards an attempt. Mirer was low-risk, no reward.

Dennis Erickson took over as head coach in 1995. Mirer reverted to 1993 form. His sacks and interceptions skyrocketed. He was three years into his professional career and on his second head coach. The Seahawks were giving up on him. Journeyman John Friesz was in the mix. Friesz outplayed Mirer but had none of the supposed potential. Mirer was given every opportunity but never seized one, and eventually, his exit from Seattle became inevitable.

By October 1996 Seattle was actively shopping Mirer. They attempted to send him to Atlanta for suspended quarterback Jeff George, but George dragged his heels, and eventually the trade deadline elapsed. Seattle was spared. It had offered George $30 million over six years. That trade goes down, and a lot of great Seahawks history is unwritten. SoCal Seahawks history.

The Legend of Charlie Frye

Things got so bad in 2008 that the Seahawks started Charlie Frye. Frye was a failed quarterback acquired from the Browns for a sixth-round pick. Seattle overpaid. The former Akron Zip was in the league for one reason, the tired concept of "prototypical." Frye looked the part of a professional quarterback, even though he couldn't throw worth a lick and sensed pass rushers from other dimensions.

Seattle was hosting Green Bay, and since it was starting Frye, it was really counting on its running game to step up and carry the offense. That is when I started to notice that the Packers were planning to stop just that, and that Seattle didn't have a hope of running with Frye playing quarterback. Every snap, the Packers linebackers crashed the line. When it was a run, Julius Jones was running into a hornets' nest. When it was a pass, well, the small disadvantage of losing coverage linebackers did not seem to hurt Frye's opponents too much.

Humans need to compartmentalize things for our sanity. We need units like the secondary and the linebackers corps, and we need to assign very specific duties and stereotypes to the players who populate those units. Football is too messy for all that. Everything impacts everything. Peyton Manning has never had a struggling run game. Who would bother defending the run when they must desperately attempt to slow Manning? Charlie Frye didn't earn that same kind of respect.

Mirer retained luster. Many thought, like Steve Young before him, Mirer was not the cause of, but victim of Seattle's futility. His sacks were evidence of the Seahawks' ineptness. Research has since shown that avoiding sacks is one of the most consistent abilities a quarterback shows throughout his career. Mirer was not taking sacks, but making sacks through a slow read and poor pocket awareness. He was busted, no good, a mistake, a botched pick, sunk cost, and Seattle knew it. The Seahawks continued to shop Mirer in the off-season and found an amazingly robust market.

Chicago has always been enamored of bad quarterbacks. Sixty years ago the Bears drafted Sid Luckman. Jim McMahon is probably Chicago's greatest quarterback since. It started a Lujack, a Romanik, signed George Blanda for $600, demanded a refund the day he reported, and ran him out of the league by playing him exclusively as a kicker. Chicago had a Bukich, a Concannon, and later, a Kramer, a Miller, a McNown, and a Grossman. It had a place for Mirer. The Windy City needed Rick Mirer. Dave Wannstedt needed Rick Mirer. And Mirer, them.

On February 18, 1997, Seattle sent Mirer to Chicago along with a fourth-round pick for the Bears' first-round pick. Wannstedt had his man, and together with Mirer, the two crushed Chicago between their iron jaws, rendering the Bears lame and lifeless and easy prey. That pick became cornerback Shawn Springs. And now you know the rest of the story.

54 The Expansion Draft

In an effort to make an expansion team less pathetic, the NFL holds an expansion draft. In an effort to punish and exploit those expansion teams, but in the name of goodwill, the expansion draft is populated by players other teams don't want. Tampa and Seattle didn't get the good players, didn't get the mediocre players, didn't get the proven players or even the players with pro potential. Tampa and Seattle got the old players, the talent-poor players coaches didn't have the heart to cut, the injured players, and the malcontents.

Teams could protect 32 players—*32!*—and each time Tampa or Seattle selected one, that team could protect another player. It wasn't even the extras from the best teams. No, no. As good teams were plundered, they could protect more and more, and eventually

The First, Worst Seahawks

Before there were the Seattle Seahawks, there were the Miami Seahawks. They were an inaugural member of the All-America Football Conference. The AAFC eventually merged with the NFL, but long after the Seahawks had disbanded.

The team ran through two coaches and finished 3–11. Their first regular-season game was against Paul Brown's Browns, and it was a lopsided shutout. Miami lost 44–0 and totaled only 27 yards. Before they could fold, the Seahawks faced Brown's Browns again and lost 34–0. This time they squeaked out 46 total yards, but also gave up nine turnovers. Still, however inept, and however short-lived, in 14 games the Miami Seahawks outscored Tom Flores' 1992 Seahawks 167–140.

Seattle was forced to add talent from the bad teams, too. Could you imagine a modern day team constructing a roster from the Houston Texans' 33rd best player? Why not spray the team lockers with MRSA contagions while you're at it.

If this process wasn't insult enough, the Players Union nearly filed suit to stop it entirely. That would have made the Seahawks and Bucs little more than college all-star teams. But it might have helped. Sure, it would have been ugly to start. It *was* ugly to start. Tampa lost 26 in a row. But instead of the aged, rejected, broken, and soon retired, at least the Bucs and Hawks could have grown up together.

Instead, it went like this: Seattle selected Wayne Baker. Baker was a lumberjack's son, so you can see the allure. Baker never played another down of organized football. Seattle selected Carl Barisich, and Barisich lasted one season. Seattle drafted Dwayne Crump and his mean Afro, but Crump couldn't make the squad. His helmet wouldn't fit. Haha. Ha. Because the hair, you see? His hair. His um this is on? I'm typing right now? It added young Bill Olds, but Olds' pro career was ending. Seattle drafted Neil Graff, and really, no one knows who Neil Graff is. And so forth.

It wasn't all bad, of course. There was "Happy Days" Ron Howard. I'm sure he appreciates that nickname. He stuck for a while and wasn't terrible. There was "Sudden" Sam McCullum, and Sam was excellent for a little while and facilitated the exit of Jack Patera. Thanks for that, Sam. There was Dave Brown, and Brown turned into a pretty special player for the Seahawks. Maybe never great, but good and for a long time.

The expansion draft. Sure, it wasn't the right or fair way to start a franchise, but it was the way it was done. Seattle and Tampa Bay took other teams' scraps, slapped a logo on them, and called it a team. They weren't proud, they weren't skilled, and they weren't great—heck, most of them never even made it—but they were Seahawks and Buccaneers. Those players scrapped and fought through some of the worst football the NFL has ever seen. Those players took the dream and promise of NFL football, nurtured for so many long years by desperate football fans in Seattle and Tampa Bay, and made an absolute mockery of it. They left it all on the field and didn't clean up after themselves. They got no respect and earned no respect but were probably paid pretty well. They retired to jobs as insurance salesman and gym teachers and bouncers, but they could always say, "I was almost good enough to be a Buccaneer."

The Kingdome

For my generation, the Kingdome was a dilapidated piece of garbage. Its finest moment was its implosion. That day, the first home of the Seahawks and first home of the Mariners reached self-actualization. Always an eyesore, a burden to its teams, an architectural blunder, noted for its falling roof tiles, noted for the repair of those roof tiles killing two men, noted for being the physical manifestation of years of losing, bad management, and irrelevance, it emerged from its impermanent shell and metamorphosed into a pile of rubble; became actual garbage. That, my friends, is self-actualization.

Was it ever anything else? At some point, someone not only authorized the building of the Kingdome but poured millions of dollars into it. Someone, sometime, like the mother of Jeffrey Dahmer, must have looked upon the still-fresh, still-clean Kingdome and felt some kind of pride. Even typing it, it's hard to believe. The millions: $67 million to be exact. Inflation-adjusted, the Kingdome would cost $275.4 million today. Numbers like that are sure to inspire a little working-class outrage, but stadia cost money, even the ugly ones. So let us not fret or sharpen our pitchforks, not yet.

Construction ended in 1976, when we must assume engineers stood a second to look upon their great creation, sighed with the sadness of passing joy, took a long, memory-destroying rip from a flask of Monarch Vodka, decided money still spends, success or failure, speedily fled the scene, and remembered to leave the Kingdome off their résumés.

It had one good quality: the Kingdome was loud, crazy loud. Sixty-six thousand football fans could get the walls shaking. Seattle fans screamed like the buried-alive, and the Kingdome reverberated like a concrete sarcophagus. It was a home for prayers. People prayed for field goals, free throws, and strikeouts. It was a home for great players, great plays, Dan McGwire. It was the site of Bo versus Boz, Refuse to Lose, losing, and a thousand more times, losing. It housed a great valley of Astroturf, and that horrible pseudo grass probably cost Junior his hamstrings. It certainly made it impossible to sign free agents. Turf burned knees, buckled knees, and invented the phrase "turf monster." The turf monster drags careers to their graves.

The Seattle Kingdome was the home of the Seahawks, Mariners, and SuperSonics from 1976 to 1999, before being demolished on March 26, 2000.

I'm sure it had a homey kind of charm for the regulars. Like many a young man, I know the joy of kicking away a beer can to reveal another beer can, in which are my car keys and knowing I am home. Maybe if I sat inside that great domed testament to technology outpacing aesthetics and lived with the team, I could look back at it with nostalgia. Instead, I will forever see the Kingdome as an ugly mistake that needed to be replaced little more than 30 years later. The Kingdome was the stadium that best represented the teams that lost there. The Kingdome almost cost Seattle the Seahawks. It wasn't just Ken Behring, after all, who demanded a new stadium; Paul Allen held out on purchasing the team before a new stadium was approved by the state. I will forever see the Kingdome as not only one of the ugliest and least successful stadiums in American sports history, but as the worst-case scenario for Qwest Field. If 20 years from now, the state is again forced to demolish and replace the Seahawks' stadium or face relocation, I will cry. Literally, in my drinking glass full of false teeth and Efferdent, cry.

56 When in Revelry You Drown Your Sense

Coaching an expansion team is a career-killer. Ownership says nice things, the right things, about patience and buying into a philosophy, but when that invariably fails, when fate crushes a newborn franchise under its wheel, it's always the coach who goes. That should be in the job description: "Professional sports franchise seeking coach and future scapegoat."

Since the Seahawks joined the league in 1976, the NFL has added four franchises: the Jacksonville Jaguars and Carolina Panthers in 1995, the Browns in 1999, and the Texans in 2002. Jacksonville began under head coach Tom Coughlin. Coughlin had some success in Jacksonville and later won a Super Bowl with the Giants. He's the exception. Carolina started under Dom Capers. He succeeded in his second season and was fired after his fourth. Four years later, he was hired to coach the Houston Texans. Four years later still, he was again fired. Chris Palmer coached the expansion Cleveland Browns and was gone after just two seasons. Who? You might ask. I don't know, I can sincerely answer. Must be some guy's name. Some guy named Chris Palmer.

Seattle entered the league along with the expansion Tampa Bay Bucs, who had John McKay at the helm. He suffered a longer career filled with more losses and more heartache than an average expansion coach, but like most, it about finished him. He never coached again. After his death, his son told the *Los Angeles Times* that he knew within the first week that he had made a mistake leaving USC. Money—when it seems like you're being paid too much, it's only because you've underestimated the enormity of the task.

Head coaches of expansion franchises are paid handsomely to lose, and lose, and after an arbitrary grace period, be blamed for losing, be vilified by fans and media, be fired, and often, retire. It's just the way it is. Maybe it's league-mandated. One gets their few years of prominence and pay, then one day a knock comes at the door, and from under it a sulfurous smoke pours in. Next thing you know, Rod Serling is in your entryway moralizing about the dangers of getting what you want. You say, "Hi Rod," but it's like *you're not even there.*

Jack Patera played the Seahawks' Faust. He was signed after making a name coaching the Purple People Eaters. He taught advanced techniques like running and running toward the quarterback. Patera packed Benchwarmer Bob with him and set off for Seattle, ready to undertake the task that would grind him down and end his head-coaching career.

He was a great fit for Seattle and a surefire failure. He was quotable and projected the steely resolve of a general. Patera was creative and knew that winning in Seattle wouldn't happen because of three years of talent acquisition, but by exploiting every angle. Trick plays became a staple, and trick plays always have entertainment value, even when they fail. But for the most poorly executed plays, fans typically enjoy razzle-dazzle. Seattle became a respectable franchise in just its third season, finishing '78 and '79 with 9–7 records.

Then, as always happens, the old players acquired through the expansion draft began to fade or retire, and the young players were not ready to step in. The offensive line turned over multiple starters, and players like Louis Bullard, Tom Lynch, and Bob Newton were at or near the end. Lynch went on to Buffalo, but was a backup. Jim Zorn took sacks, threw picks, was harassed, and struggled.

Things didn't get better the next season, and part way through the strike-shortened 1982 season, Patera was fired. Losing facilitated the move, but problems cut deeper than that. He had an adversarial relationship with the press and was very private at a time when people expected greater and greater access. He once infamously started a press conference by saying, "Let's get it over with. I don't want to be here any more than you." Maybe he didn't get that becoming a head coach also meant becoming a celebrity. As Marshawn Lynch recently learned, it never pays to antagonize the media. Patera made himself an easy target with a drunken driving arrest on September 11. By the time the case went to trial, Patera was defamed and jobless and any hope of a fair trial was likely lost. His attorney, Doug Cowan, even went as far as accusing the prosecution of aiding in Patera's dismissal.

He had problems with players, too. He refused water breaks during training camp. Less outright stupid but more inflammatory, he cut Seahawks Players Union representative Sam McCullum and provoked Seahawks' players into threatening a team-only strike. McCullum was in his peak seasons, and his replacement, Roger Carr, was on the decline. Patera's steely resolve and old-school style were backfiring on him, and just in time, because his expiration date as an expansion team coach was at hand.

57 Play Catch

My wife throws a mean spiral. Alanya doesn't have a gun, but she could make a great quarterback in a West Coast Offense. Slants, digs, quick outs: she's nails. We don't play contact, and we can rarely coordinate enough people to play a game, but we get out and toss the ball around every few weeks. It's fun, like watching football can never be, and it keeps you engaged with the game even after your cleats and pads days are long over.

Yeah, I've played Madden, I've beat the system and abused the computer, spent hours and hours, and winning 98–0 is not as fun as one well-thrown pass. One run and reach and dive and, oh yeah, I caught it. Before it was our obsession, we were kids, and we probably looked at our dad all hunkered down on the couch, chip bowl and beer nearby, and wondered, *What is he doing? If he likes football, why not play?*

It's a great question. I am passionate about the Seahawks, and, man, when they win, I soar. But no touchdown, no sack, is ever as fun as winging the ball—as running, jumping, striving, playing football. You don't have to be athletic. You don't need equipment and pads. Just get a ball and some friends, or a friend, find a field, and let loose.

Some years back, in some Portland neighborhood I scarcely remember, sometime late, 3:00 AM, I was party to a party departing a party, pigskin in hand. We found a field and started to play. We weren't in our best minds. Some of us were in no shape to drive (we didn't). Some were worse off than that, and when I evaded a rusher and scrambled for 20, yeah, I stiff-armed a butch, and that was a little awkward, but it was cool, because it was in the name of sport, play, and it was fun. And fun is impervious. Fun knows no shame.

Nowadays it's mostly just my wife and I. We don't walk too far, and what little speed I ever had, well, I still mostly have, but I'm sure it's fading. We have no score or rules or goal or time clock, but the soreness in our shoulders. It's fun and light and contagious: catch attracts strangers. Then there's more hands and more running and different throwing styles, and that one dude that's way too good, and the kid—better not swear (much)—and throw together a game of touch football, and that one dude dominates, and after a while people break off and leave, and maybe they're replaced, or maybe you thank everybody and go home.

58 Specialization

Hall of Fame enshrined running back Curtis Martin started playing organized football his senior season in high school. He did so at the insistence of his mother, who just wanted him to participate in an extracurricular activity "to stay out of trouble." Martin ran for 1,705 yards and 20 touchdowns his first season.

This is all well-known. It is also semi-well known that the greatest Olympic swimmer of all time, Michael Phelps, is blessed with a particularly weirdly shaped body. He has short legs, long arms, a long torso, etc. Martin and Phelps are specialists—fundamentally normal people whose bodies and minds are constructed in such a way to make them among the greatest in the world at one single thing.

Most team sports are comprised of generalists, more or less. Each has their specialists, perhaps no more specific than the so-called LOOGY (or Lefty One Out GuY, an acronym coined by baseball writer John Sickels), but by and large, there isn't too

too much that separates a midfielder from a forward, or a left fielder from a right fielder, or a small forward from a shooting guard. Baseball is known for its defensive spectrum. A first baseman cannot play a competent shortstop, but most shortstops would have little trouble playing first base, so there isn't so much specialization as ability. Some baseball players are world class athletes comfortable in almost any athletic competition. Some are professional hitters with legs and feet that move and articulate in a running fashion. In basketball, guards can't play center, and centers can't play guard, but all players jointly set picks, rebound, shoot, etc. There's minor specialization mostly dictated by height, but differentiation of duties is somewhat subtle, and almost anyone could be called on to do almost anything in a specific situation.

Russell Wilson and other Maori War Gods notwithstanding, quarterbacks cannot do a damn thing but play quarterback, yet they are the most valuable player on the roster. The offensive line has a spectrum, sort of, and the defensive line to an extent too, but mostly football is a sport of specialization. And no coach perhaps ever has so completely understood this like Pete Carroll.

The 20 Positions Played on the Seattle Seahawks Defense

When we think of athletic talent, we think of strength, quickness, agility, and coordination. General things. Those qualities that make some people athletic and others not. And sure, most great sports stars are also great athletes, some exceptionally so. People like Deion Sanders and Bo Jackson are so generally athletic, they were able to excel in two sports. But when I say "excel," I really mean just play at the top level of competition. Both Jackson and Sanders were fairly mediocre by the standards of Major League Baseball. That's because the more specific the rules of the sport, the more specialized the abilities it takes to excel at it. Someone like Edgar Martinez may not match the quickness of Sanders or the power of

Everyone's a Scout

Amateur scouting has become a big deal on the Internet. It's something I both love and hate. Expertise is hollow. Anyone who attempts to convince you their own opinion holds more weight is trying to sell you something. A fundamental idea of logic is that ideas can be true, but an idea cannot be true because of who said it.

However much I love the concept of a wide-open and free scouting community composed of hard-working people instead of experts, the execution is often very poor. For whatever reason, everyone wants to be the next Mel Kiper, and instead of taking a quiet and patient approach to evaluating players, they attempt to match his moxie and certitude. The product is a black-and-white view of the NFL Draft. Some players are certain busts, while others are undiscovered stars.

It might surprise some, but the NFL Draft is actually a pretty efficient process. Brian Burke of Advanced NFL Stats ran a survey of every draft pick and found a strong correlation between round and future success. We tend to think otherwise because exceptions stick in our memory, but trust me, not every Mike Kafka will become Kurt Warner.

Jackson, but his amazing eyes, which read the spin and direction of a baseball better than anyone maybe since Ted Williams, allowed him to perform as a hitter like neither of the other two could. They may have been better athletes than Martinez, but they were far inferior batters and baseball players.

But batting, and all its constituent skills and talents, is an ability that must be mastered by all but pitchers. Someone like former Mariners shortstop Brendan Ryan may seem bad, but he's only bad relative to other major league hitters. So baseball players are specialists, broadly, but generalists, specifically.

The hitters of Seattle's best in the NFL defense are a motley bunch, all generally athletic, but within the Carroll and Quinn's scheme assigned incredibly specific responsibilities. All defenses have some degree of specialization, but Pete Carroll, defensive coordinator Dan Quinn, and former defensive coordinator Gus Bradley took that idea and absolutely ran with it.

During their Super Bowl run, Seattle had a Leo end (Chris Clemons), a nose tackle (Brandon Mebane), a pass rushing nose tackle (Clinton McDonald), a pass defending undertackle (Tony McDaniel), a pass rushing undertackle (Michael Bennett), a 3-4 style strongside end (Red Bryant), a pass rushing strong side end (Bennett), a situational end in its NASCAR package (Clint Avril), and two bear end/tackles (Bryant and McDaniel).

It has a weakside linebacker (Bruce Irvin), a strongside linebacker (K.J. Wright), a middle linebacker (Bobby Wagner), a pass coverage weakside linebacker (Malcolm Smith), and a rush linebacker (typically Irvin, but also Wright and Wagner).

It has a shutdown corner who, well, shuts down half of the field (Richard Sherman), a big corner (formerly Brandon Browner, but now Byron Maxwell) for bigger receivers like Larry Fitzgerald, a nickelback (Walter Thurmond III), a dimeback (Jeremy Lane), a strong safety (Kam Chancellor), a free safety (Earl Thomas), and formerly a situational safety they called the big sub (Atari Bigby).

On the Advantages of Specialization

Each person can be good at many things, but most people can only be great at a few things. Specialization in football allows players to master positions they excel at and overcome their weaknesses through teamwork. McDonald struggled against double teams, but Mebane didn't. McDonald, however, was the better pass rusher of the two. A more vanilla system, without specialization, demands rare talent. In another system, either McDonald or Mebane would be counted on to do both, and both would suffer, and so would their team. In the Seahawks system, each could make a tidy career out of just doing what they're best at.

Seattle had the best defense in the NFL in 2013. It was not the greatest defense of all time, but adjusted for era, it was indeed historically great. But many of its players were no more than good or very good. Only Thomas and Sherman were truly great players. But by emphasizing what they could do, seeing how their brains and bodies interacted, the distribution of their weight, their hand fighting skills, their arm length, and jumping ability and ball skills, etc. Carroll and Quinn were able to maximize every player's potential.

59 The Bit Players

Franchises need both great people—great personalities and great players—and minor actors, forgotten but essential. For example, Rod Rutledge, the starting tight end for the 2001 Super Bowl–champion New England Patriots, caught Tom Brady's first pass. Had he dropped it, Brady would have gone 0-for-3, maybe fallen back behind Michael Bishop, maybe never had a chance to prove his greatness.

Mike McCormack was an offensive tackle who played in the '50s and early '60s. He was one of those old-school run-blocking road graders who could dominate the pre-modern era. He went to six Pro Bowls, five as a right tackle for Paul Brown's Browns.

McCormack was elected to the Pro Football Hall of Fame in 1984, two years after he relieved Jack Patera and became the Seahawks' head coach. He was instrumental in signing Chuck Knox. He reached out to Knox, and Knox was happy to work for a former offensive lineman. Until 1989 he was the Seahawks' general manager and worked with Knox to create the first consistently successful Seahawks teams. That was when it was assumed general managers and coaches would work together to determine a roster.

Of course, it was McCormack who wagered a first-round pick to draft Brian Bosworth in the 1987 supplemental round.

Randy Mueller worked under McCormack from 1983 to 1989. He would stick with Seattle through the 1999 season. Mueller did two things that forever changed Seahawks history. He traded Rick Mirer to the Bears for a first-round pick, an accomplishment that startles me every time I type it. And he helped Seattle wheel and deal to move up and draft Walter Jones. Bob Whitsitt made his name as the general manager of the Portland Trailblazers. It was not a distinguished name. Nor is he remembered for his great work with the Seattle Seahawks. But if he was never great, and if his moves never helped make Seattle a contender, he was nevertheless vital.

Maybe Whitsitt was just a better businessman than talent evaluator. His draft classes were weak, but his deeds were great. He helped negotiate the creation of Qwest Field, and Qwest Field is a jewel on the NFL landscape. He also signed Mike Holmgren.

McCormack, Mueller, and Whitsitt did great things for the Seahawks. They also committed great folly. They were not the stars, they were never revered, and I am sure even most diehard fans hardly know their names, but they were power players in the annals of team history. Each one was minor but essential.

60 Record a Game and Rewatch It

I know what you're thinking. *That dude totally dropped the pass.* Rewatch it. The pass was behind him. *That tackle totally blew his block.* Rewatch it. The quarterback ran into the defender. *That end was shut out.* Rewatch it. He was playing in the offense's backfield.

Football is chaotic. Football is visceral. It's felt, not understood. Add a little beer to the mix, a little company, maybe a kid, someone who asks too many questions, and you're liable to miss the whole thing. A whole game unfolds in about 11 minutes. Twenty-two players with 22 separate jobs, all competing, winning, and losing play by play, in increments of seconds, split-seconds, and Bill in maintenance has opinions to last the week. The wide receiver's a bum. That linebacker's a gamer. That rookie quarterback, total bust.

Love is understanding, right? Didn't Hallmark copyright that? Or did I read it in *Chicken Soup for the Leper's Soul?* Wait, no, love is never having to say you're sorry.

No, love is that delicate line between knowing and not knowing: the place where we settle when we understand enough to love but stop before the autopsy. Most football fans are merely infatuated. Infatuation is capricious. Infatuation is heartsick for someone one second and sickened by that same someone another. Most football fans know, broadly, what it takes to win or lose, know, for sure, that they like winning, but know nothing about what it takes to win. Instead, they resort to empty platitudes about heart, grit, and the spirit of a champion. It's really quite revolting.

So if you love, truly love your football team, stop a second, put aside your judgments, and instead do what true love does: ask questions. Record a game and rewatch it. Pick a player, and focus on him for a series. Rewind, watch that same play, but watch another player. Who finishes their blocks? Who finishes their routes? Whose fault was that drop?

I started football commentary the easy way: bad statistics and overwrought opinions. Speak strongly and you'll blunder into a few truths, and those seeking easy answers will remember your accuracies and forget your failures. (2014: nothing's changed.) But opinionated and ignorant is no way to go through life. So I decided

Best Game Ever

If anyone ever asks you what the most exciting game in Seahawks history is, you can provide them something approaching an objective answer. In 2005, after falling to 2–2, the Seahawks ripped off a six-game win streak. People were really starting to believe in the team, but at the same time, it wasn't like Seattle hadn't been here before. In fact, 8–2 was exactly how Seattle had started in Holmgren's first season.

The NFC West was already declining into a pitiful division, and though the Seahawks were 8–2, they had fattened on teams that could not tie their cleats without supervision. The 7–3 Giants were the exact test Seattle needed to prove their playoff mettle.

The game turned out to be not just important, but exciting. Win probability assumes 100 percent is sure victory, but between a 50–50 starting point and the inevitable victory, the probability itself can move wildly or almost not at all. Consider the butt-kicking the Vikings gave Seattle in Week 11 of the 2009 season. The game was over before the half, and so the sum movement was only 160 percent, or a little more than three times the minimum. Seahawks-Giants moved an astonishing 1,030 percent.

Well, astonishing if you did not watch it. Each team owned a lead for a little bit, but New York looked like it would prevail with a late drive to end the fourth quarter. The Giants closed to within the Seahawks 22, and with four seconds on the clock, attempted a 40-yard field goal. Jay Feeley hooked it wide left, and the game went into overtime.

Overtime only upped the excitement. The ball changed hands multiple times, and Feeley attempted another field goal but missed again. Eventually, Josh Brown nailed a 36-yarder to end it. The game not only gave Seahawks fans the quality win they needed to believe, but determined something more tangible. The Giants hosted Carolina and lost in the wild-card round. Had they won, they would have owned the tiebreaker with Seattle, the No. 1 seed, and a first-round bye. No one knew it then, but the Seahawks were playing for the Super Bowl.

to hold myself to my own standards. I started recording games and piecing through them.

The first thing you notice is how amazingly complex everything is. Every play involves incredibly delicate and complex interactions. I had to create new ideas just to know what was happening. And those ideas survived or died with more and more exposure. I was attempting to unravel the game and forced to learn it by doing so.

It may not appeal to everyone to attempt to know everything about a game. It should appeal to every fan to attempt to know what really happened in a game. Somewhere between a first viewing and a 15th, I think every fan can find a point that satisfies their needs. Maybe you just need to audit the officiating. Maybe you just need to watch the final minutes again, and see if it could have ended differently, better. Whatever you need, the answers are on the tape. It's free, but for the time and effort. And it will save you from being the guy who trades loudness and the semblance of certainty for actual knowledge.

61 Lawyers, Puns, & Poison Pills

Tim Ruskell made a habit of waiting until the off-season to negotiate contracts. If you can command the English language, and, by command, I mean string together words into a halfway intelligible whole, you could postulate on why he did this. And, by postulate, I mean speculate. And since we're speculating, what matters most is our internal biases toward the man.

If you respected Ruskell, went so far as to express an "in Ruskell we trust" mantra—*you know who you are*—you might extol the virtues and pseudo-virtues of waiting. Waiting allowed Ruskell to have the full picture of the player. It supplied the most important evidence to predicting their future ability: their most recent performance. It allowed Ruskell to sign a player when their health had stabilized and wasn't in permanent flux as a playing player's is. Sign someone to a million today, and they blow out their knee tomorrow. Oops.

If you had a rosy but realistic picture of Ruskell, you recognized the above, but also understood that it shouldn't be a rule. Ruskell was pretty cutthroat, fully willing to go back on his word if it was prudent. Before releasing Shaun Alexander, Ruskell gave the broken running back his public support. He would share his opinions of players, unfiltered, gave a less-than-glowing assessment of Marcus Trufant before signing him to a long-term contract, and knowingly used the media and its ability to shape opinions to leverage negotiations. It might be a rule of thumb to sign most players only after their contract had expired, but certainly there should be exceptions. That was just good business.

If you had a jaundiced but fair opinion of Ruskell, it was obvious that he sometimes leveraged against his own sometimes incorrect opinions. He had a figure for his player's value and would rather not overspend if he could let the market reinforce that figure. Ruskell was notorious for letting a player test the market, sure that player would crawl back discouraged and willing to negotiate. It worked sometimes. He got a deal on right tackle Ray Willis and pulled an absolute negotiating coup in the signing of LeRoy Hill. It also failed miserably sometimes.

If you hated Ruskell's guts and wouldn't sit in the seat he vacated because the warmth of his backside turned your stomach, you thought he was a moron, and whatever plausible explanation there was for his actions, it was nothing more than further proof of his half-smart scheming and abundant arrogance.

That particular opinion was sewn into many a Seahawks fan's heart after Ruskell lost Steve Hutchinson to an elaborate bit of back-door dealings. And at the hands of an arbiter who rivals Roger B. Taney for judicial miscarriage and overall buffoonery. No, arbiter Stephen Burbank wasn't a "stooped, sallow, ugly…supple, cringing tool of Jacksonian power" as Connecticut law professor R. Kent Newmyer described Taney, and he didn't set the civil rights movement back a hundred years or unleash a corporate monster still unvanquished, but he did deprive Seattle of a Hall of Fame–bound guard, the best of his generation, and render the transition tag impotent.

In football terms, Ruskell called a controversial play, one with moderate upside and potentially damning downside, and managed to fumble, watch his quarterback toted out on a stretcher, and then lose half his fan base to spontaneous combustion. Ruskell envisioned a Super Bowl contender he could improve into a dynasty. It's not unprecedented. The 1971 Dolphins lost the Super Bowl but rebounded to win the next two.

Marcus Trufant's Peak Season

For a long time, Torry Holt was the bane of the Seattle Seahawks and especially Marcus Trufant. He had five 100-yard receiving games against Seattle and four since Seattle drafted Tru in 2003. His most thorough butt-kicking was in 2006, when in Week 6 he had eight receptions for 154 yards and three touchdowns.

Things change, though, and sometimes suddenly. In 2007 with the Rams and Holt fading, Trufant emerged as a complete corner. Long known for his pure cover skills but not for his ability to snag picks, Marcus combined the two skills and began showing the rare ability to play the ball without losing the man.

Instead of facing Holt, Trufant mostly matched up against Isaac Bruce. On one play, he ran Bruce up the sideline, maintaining his normal close cover, but when the pass arrived, he showed a new ability, something tantalizing. He broke cover, leapt, and intercepted the pass. It was all part of a spectacular season for the corner. It's too bad that might be as good as it ever got.

Trufant announced his retirement in 2014.

Ruskell was never shy about spending his owner's vast fortune to add talent through free agency. He believed he could retain Hutchinson and also add elite talents in defensive end John Abraham and linebacker Julian Peterson. If he did, he would no doubt have been deemed a genius of Newtonian proportions. That team could find the playoffs blindfolded and would have been a clear-cut Super Bowl favorite. But Ruskell became Homer caught in the vending machine, stuck because he wouldn't let go of a soda and candy bar.

Hutchinson made it clear he didn't find Ruskell's decision to wait until the off-season particularly complimentary. Like many athletes, he equated pay with respect, and Ruskell's unwillingness to sign him ASAP was an indication that Ruskell was not that enthused about signing him at all. It's possible he was right. It's possible Hutch was tying together a loose straw man to deflect his own desire to leave the Pacific Northwest, it's geographical location opposite his home in Florida, and far away from his adopted home in Michigan. Peel a fable back, and one often finds no bad guys, only bad situations.

Ruskell sealed his fate when he applied the transition tag to Hutch. The stated purpose of the transition tag was simple and elegant. The transition tag allowed the recipient to test the free-agent market by being able to negotiate a contract with other teams, and the team applying the tag the right to match any contract and still sign their player. In theory, it was a masterful application of Ruskell's belief that even the best player was not priceless, and that instead of competing with oneself to sign a player, a general manager could allow the market to determine the player's worth.

In reality, it was Ruskell waxing the slue on Hutchinson's farewell slide to Mosquito Boot—which is my little colloquialism for The Land of a Thousand Stagnant, Glacier-Dredged Larvae Incubators, aka Minnesota. Seattle did its best to overcome that first blunder, appealed to NFL commissioner Paul Tagliabue ('bue was sympathetic to Seattle's plight. The Seahawks weren't, after all, attempting to expose a massive brain injury cover-up or anything), and appealed the contract to arbitration, but the Seahawks franchise and Ruskell had already extended themselves too much. Burbank was likely to rule as a litigator should, to the letter of the law and not to its intent. He did, and Hutch was a Viking.

Seattle cleverly negotiated themselves into an imploding stellar core on the offensive line. Such blunders are rare, wondrous, and franchise killing. Abraham signed elsewhere, and of Ruskell's targets, only Peterson and Shaun Alexander were attained. One was good. Another was the pyrotechnic ash of a copper halide prime.

Mike Holmgren never recovered from the trauma, and his relationship with Ruskell threatened mass extinction. Now nearly a decade later, I can draw a few conclusions with a fair amount of confidence. Ungodly blunders find the arrogant it seems but only sometimes. So Ruskell was both probably too sure of his strategy but also very, very unlucky. Rob Sims, Hutch's replacement, ended up being a good guard but poorly fit for Holmgren's system. Some of the run game's collapse was surely on Sims and by extension Ruskell. Seattle in the later 2000s showed the world how truly dysfunctional a team becomes when a general manager chooses talent irrespective of his coach's scheme just as Seattle in the early 2010's has become the absolute model for executive and coaching interaction. And, finally, maybe hastening the collapse wasn't so bad in the long run. Matt Hasselbeck didn't age well. Walter Jones was near the end. Alexander had a time share reserved in Washed Up that he didn't remember buying. Ruskell's unorthodox but surprisingly good eye for defensive talent eventually proved why orthodoxy is often wiser than it seems. Lofa Tatupu, Darryl Tapp, Josh Wilson, et al., burst onto the league but declined when elite talents are just breaking out: in their mid- to late-20s. The 2006 Seahawks were set to detonate, Hutch or no Hutch. Had Hutch been forced to re-sign, that eventual collapse may have been delayed, and everything would be different.

For once in my decades of Seahawks fandom, I can say that I wouldn't change a thing.

Engram

It will shock latter-day Seahawks fans to read, but Bobby Engram entered the league a true No. 1 wide receiver. The Bears drafted him in the Greatest Wide Receiver Draft Ever, as determined by God and Kiper. He was not drafted in the second round because he fit the position of slot receiver and third-down specialist but because superstar talents like Keyshawn Johnson, Terry Glenn, and Marvin Harrison hogged the first. Receiver talent drowned Engram's class like water over a flood plain: Eddie Kennison, Eric Moulds, Amani Toomer, Terrell Owens, and Joe Horn—afterthoughts and consolation prizes in the Johnson-Glenn sweepstakes.

Had Engram declared a year earlier or later, he could have breached the hallowed first round. It's laughable to think of Michael Westbrook or Ike Hilliard topping their respective draft classes when Engram was the 10th receiver drafted in 1996. Westbrook and Hilliard made a career out of what Engram declined into: a possession receiver.

See, the kid was good. Trawl the Internet, and one can still find love letters written to Engram by former Penn State students. Men enwrapped in appreciation for Bobby. Bobby Engram, the man who dusted off the record books and scrawled his name atop:

first in receiving yards (3,026), second in receptions (167), first in receiving touchdowns (31), and second in punt-return yards (786). Engram was the first-ever Fred Biletnikoff Award winner in 1994. Penn State was undefeated that season, but fell short of a national championship in a split vote. He had the athleticism, achievement, and production of a first-round pick, but fell, fell, fell to the Bears.

Engram never broke out in Chicago. Dave Wannstedt, and later Dick Jauron, wanted Engram to be a star, a stud, a difference-maker, but paired him with busts, retreads, and Kramers. Well, just one Kramer, but one is enough. Engram caught for Dave Krieg on Krieg's farewell tour. It was his last stop starting. Engram received for Shane Matthews after Matthews returned from the balmy climes of North Carolina and back to the team foolish enough to make him a pro. That same team later drafted Cade McNown, and McNown fluttered a few passes toward Engram before benching himself, being benched, benched again, banned from the Playboy mansion, and finally traded to Miami. You know what they say in Chicago about Cade: he's no Akili Smith.

Bobby tore his ACL in 2000 and for that effrontery was cut August 29, 2001. Mike Holmgren signed him two days later. Engram signed a two-year contract that paid him less than $500,000 annually. He was the 101st highest paid receiver in 2001. He got a $60,000 raise his second season and took on punt-return duties to compensate. He averaged 10.7 yards per return and returned one to the house. That was the season Engram became the darling of Football Outsiders metrics. Targets to Engram ranked 26th in total value and 13th in value per target. He was ninth and second in 2003. Engram received a raise before that.

The Outsiders crew came to call Engram "first-down machine," and the title was earned. Engram didn't waste a reception. He didn't receive for six on third-and-7. He packed value into every curl, slant, and out. In his first five seasons in Seattle, 77 percent of his receptions achieved a first down or touchdown.

Bobby Engram gains 14 yards on a reception before being tackled by New York Giants cornerback Ralph Brown during a game at Giants Stadium in September 2002.

It was more elegant than stats can describe. Hasselbeck-to-Engram took on pneumatic precision. Hasselbeck would drop back, throw, and as surely as the camera panned to his target, there was Engram snatching the pass, continuing the drive, bewildering the defender, all unassuming and easily athletic, death dealt seven yards at a time.

Engram's 1,000-Yard Season

Mike Holmgren was always able to create incredible value through his slot receivers. When the Seahawks would split three or four wide, opponents were in a true fix. The power of the Seahawks' rushing attack made them want to avoid nickel coverage, but assigning someone like Bobby Engram or D.J. Hackett a linebacker or safety was a bad mismatch.

It didn't matter if it was James Williams, Jerheme Urban, Bobby Engram, D.J. Hackett, or Jerry Rice. If Holmgren could play you out of the slot, you were almost unstoppable. His greatest accomplishment was in 2007, when the Seahawks abandoned the run and attempted to create an offense through Holmgren's vision of a spread. Thirty-four and recovering from Graves' disease, Engram had the first and only 1,000-yard season of his career, and became the Seahawks de facto No. 1 receiver, one 10-yard curl at a time.

And so it was for the next five seasons. B-Easy was the biggest little thing in Seattle: a watermark indicating true fandom, the glue in Seattle's greatest offenses—so steady, his full name became "First Down Bobby Engram." As in, Hasselbeck drops, looks right, sees, and fires. First down, Bobby Engram.

Then 2007 arrived, and Engram, the surviving stalwart on those great Holmgren offenses, returning from Graves' disease, took on the role he was drafted to play. He became the Seahawks' No. 1 receiver. Perhaps the first-ever No. 1 receiver to play primarily out of the slot. Deion Branch couldn't stay healthy and never developed trust with Matt. Shaun Alexander was a shadow of himself. The team needed an anchor, something to give its offense mooring, a counterbalance to a defense that was suddenly developing, a means to the end zone that didn't travel through Branch, Alexander, Nate Burleson, Maurice Morris, or Marcus Pollard. And so Engram, 34, caught for 1,147 yards on 94 receptions. Through him, Seattle had one of the best passing offenses in football.

Everything after is dross. Engram lost much of 2008, and the Seahawks' offense splattered like Blitz droppings. He wasn't retained in 2009 and did what soon-to-be-retired players do: signed with another team and suffered a brief and ignominious finale. But for a little while, and in his own way, Engram was great, an inseparable piece of the second greatest run in Seahawks history.

63 Share the Team You Love

No one ever owns a football team. With all his money and all his influence, Paul Allen can no more own the Seahawks than I can. Need proof? Watch the Lombardi Trophy ceremony. Players: elated. Carroll: jacked, as always. John Schneider: giddy. Allen: almost somber, perhaps realizing great achievements you more root for than accomplish are innately hollow. A local sports franchise is community property. Fans go when we can, give what we can, take what we can, and love it like a child. But fans, fans away from Seattle, can suffer distance that's not entirely geographical.

I live in an apartment. I see my neighbors not at all. Maybe we exchange a polite hello; maybe I see a hand closing a curtain as I walk by. I think I have a neighbor who's a Seahawks fan, but it's so hard to say sometimes. Fans shrivel or disappear entirely when the team goes bad. This was originally written when the team was very bad. Over the years since as the franchise picked itself up and eventually achieved immortality, that fan I live next to has never said more to me than "it's gonna be a good season." His son's been seen wearing 49ers gear. I've certainly never had a meaningful conversation with a stranger about team needs, or defensive strategy, or James Carpenter versus Paul McQuistan. Maybe more gregarious, less frightening looking Seahawks fans do all the time. Fans multiply and metastasize when teams win. Conversations are certainly out there to be had. New business in Seahawks crap is surely through the roof—all irony intended. But what I want is connection not a new hoodie.

If you are separated from Seattle but still bear a passion for the Seahawks, you can follow the news, you can listen to the radio, and in most places, you can even watch the team play, but you can also talk about the team. You can fulfill the second need of a fan: community. Without community, there is no Seahawks, not really. You can savor the action, but with whom can you celebrate? You can die with the ending of the game clock, but with whom can you commiserate? You can summon all the joy and excitement you've stifled, protected but also feared and let it explode out of you, go effing bananas the day the Seahawks finally won, finally won, finally won the Super Bowl! But who's gonna help you flip that car?

For me, down here in suddenly trendy Portland, Oregon, community meant online community. I would be a liar if I told you I enjoyed every second I spend online talking Hawks. When I started writing about Seattle, I honestly bristled at being called a blogger. The word sounds stupid. I worked for a long time without compensation of any kind. And now that I make money if not much, the experience feels somewhat compromised. This book like so much slag merchandise profiteered from newly avid Seahawks fans will sell because the team is winning. I want the team to win because I love the Seattle Seahawks. Now, the team winning keeps the heat on, kind of. Cry for me, I'm sure you want to.

I would be a liar if I told you I understood or appreciated every opinion from every Seahawks fan I ever encountered. I think many are entitled. Maybe they signed on in 2005 and never loved football until the team started winning. When the Seahawks began to sink, fingers emerged for pointing, and blades for goats sharpened. Now that they are good again, now that they are in fact great, the best team in all the world, the very best professional gridiron football team on Earth, and one of the greatest ever to grace this rare life-giving planet, people all over wear shiny, store-bought new regalia, because *winning*. And to them I say "welcome." No snobbery here. Some light hazing? Maybe. But there's always room for new 12, new maniacs to scream their lungs out and pump their fists and shout loudly profanities at offensive coordinator Darrell Bevell.

I would be a liar if I told you that reaching other fans, having somewhere to celebrate Richard Sherman, somewhere to bash Bevell, somewhere to stop every day and talk Hawks, did not take me from fan to disciple. It saddens me how modern man is Balkanized. Maybe it's a West Coast thing, but all this land, this separation makes life feel very desultory sometimes. I'm in the car, I'm somewhere else. I'm in the car, I'm somewhere else, never a moment of empathetic eye contact between. It's important to have somewhere to feel comfortable, to relate, and to connect with people who think obsessing about K.J. Wright and Jon Ryan is not so dang foolish.

I cannot speak for everyone, cannot tell you that finding a community will make being a fan more fulfilling. I can only invite you to find others, connect. I would be a liar if I told you it does not still sound kind of foolish to me, but it's the truth: sharing the team you love makes you love it more. Maybe there is something innately less substantial and satisfying about toasting Twitter mates, I don't know. But this last Sunday, I took a hearty swig and toasted you, distant but fellow Brothers in Blue.

64 The Joey Galloway Trade

The Dallas Cowboys' dynasty was collapsing. Oil tycoon and celebrity football team owner Jerry Jones couldn't stomach it. Guy's rich as a sultan, was given every break by Daddy and luck, and has spent the better part of two decades smashing Duplo blocks into Lego holes and calling it a billion dollar professional sports franchise. Jones' beloved quarterback needed help. Troy Aikman was winding down. He was entering his mid-30s, had swapped Michael Irvin for Raghib Ismael, Jay Novacek for David Lafleur, and Emmitt Smith for old Emmitt Smith. His completion percentage was down, his health failing him, and the dynasty he quarterbacked was crushing Aikman as it crumbled. Soon he would be honking pedantic beside Joe "please God let this game be over" Buck. But wallet agape, Jones was in a panic to spend ill-gotten gains on chasing the past. The Seahawks were only too happy to rob a pensioner blind to fund that which Jones will never again have: a promising future. By Jerry's logic, Aikman didn't need a time machine but "weapons." Joey Galloway, disgruntled and poorly fit for his new coach's scheme, needed out. Mike Holmgren needed an exit strategy and maybe aspirin too. He had inherited Galloway and all his airs. Galloway was a star on a star-crossed team. He had elite speed. He could scare defensive coordinators, if never crack the Pro Bowl. He could catch anything and had to, receiving for busts and retreads—saved, *saved*, by quatragenarian bomber Warren Moon.

Galloway was the kind of player a kid like me loooved. He was a one-man team on the highlight reels. Galloway for 59. Galloway for 81 and the score. Galloway for 86 on the end around. No one's catching Joey. All deep routes and burnt corners. All busted coverage and touchdowns. All highlights every play, and not an ordinary completion between them. (Highlight reels edit out the drops, rounded off cuts, and dropped routes.)

In four years in Seattle, Galloway was targeted for more incomplete passes than completions. He never cracked even a 50 percent catch rate. Galloway could take it to the house but rarely sustain a drive. He didn't play Holmgren football. He was a Cowboy by birth and a Seahawk by accident.

Paul Allen offered Joey an impressive salary, enough to make him the second-highest-paid receiver in the NFL, but never enough. Galloway held out through training camp and into the season. It was a godsend. Seattle traded Galloway to Dallas on February 12, 2000. Seattle traded Galloway to Dallas for their first-round picks in 2000 and 2001. It was lunacy. Unforgivable the second it happened, and it only got worse.

Seahawks wide receiver Joey Galloway pulls away from the Dallas Cowboys' Kevin Smith for a 44-yard touchdown reception at Irving, Texas, in November 1998. Galloway was a good receiver who could have been great in the play-action, deep-passing game of eras past.

Galloway tore his ACL in the fourth quarter of his very first game. Boom, pop, burner broken. It's not like I ever wished harm on Galloway, but there's a shameful satisfaction in not only winning a trade, but dominating. Galloway was gone for the rest of 2000. Aikman suffered his 10th concussion…ahem, *diagnosed* concussion. He was waived before the 2001 season and retired.

Maybe if it wasn't the Cowboys I wouldn't feel such warmth and smug satisfaction typing this, but it was the Cowboys, and screw them. Jones decided that he would replace Aikman with a series of surprise quarterbacks, each more surprising than the last. He drafted Quincy Carter, and Carter introduced himself to the league with two sacks, two fumbles, two picks, nine completions and a benching in Week 1. Carter was No. 2 incarnate. Then there was Anthony Wright, but Wright went wrong, and so Carter returned, briefly. Eventually, Clint Stoerner and Ryan Leaf joined the mix. Galloway threw a pass and completed it for one, and everyone agreed that apart from punter Micah Knorr, Galloway was the best quarterback of the bunch. He understandably struggled as a wide receiver.

Seattle turned those picks into Shaun Alexander—*hooray*—and Koren Robinson—*glug, glug*. Alexander was sensational, good enough to be underappreciated, and Robinson, well Robinson careened off the straight and narrow and eventually out of the league, but before all that liver damage, accomplished more than Galloway ever accomplished in Dallas.

And so it was, for one transaction, the good guys won, and the hated Cowboys lost, and it was good. It wasn't Tony Dorsett good, but it was good, and deserved, and may I end with: screw the Cowboys.

The Pyrrhic Victory That Wasn't

6–9 entering the final week of the regular season is commonplace for bad teams. Some will end 6–10. Some will end 7–9. But not until January of 2011 could a 7–9 team call itself Super Bowl contender.

Since 2002, the debut of the Texans franchise and the first year the NFL fielded 32 teams, 131 or 31.5 percent of teams have finished 7–9, 8–8, or 9–7 (or records near about but including one or more ties). If wholly random, only 18.8 percent of teams would be expected to finish within that range (or any range of three). So there's a regressing force at work. The distribution of all final records is a very common bell curve. It's also not at all uncommon for a team with a 9–7 or 8–8 record to make the playoffs, and despite eking in with seemingly the lowliest of performances possible to make it, the set of those teams is 19–20 in playoff competition (again, since 2002). Now, if I wanted to shoehorn an ultra-naive and totally intellectually dishonest comparison here, I might point out that the difference between a 7–9 and a 9–7 team is slight. And I could back it up with many fine and shiny statistics. In truth, though, Seattle was 7–9 and *bad*.

What's more, they were bad but most of the way to a non-tank tank job that could land them a prime position in what was supposed to be an excellent draft for quarterbacks. Imagine being offered $10 million to throw a basketball game and refusing but never saying as much. Imagine the offer was still on the table before the game started. And playing good not great, in line with expectations and no more, but approaching the final seconds of the game down one and with the ball in your hands. All you'd have to do is miss, and you'd be a millionaire. Well, in the partially mangled words of Doug Martsch, Seattle did the stupid thing and kept on living. Swoosh.

This was the second time in four years that Matt Hasselbeck was nearing free agency. A player older than his years despite having started only 131 games in 12 years, Hasselbeck was out Week 17, the deciding game of the season, after injuring himself scrambling untouched into the end zone against the Buccaneers. Last time Hasselbeck was approaching free agency, Seattle sort of punted and sort of doubled down on a bad decision. Tim Ruskell re-signed him, assuring all that he *was not* the problem, etc. Which he wasn't and he was, and which clarity of Ruskell's thought chills me to the bone. It must be so quiet in the brains of the chronically certain.

This time it was assumed Seattle had better leadership, but that particular leadership's ability to assess quarterback talent was in serious doubt. They had traded a not insignificant combination of draft pick and draft position for Charlie Whitehurst, the former third-string/current second-string quarterback of the San Diego Chargers. Whitehurst had not looked the part in his preseason performances with San Diego. He had not looked the part but for a brief time in his first preseason with Seattle. And despite being traded for to compete with Hasselbeck for the starting position and Hasselbeck seemingly resoundingly washed up, Whitehurst had not been a serious contender since it was announced he was a serious contender. His two starts, one in Cleveland, the other home against the Giants, seemingly confirmed everyone's worst doubts. And though that's a hell of a way to evaluate a quarterback, it was at least enough to force coaches, executives, and fans to acknowledge adding another talent was necessary. Seattle absolutely could not enter the 2011 season with Whitehurst unchallenged atop the depth chart.

Further mucking up the rah rah, "always compete" stuff was the fact that the 2011 draft looked particularly deep for quarterback talent. At the time of this game, Andrew Luck had not confirmed he would stay another season. Cam Newton was declaring himself as that ultra-rare one-year wonder that's just too extraordinarily talented to write off. Many Seahawks fans were crazy about local talent Jake Locker. And should Seattle win, their draft position would plunge at least from ninth to 24th—and maybe even from ninth to 32nd—*the horror.*

But this was also a time of weird playoff performances. The 2011 Giants, who finished 9–7 and were outscored by six points in the regular season, beat the 16–0 New England Patriots to win Super Bowl XLVI. The 9–7 Arizona Cardinals nearly beat Pittsburgh in Super Bowl XLIII. Seattle did not seem quite as good as either of those all-time underdogs, but then so much better the story. And making the playoffs is life, no matter how flickering or fleeting, and missing the playoffs is death. Could prudence ever dictate trading a shot, however red-shifted, at four wins and immortality for an improved draft pick?

Was this a clouded and ambivalence-inducing time to be a Seahawks fan? In the immortal words of *Arrested Development*'s T-Bone, "Oh, most definitely."

It was truly weirder than all that, too. Hasselbeck was out because of a mysterious injury, one that he had fully recovered from by next week in time for the wild-card round of the playoffs. He did seem hurt. You could watch him grab for his back after running into the end zone. But players play hurt. Typically the criteria for playing hurt is: will playing make the injury worse? And: does the injury diminish the player enough that it would be better if his backup started instead? Hasselbeck had what was described as a "hip injury." What I am trying to say is, hypothetically, if Hasselbeck were still good, still healthy, if the quarterback position were stable and good and the Seahawks a good team with a good chance and no ancillary "embarrassment" or meaningful draft position lost by winning, would Whitehurst have started?

I'm not picking for conspiracies or sowing scandal—especially not in such barren soil, but Week 17 of the 2010 season was easily among the weirdest regular season games in Seahawks history. Whitehurst started and was bad. Sam Bradford started for the Rams and was worse, which was bad for Bradford because short of his team winning with him under center he was looking every bit a bust. Seattle won 16–6, and there's this image burned into my head: Carroll congratulating Whitehurst but not like, "Damn, son, we're headed to the playoffs!" Instead: "Damn, son, you won a game!" And healthy again and despite another pretty rotten season overall, Hasselbeck was immediately reinstated the starter afterward.

So divisive was the outcome that I created separate posts and adjoining separate comment sections in preparation for the game. Some people abhorred victory, invoking that notion of a Pyrrhic victory, which idea can be best captured by King Pyrrhus himself "one more such victory would utterly undo" the Seahawks. Some people abhorred losing on purpose, arguing the very notion could so infect and debase the organization, that it would become curse. Ever committing the great refusal, as Dante would say, I understood both arguments. But partway through the game I felt, as singer Dan Bejar would say, "Somethin's telling me it's time to take sides." And I just couldn't root for a loss, future be damned.

Seattle's pick plummeted and then fell further after the Seahawks beat the Saints. That pick became sometimes-for-a-series left guard James Carpenter. One of the lesser in the ranks of Cable's Cabal and probably a busted pick. But, as if by extreme poetic justice, Seattle, by winning and missing an opportunity to draft a quarterback in 2011, missed too a raft of busts and a year later drafted Russell Wilson.

This I think is the ultimate problem with critiquing "process." It's sort of a ludic fallacy, in a way. If we could know exactly what a good process to constructing a good football team was, and that good process was more or less free of the wild variability inherent in assembling and maximizing human resources, if building a sports team were like building an automated factory, then scrutinizing and critiquing process would be okay. By that thinking it's almost impossible to argue against the Seahawks tanking Week 17 of 2010 against the Rams. We can look at all possible outcomes quasi-objectively and say since the Seahawks had such an insignificant chance of competing for the Super Bowl and since the Super Bowl is the ultimate goal that trading hugely valuable draft position for that insignificant chance is bad process. And that Seattle ended up with a good outcome is nothing more than dumb luck.

January 2, 2011: the Seattle Seahawks had a decision to make: try their best to win or tank on the down low and for some speculative reward. They chose to win. And on down that chain of events, they eventually chose to win it all and become Super Bowl champions. Seems like a hell of a good process to me.

66 Care About the Kicker

Care about the kicker,
the return man,
the punter,
the gunner,
the up back.
Care about the backup fullback,
the emergency quarterback,
the emergency punter,

the emergency kicker.
Care about the depth,
the practice squad,
the reserves,
the next man up.

Care about the assistant head coach,
the quarterbacks coach,
the running backs coach,
the wide receivers coach,
the offensive line coach,
the defensive line coach,
the linebackers coach,
the secondary coach,
the special-teams coach,
the offensive quality control coach,

A Kick in the Teeth

Josh Brown went from hero to villain in record time. He was Seattle's kicker for most of the good seasons and enjoyed the halo of success. In 2006 he set new standards for good timing and was perhaps the most important part of Seattle making its fourth consecutive playoff.

Brown was known not only for his clutch kicking, should such a thing really exist, but his tackling ability. Brown was that rare breed of macho kicker who seems to savor contact. His most famous tackle came against the inimitable Devin Hester. He threw down and then hulked out.

Ruskell offered to make him the highest paid kicker in the history of football that off-season. Brown declined and instead signed a similar contract with the rival Rams. The move was met with boos and hollers. Funnily enough, it worked perfectly for Seattle. Brown brought his kicking to a team that needed everything but, and Seattle signed Olindo Mare. Mare, then derided for his accuracy, not only outperformed Brown as a field-goal kicker but wiped the floor with him as a kickoff specialist.

the defensive quality control coach.
Care about the head of strength and conditioning,
the assistant strength and conditioning coach,
the team physicians.

Care about the CEO,
the president,
the general manager,
the head of scouting,
the vice president of player personnel,
the director of pro personnel.

Care about the Southwest scout,
the Midwest scout,
the Northeast scout,
the Southeast scout.

Care about every single one,
because winning takes the kicker,
the punter,
the return man,
the gunner,
the up back…

Dan McGwire

Dan McGwire burned up on reentry, which is to say he stooped to tie his shoes, and cost Seattle Chuck Knox, maybe not in that order. Draft experts come in the proclaimed, the bona fide, the unidentified, and then there's the unassuming but prophetic. "He's an easy target. If you beat the line, get rid of the center and try to fight off the guard, you've got him, and he can get hurt. He's there. A big guy. You can't miss him."

Spartan defensive tackle Bobby Wilson was right. McGwire was a sack waiting to happen. Once in every eight drop-backs, McGwire was sacked. That is almost beyond comprehension. A quarterback regularly passes eight or more times in a single drive. McGwire only had 169 drop-backs in his entire professional career, but 21 ended with him under a defender. If he'd lasted long enough to qualify, McGwire would have ranked 183rd all-time in sack percentage. Only Steve Fuller, Bobby Douglass, and the inimitable Rob Johnson were sacked more often among qualifiers.

Johnson was truly amazing. In 1998 Johnson suffered sacks in 21.3 percent of all pass attempts. Lest you think he was playing a man short, or behind a sadistic offensive line, teammate Doug Flutie was sacked in only 3.3 percent of all snaps. Consider that— the 6'4" Johnson, waiting and waiting, defenders closing on all sides, and the 5'10" Flutie, bobbing and weaving, scrambling away and keeping the play alive.

But Johnson had something resembling redeeming value, because he continued to start. He took his licks, got comfortable with his horizontal, picked himself up, and was entrusted to try again. McGwire was sacked into dust and then abandoned. You may never see another first-round quarterback who elicited less faith in his head coaches than McGwire. There have been bigger busts, but few bigger failures.

Regarding Knox: Chuck, like any decent human being, had a chilly relationship with new owner Dan Behring. Knox was on his last year of his contract but wanted an extension. Negotiations lasted for months. It was reported that Knox wanted to extend his contract another three or four years. He settled for one year and an option.

Knox didn't like McGwire and didn't want to draft a quarterback in the first round. McGwire was all Behring. Knox favored a player he thought could be had in the second round, but only two quarterbacks were selected in the second round of the 1991 draft: Browning Nagle and Brett Favre. It's a fun fantasy to envision Favre in the Silver and Blue, but Favre was long gone before Seattle got to pick again. More importantly, the fissure between team ownership and Coach Knox opened after that draft and, after the public showing of disrespect, never healed. A year later, Knox was gone.

McGwire stuck around. Took more sacks. Got injured. Had whatever media-created luster stripped from him. Finally, under Tom Flores, McGwire finished out the 1994 season, playing extensively in the final four games. It was crazy, really. Seattle had already replaced McGwire with a comparable bust, Rick Mirer. Mirer went down with a broken thumb, and there was McGwire, all ostrich-like, ready to begin again, rewrite his unwritten legacy, and he did. He did. He did. He wrote 13 sacks onto the field, and punctuated his work with nine fumbles.

That ended Dan McGwire. Not as excruciating as Mirer, but his own kind of awful, on the down low.

 **Better to Reign in Hell**

14 Jan 2009
Aaron Curry was supposed to eat dynamite and belch thunder. He was supposed to be Lawrence Taylor combined with Derrick Brooks, including all constituent parts. Aaron Curry, four arms and four legs of pure, linebacker badassery. He was supposed to be a rookie sensation, the greatest linebacker prospect of his generation:

a mutant, cyborg, zombie, vampire, Frankenstein composed of Butkus and HAL and Lucifer, but not fey Lucifer, but butt-kicking, sword-wielding, fallen-angel Lucifer. He was supposed to be that, because that is what a fourth overall pick is: Roger Goodell's boo-boo kiss for your team getting smacked around all season.

Aaron Curry was supposed to be that, because when you're bad, and you know you're bad, and you know you're not going to escape anytime soon, you want to be bad, but cool. Seattle selected Aaron Curry after finishing a 4–12 season. It suffered a historic wave of injuries. It lost most of its offensive line. It lost Walter Jones forever. It lost Lofa and LeRoy and Hasselbeck, and about anyone else you care to care about. It was a broken season, and it was Mike Holmgren's last in Seattle, so it lost Mike Holmgren, too.

Aaron Curry was long-limbed and powerfully built. He had a mean streak that began and ended on the football field. He could fly around and propel 260 pounds of ripped muscle into anyone, anywhere, anytime. Some said he was an excellent pass rusher, but he wasn't really. Some said he knew a lot about cover, but a couple fluke picks can confuse. About no one said he'd bust.

Curry was safe. Maybe he was just a linebacker. Maybe a linebacker never won a championship for a team. Maybe the Hall of Linebackers is half-filled with great players who never grasped glory. But if he wasn't going to put the team over the top, he would at least be awesome to watch.

Like Cortez in the '90s. Cortez Kennedy was an indisputable point of pride for a run of Seahawks teams that frustrated and embarrassed. Tez was enviable. Any fan would want Tez. Any team could sign Tez and improve. But he was ours. And through him projected the dim rays of a better future.

Aaron Curry didn't do it. He looked lost at times. He didn't trade rookie boners with moments of great promise. Jim Mora spoke of him in veiled putdowns. Mora began limiting his snaps.

Established players began accusing him of being dirty. Elder fans invoked "the Boz."

Aaron Curry was just a rookie. So no one worries too much. Speaking worries is blasphemy. First spoken and then truth. Could he be a bust? Could he be all prototypical body and bad football? Don't say it.

Don't say it.

4 Feb 2014

No one ever needed to. Curry busted out of the league with the kind of speed you can't coach. If the primary athletic talent, the primary tool (in the jargon) is size, then a close second would be health. Aaron Curry was fast. Aaron was strong and agile and powerfully built. But "agile," "strong," "fast"—these are outputs. Products of an intricate machine still only partially understood made of bone and tendon and ligament and muscle.

Carroll and Schneider wisely traded Curry to the Oakland Raiders before his value had bottomed out. Likely it is easier to overcome the sunk cost fallacy when it wasn't you that sunk the cost, but Carroll and Schneider have showed equal prudence in trading their former third-round pick John Moffitt. A seventh-round pick from Oakland in 2012 became J.R. Sweezy. A fifth-round pick in 2013 became Tharold Simon. After getting cut by the Giants in 2013, Curry retired from football.

Curry busted out of the league with an alacrity Boz couldn't touch.

Soon after the Seahawks won the Super Bowl.

So the particular disappointment created by one failed pick, no matter how hyped or how expensive, doesn't matter too much it seems. But for the sake of posterity, let's remember one indispensable lesson, one small but redeeming bit of wisdom Seahawks fans may glean from Curry's failure: There are no safe picks in the

NFL Draft. And until someone proves otherwise, I am not going to believe there's even much element of "safer" or "riskier." At least not in a way supposed experts can detect and forecast.

Thankfully Carroll and Schneider like a little risk and love a big reward.

Bo Versus Boz

The unsung hero of Bo versus Boz was Marcus Allen. Allen, a feature back in his prime, was relegated to not only splitting carries but lead blocking. He did, with heart, and he threw some beauties. On the famous 91-yard rush Bo Jackson ended in the Seahawks tunnel, Allen cut-blocked corner Patrick Hunter to free Jackson to the sideline.

The unsung goat of Bo versus Boz is Kenny Easley. He fell, allowing Jackson an easy touchdown reception earlier in the second. His athleticism fading, Easley's sometimes poor instincts in coverage were exposed. On Jackson's long run, Bo exploded past Easley easily, provoking Dan Dierdorf to comment that Kenny was "not a burner." Dierdorf was always a little loose with the facts, but that day he was right. Easley was not just easily eclipsed by Bo but caught from behind by a hustling Brian Bosworth. (A reminder to not believe the hagiographic mythmaking of invested parties. No one's quite as unqualified to properly assess, say, Leonardo Da Vinci as a Leonardo Da Vinci biographer.)

The story of Bo versus Boz was not about Bo or Boz—both were gone from the league before they could justify their hype—but the fading Seahawks. It was 1987, and Chuck Knox thought the Seahawks were favorites. They beat both of the Super

Bowl–bound teams the season before, and that meant a lot to Knox and the media.

That kind of logic just does not translate to the football field. No one knew it then, but Easley was near his end. So was Steve Largent. Jacob Green had turned 30. Curt Warner wasn't old, but his legs were. The team was at the precipice, and maybe if things had broken different, 1987 could have been their 2005.

Knox blamed the strike, but the Sea-Scabs finished 2–1. They had a ringer, too. Largent crossed picket lines to play in Week 5 at Detroit and caught 15 passes for 261 yards and three touchdowns. Knox thought the strike hurt team unity, but it wasn't unity, or the lack of it, that let Jackson run all over the Kingdome.

Jackson was turning the corner with ease, and only Bosworth was quick enough to get near him. He was bowled over attempting to do something no other Seahawks seemed capable or particularly inclined to do: attempt a tackle. Ultimately Boz may have failed, but it was the overall failure of the Seahawks defense that set him up for the fall. Knox's defense was getting old, and it showed against faster opponents.

The idea of Bo versus Boz is a Bosworth-worthy fabrication. The entire Seahawks defense was crumbling. Boz could neither save nor destroy it. In 1987 the team allowed the most rushing yards per attempt in the NFL. It was not just Bo. Eleven opponents topped 100 yards rushing, including the Oilers in the wild-card. I guess "Boz versus Alonzo Highsmith, Mike Rozier, and Allen Pinkett" does not have the same sex appeal—that group of Oilers helped Houston run for 178. And when we say "sex appeal," what we really mean is marketability. Where there is money to be made, there are lies to be told.

It is easy to make sense of it in retrospect. Back then, no one knew Easley's kidneys were failing, or how bad Bosworth would bust. No one knew the Seahawks were winding down their best run in franchise history, or that it would be the defense that

243

betrayed them. They just knew a two-sport athlete and overblown hayseed and how one ran his mouth and the other ran all over him.

70 Make Football an Event

Multitasking is dead. Long live the pure experience.

Maybe I am at odds with my generation, but I find multitasking to be shallow and insubstantial. Research has proven that the underlying premise of multitasking, the ability to do multiple things at once, is in fact a lie. We never do multiple things at once, but instead quickly shift from thing to thing. The quality of each thing we do is reduced, as is our ability to understand, appreciate, and enjoy each thing we do. We are not accomplishing or experiencing more. Each endeavor and stimulus blaring and dissonant, competing for your compromised attention, the result is cognitive noise. A constant coming to; watching football intently is to watching football while multitasking, as Jimi Hendrix playing "Purple Haze" is to a YouTube "Shreds" videos.

I am not an old-fashioned guy. I do not believe in a Golden Age, a centuries-old myth; I do not pine for an era when most humans were repressed. I don't miss oil-slick hair and casual racism, something that's been a vogue reaction to our often stifling need to tolerate. (Chemotherapy is tolerated. I love and accept other people. Some I like. Some I don't.) No, no, I am, ladies and gentleman, a futurist.

Multitasking is dead. Maybe we don't see it yet, but it is. Lag or something. Multitasking is dead, because multitasking is not progress. It is a detour, a distraction, a cowardly retreat from experience.

Yes, you can appreciate more taste in your food if you turn off the TV. You can better understand music if you close your eyes and listen. You can better enjoy football if you close the laptop, quit flipping channels, and sit agog at its beauty and complexity. I know this firsthand. I have twittered and checked email and even attempted to install a heat sync in my now dead laptop, and all while nominally watching football. Like a speed reader, I gleaned the plot, characters, and general tone of a game, and missed all that makes it worthwhile.

It's true. We get what we put in. Not because of cosmic justice, no, that's BS. We get what we put in because the more we look forward to Sunday, the better we plan, the more we invest, the more we care, the more it can hurt and the better it can feel.

So make football an event. Prepare a good meal. Get a grill going if that's your thing. I love a well-crafted sandwich. Get some snacks, too. Don't just get crap to munch on, but find something that really satisfics. Spend money. Everyone has some money. Money we blow on Mountain Dews while buying gas and lottery tickets and other ephemera and crap. My first roommate spent himself broke with these incidental purchases.

Pool your wasted cash and buy some good beer. Some expensive beer. Get a beer for every quarter, not some domestic crap, but how about a wit beer for kickoff, and a stout for the third quarter? Get the beer you love, and drink like you enjoy the beer, not like the beer is a means to an end.

Love football like it's not a means to an end. Love the moments stretched to breaking. The snap. The good block on the bad run.

Invite friends. Make Seahawks friends and get together and get loud and ribald. There is no substitute for shared fandom.

Treat every game like it's special because it is. Know your opponent and know the match-ups and the storylines and the implications. Anticipate. Get nervous. Concentrate on every moment. Savor. Don't dabble in football and disappear when things get tough. Commit. Care. Believe.

71 The Whole Sick Crew

History remembers the stars, the victories, and also the epic failures, but it tends to glance over the screw-ups, the jobbers, the last line of defense, the sycophants, the favored, the bad, the players who made those failures possible. To fans, the bad players are almost as important as the good. Invariably, a team is going to lose—and if you're a Seahawks fan, a lot (editor's note: Hahahahahahahahahaha)—and losing produces grief. Grief is a miserable thing for a sports fan to endure. Sport is leisure, an escape, and suffering through your leisure is better left for ascetics. My leisure comes with beer and swearing and stomping on the ground and yelling: whooping, hollering, onomatopoeia of all shapes and sounds.

So how about the bad guys, the schmucks, the players whose name are most often bookended by profanity? Let's give it up for them. It wasn't always their fault, but, holy hell, how does a football split your outstretched hands and bonk off your facemask, Kelly Jennings!?

To be a true scoundrel, you can't just fail and get cut. Sports fans have little concern about the fodder that briefly graces a roster and is replaced just as quickly. No, you have to have some staying power. The true thorn of a sports fan is the player who not only sucks but inexplicably sticks, sometimes for seasons.

Seattle was short on talent of all kinds in 1976, so when Jack Patera signed his former player Bob Lurtsema, it probably seemed like a sensible acquisition. Minnesota was a contender in the '70s, and their strength lay in their defensive line: the Purple People Eaters. Lurtsema had earned a spot in Vikings fans' hearts as "Benchwarmer Bob," situational end and minor celebrity.

He had all the markings of an absolute pain in the ass. He had earned favor from his coach and was acquired not because of obvious ability but connections. Patera made the 34-year-old man and nine-year backup an immediate starter. He stuck for two seasons before gifting the franchise with his retirement. The Seahawks contended the very next season. That isn't to imply *post hoc ergo propter hoc*, only to say: We all must spit out our binkies some day, Mr. Patera.

If you can't insert yourself through connections and good press, vengeance works. Patera signed Roger Carr to replace Sudden Sam McCullum. McCullum was the Seahawks' union rep and among their best and most respected players. Carr was on the downswing, every bit of what you'd expect from a middling, oft-injured wide receiver turning 30. He only lasted one season, but it was an arduous season, and his suckiness seemed especially glaring because of it.

After Carr and after Patera, there was Chuck Knox. Knox was good about starting the best players instead of the best-known, but even Chuck had a soft spot for veterans and legends. And so Seattle signed Franco Harris. Harris was every bit the burned-out shell of his former self the Steelers cut. Knox could be forgiven for signing Harris—after all, it wasn't the plan. Seattle had its star rusher, Curt Warner, but Warner blew out his knee in the season opener and was placed on IR.

Harris brought national attention. He was a Super Bowl legend and only a few yards short of Jim Brown's all-time rushing record. Harris had rushed for 1,000 yards the season prior, and that, my friends, is an immutable achievement. Sure, Harris was plodding where he once was powerful, and he had not had a run longer than

21 yards in two seasons, and, sure, maybe his fumbling problems were no longer excusable when his rushing couldn't match, but *this was Franco Harris*. A legend in pursuit of history.

His arrival was met with ludicrous expectations, as if he carried the Steel Curtain to Seattle atop his broad shoulders. Guard Reggie McKenzie was psyched: "When Franco came here, the first thing he talked about was us winning the Super Bowl. Not going to the Super Bowl; winning it. Oh, it's going to be such a great year." It was. It was. Right after Seattle cut Harris and his 2.5 yards per carry.

Looking backward, there was Norm Johnson, who somehow earned the eternally trite nickname "Mr. Automatic." One wonders if it was meant ironically, as Johnson, somehow, despite kicking at least half his games in a dome, finished with a 69.7 percent field-goal percentage. That's not fair, though. Johnson kicked during a time when all kickers were less accurate for various reasons. It still looks wonky to me. Even in the most hostile environment, Johnson's 36-for-60 run from 1985 through 1986 must have been hard to swallow.

The next big disaster was probably the Boz, but Brian deserves his own essay. Seattle then crawled from a period of relevance, where disastrous players could actually stick out, to a point of complete failure, where singling out any one failure is petty and beneath me. Rick Mirer.

That Mirer somehow won AFC Rookie of the Year speaks volumes about the award. He was a sack-prone check-down artist who somehow arrested coaches' interest—first Tom Flores, then Dennis Erickson, Dave Wannstedt in Chicago, and after all that failure, Bill Parcells in New York.

Almost any member of Holmgren's defense fits the Crew. There was an Isaiah Kacyvenski and a Rashad Moore. Bob Whitsitt added a couple players who put an ironic spin on their position title: safety Ken Hamlin and safety Michael Boulware. They were all pretty forgettable, though. Bad players, soon replaced, sooner forgotten.

It was not until Brian Russell that the Sick Crew got its team captain. Russell had it all: grit, determination, a fluke good season many years removed, a rapport with coaches, good interview skills, and the favor of local media. Most importantly, Russell had a secret weapon: the overseer zone. Russell took the axiom of keeping the play in front of him to absurd lengths. Every play started a minimum of five yards in front of him. He was seemingly never involved in anything but cleanup tackles. He played in 32 consecutive games and broke up nine passes. Russell had little range, and that made it seem like he was never burned, like the receiver would pop open from thin air, or the corner was just supposed to be isolated in single-coverage. He took confusing angles to the ball carrier and tackled like a Crisco-glazed fourth-grader. He hit late and often, and padded his stats by jumping on every pile no matter how dead the play.

But Russell played and played and even convinced some people he was good. Some took an agnostic stance; others attempted to prove his quality through negative proof. Russell was terrible when we saw him, but when we did not, he was Ed Reed/Ronnie Lott. How else could he continue to start? Maybe the coaches saw something we couldn't. Maybe fans suffered Stockholm syndrome. Maybe Brian Russell was good.

Maybe they all were.

Synthesis

There's a movement toward bookishness in roster building. Data, the days of Big Data, sports have been swept up in it, and I for one am happy about that. As counter-movement becomes movement, and establishment becomes outsider, in true Hegelian fashion, movement becomes counter-movement—reformer informing the better way, what maybe was lost because of their ascension. What does big data maybe not know? Where are its blind spots?

Maybe the wise words of 2012 NFL MVP Adrian Peterson might help us find out: "I know talent. I can watch Michael Jordan and Scottie Pippen and see the difference," Peterson told ESPN. "There are two Jordans on this team. I'm not trying to be cocky. I'm just very confident in my abilities," Peterson said, calling [Percy] Harvin the "best player" with whom he's ever suited up.

How do we quantify Jordan talent versus Pippen talent? Basketball Reference, naturally, assigned the higher Win Shares overall to Jordan. But what about in a sport where "individual" statistics is an absurdity?

A favorite kind of analysis for the statistically inclined is comparing a player to a representative sample of similar seeming players. The website Football Outsiders attempted this type of analysis and produced three historical comparisons for Harvin: Danny Amendola, Al Toon, and Andre Johnson. That might seem like best case, worst case—and who again is Al Toon? But what it is, is a shot in the dark. There is nowhere near enough information found in a box score to accurately compare players' abilities. Some dreaded qualitative analysis must be done, biases and all.

For the sake of argument, let's make some distinctions that probably do not exist, strictly speaking. Let's say the coaching side of Seattle's front office, headed by executive vice president Pete Carroll, but informed by his entire coaching staff, handles the Peterson side of evaluations, along with more granular stuff like scheme fit and chemistry with existing talent. And let's say the executive side of Seattle's front office, headed by general manager John Schneider but extending through senior personnel executive Scot McCloughan, director of pro personnel Tag Ribary, director of college scouting Scott Fitterer, assistant director of pro personnel

Trent Kirchner, etc., handles the data analysis stuff, along with more granular stuff like market value, value of picks in any given draft, etc.

The calculus of the Seahawks trading for Percy Harvin becomes something like this: $x + y + z < a$

With "x" equaling the projected value of players likely available and useful to the Seahawks and who would be available in the first round of the 2013 NFL Draft and the third and seventh rounds of the 2014 NFL Draft.

"Y" equals Harvin's impact on Seattle's salary cap—specifically, who Seattle can retain, who Seattle can sign in free agency, and who those free agents may be.

And "z" equals the cost of having Harvin take a spot on the 53-man roster—which may seem slight but became onerous after Harvin missed week upon week recovering from injury, including missing the NFC Championship Game.

"A" of course is the value of Percy Harvin, and though Schneider et al. can probably pretty safely project "x," "y," and "z," "a" is not so easy. And that's where PC et al. come in.

Receivers have somewhat consistent value within a team (because of the quarterback and other surrounding talent, because of the scheme, and maybe too because the team has *chosen* to keep said receiver, which imparts some selection bias) but no consistent value outside of a team. That is, in reality, *passes to that receiver* have somewhat consistent value within a team but no consistent value beyond it. So that big magical all-defining "a" variable up there must be, assuming front offices do not have access to a much, much better absolute rating of individual players (which there's no evidence they do), determined by simple human judgment—by the Peterson scale of Jordan or Pippen, and everyone in between, and everyone outside that narrow spectrum.

And, in many ways, this is the quintessential Carroll-Schneider decision. I presume Schneider evaluated the likelihood of landing a player like Harvin through free agency (unlikely because of the league's very restrictive franchise tag system and unlikely because I've watched football 20-plus years and never seen another Harvin), what his cap hit would mean to the team, how potentially rich the 2013 NFL Draft class would be, etc. But Carroll had to confer with his coaches and make the unscientific but ultra important assessment of what the heck Harvin actually *is*.

Maybe the difficulty of that assessment is not entirely clear. Who, really, can't tell the difference between Jordan and Pippen? Let's face it, Peterson's analogy is sorta facile. Though both enshrined in the Naismith Hall of Fame, Pippen and Jordan couldn't be much more different. Pippen's excellence was subtle. Jordan's was loud, flamboyant, and maybe liable to be overestimated because of it.

The idea of beauty on the gridiron, it may seem a little wishy-washy to some, but among us non-gamblers, there must be something beyond winning or losing that makes football compelling. Or else we'd equally be fans of bowling, cross-country skiing, and high-stakes poker. We'd cheer on coin flips and Magic: The Gathering tournaments. Football, at its best, is very appealing to the senses. So much so, it can be difficult to differentiate between beautiful play and effective play. We know there is some distinction or else the league would be all DeSean Jacksons and no Red Bryants. But when we say Harvin is Jordan talented, what really are we saying?

We are saying Harvin plays with a speed, grace, and athleticism that is undeniable and undeniably beautiful.

What the Pete Carroll side of the Seahawks decision making apparatus must do is determine how that beauty translates to effectiveness.

There is no formula, no metric, no algorithm that can project what Percy Harvin will do in 2014. There is no way to project how many yards he will receive for, or how many touchdowns he will catch, or what all those catches and yards will translate to in terms of points. There are intelligent ways to determine Harvin's market value. There are intelligent ways to determine the projected market value of what Seattle gave up in exchange for Harvin. Between the two an informed decision can be made, a best guess.

What Carroll and Schneider represent is a cutting edge synthesis of the best qualitative analysis of talent evaluators and the best quantitative analysis of statisticians. It's not perfect. Harvin, it turned out, didn't contribute much in 2013. Ultimately there is no answer to the question "How good is Percy Harvin?" Because we must forever say, "Good at what?" Good at running a post pattern out of the slot—and against what defense, what defender, in what weather conditions, in what state of health is Harvin's body, and how accurate, how fast the pass? But these incalculable, seemingly unanswerable questions prove answerable to the human brain. The human brain, for better and worse, favors ideas to facts. It can understand the beauty of Harvin's play and potential, if never know the truth of his ultimate contributions.

Enough bluster, elaboration is for mythologizing. Here's how this probably really went down.

Carroll: "This guy Harvin's a player. He could be great. Let's do this. Let's bust down every door until we get him."

[Some thousand phone calls later.]

Schneider: "Here's how we do it."

Bulletin 1147

It is with great regret that I am announcing today that the NFL franchise we purchased in 1988 is leaving Seattle.

—February 2, 1996

Ken Behring's son, David, thinks that his father soured on football after the 1992 season. Man, didn't we all? Seattle finished 2–14 in its first season after Chuck Knox. Tom Flores, attempted to modernize the Seahawks' offense, and through his modernism created an existential nightmare. (Offense died today. Or, maybe, yesterday; I can't be sure.) Seattle scored 140 points, the lowest total in the history of the 16-game season. If you're looking for a record that's never likely to fall, that's a safe one.

Scoring points isn't the measure of a football team or even the measure of excitement. If Seattle had allowed 0 points, well, 1992 would have produced the greatest Seahawks team in franchise history. It didn't, of course, Seattle allowed 312 points. Still, being bad is one thing, and Seahawks fans have known that feeling pretty well throughout their history, but never even scoring 20 points in a game? Averaging fewer than 10 points scored a game? That has to be desperate and absurd. Are you still a fan when you hate your team more than your rival?

Knowing he was responsible? I'm sure that would have burned Ken Behring if he cared. I do not think he did, though. I'm sure, like most private citizens suddenly thrust into the spotlight, the hate mail was startling and discouraging. Anonymity and entitlement bring out the worst in people. Fans expect to win, and those who write hate mail typically forego the return address.

You might notice by now that this essay is short on name-calling and recriminations. Let's see if I can fix that.

Behring was a Midwesterner. He had no connection to Seattle but the Seahawks. Injury ended his college football dreams. I think he just wanted to own an NFL franchise, and when the Seahawks became available, Behring seized the opportunity. The Nordstrom family wanted out. They sold Behring the Seahawks, knowing full well he was not committed to the area.

Nashville businessman George C. Gillett was interested. Nashville was pushing hard for a major sports franchise, and the

Houston Oilers eventually relocated there and became the Titans. Had Gillett offered a little more, the Seahawks might have been relocated before Paul Allen could intercede.

In that way, Behring was a lesser villain. Maybe if he got his way, maybe if he acted earlier and NFL commissioner Paul Tagliabue had not soured on the proposed relocation, maybe I would harbor more anger toward Behring. He wanted to murder the Seahawks and steal life from the city of Seattle. Behring believed that was his right as an owner. He thought the Kingdome was a dump and pressured Seattle to spend millions in renovation or build him a new stadium entirely. The Kingdome was a dump. Paul Allen himself did not commit to buying the Seahawks before the State of Washington agreed to build a new stadium. I doubt Behring was interested in staying, regardless, but he wasn't wrong. Whoever owned the Seahawks today, the team would not be playing in the Kingdome. Maybe under it.

Some welcomed Behring when he joined the organization. He was "hands-on." He wanted to shake up the team. He demanded a winner. He wanted a more wide-open offense, and it's not like Ground Chuck wasn't getting a little stale. Time turned his intentions into folly, revealed his distance from the city, and exposed him as a selfish owner.

There is a more exciting way to tell this story, I'm sure. Maybe in the moment. Behring must have seemed sulfurous and Machiavellian at the time. Seattle could have lost the Seahawks. We didn't, though. And Behring's treachery begat Paul Allen; Allen hired Holmgren; and Holmgren helped give us 2005.

I guess that makes Behring a despicable but elemental piece in the process. He swooped in and drove out Chuck and then attempted to destroy the Seahawks but failed. The fear he wrought surely encouraged voters to ratify a stadium bill, and that built Seahawks Stadium, and kept the Seahawks in Seattle for the foreseeable future. Behring wanted to move out of Seattle but failed, and so sold the Seahawks to Allen. I guess that makes Ken Behring the fertilizer from which Super Bowl XL grew.

74 Believe

Did anyone think that Seattle would make a championship run in 1983? Of course not. The Seahawks started with one quarterback and finished strong with another, went from a castoff to a nobody, and rallied behind Dave Krieg like nobody could have anticipated.

Did anyone think that Seattle would make a Super Bowl run in 2005? I guess some thought it was possible. Seattle was a playoff team in 2004, but a paltry one. It was the year of the drops. The year Matt Hasselbeck regressed. The year that Seattle won the NFC West, only to lose its third straight game against the rival Rams. Tim Ruskell was throwing talent at the defense, and not five-star talent, but too-small players like Lofa Tatupu. If you believed Tatupu was the ingredient that would put Seattle over the top, you were a better fan than I.

Things do not follow the miserable path so many envision. Things never follow the optimistic path some seem to survive on. Mostly, though, things just do not follow the path we predict for them.

In retrospect, the shaky and weak-armed Matt Hasselbeck first appeared in 2007. Yet 2007 was perhaps the year of Hasselbeck's greatest career accomplishment. The line was no longer the league's best, and the skill-position talent was comprised of whoever had hands. The running game was frightful, and the once gliding, ankle-breaking style of Alexander was now plummeting, heartbreaking. Hasselbeck moved and distributed and used all his weapons and helped construct a top 10 passing offense. He was also slower, had lost his deep range, and needed wider and wider windows to throw through. For a season, there was a mesh point where his knowledge overcame his fading ability, and his fading ability perhaps brought his decision-making to the fore. So, though Hasselbeck was becoming inexorably worse, he was briefly in a place where he played better.

I watched every game of the 2007 season with meticulous note-taking, and though I could see he was slowing down, that his arm was weakening, I did not see that he was fading so rapidly. No one did. No one could.

Injury was to blame for the team's 2008 collapse. I guess. The team had shifted. It had realized a decline that was following it for years. Some of that decline manifested in injury, but the injury was not unnatural, a fluke. It was more like a tether breaking that had been strained so long.

As surely as that is depressing, the currents run in both directions. Seattle sprung into its own in 1983 and 2005. No one could see what it would become, but it wasn't chance or the product of great and wise decision-making. It was an emergence. It was a blooming where before there had not even been a flower.

If there is one thing every fan must do, it is believe. Believe your sorry team can get better. Dramatically. Believe it might already be happening. Believe it can happen without warning. It happens all the time. Believe, because hope and faith are a fan's sword and shield against the inevitable fact that every team but one ends the season a loser.

75 A Dreamed Realization

Day Four, Post-Super Bowl Victory

Well, I'm sober. I am no richer. I am a little poorer. I am no healthier. I am surely less well than I was before this business all started. Endorsement deals haven't yet begun to pour in. My place is... not clean. Beer bottles have gone from stacked, to surely precarious, to disintegrated and sharp and dappled in dry blood. My now five-weeks-since-last-washed Brandon Mebane jersey will require tagging and bagging. Good-bye, friend.

Seriously, when is Nike going to call me about my own line of sneaker?

My favorite sports franchise, the one I have dedicated literally thousands of hours of my life worrying about and watching, knowing in depth and never giving up on, surviving and riding high with, has won the Super Bowl. The Seattle Seahawks are Super Bowl champions.

And the beer didn't do it. Nothing else in my chemical arsenal did it either. Not the pills for my sadness, not the puffs for my wife's GERD. Nothing I could do made it quite as good as it was always supposed to be. I have not burst into flame or gained spiritual awareness. God didn't teleport me to heaven on a sunbeam. Nope. Whatever the hell happens at the end of *2001: A Space Odyssey* didn't happen. I am the same steadily aging, largely poor, professionally unsuccessful, happily married man I was before. I am the same. And right now that feels very, very disappointing.

Oh, but! Oh, oh, oh, but!

It doesn't matter.

My particular happiness and disappointment do not matter. I do not need to know how to feel this right.

Because what is not good enough today may be good enough 10 years from now. This never ends. My momentary disappointment cannot wound it. My foolish abuses cannot alter it.

The Seattle Seahawks are Super Bowl champions. The Seattle Seahawks will forever be Super Bowl champions. This outlives me. This shimmering pool I may drink of forever and never quench my thirst but forever return to drink again. It doesn't have to happen when I want it to. It will happen again and again, giving me joy and hope and a sliver of triumph, again and again, throughout my tiny forever.

76 Visit Training Camp

You drive into Renton, but it gets better. You drive into Renton and find a shopping mall, never a challenge. You drive south and then north, and you enter Renton, but you stop there, yes, and I know that's crazy talk, but you drive into Renton and park at a place called The Landing. At The Landing, you're going to want to find parking, and it's going to be tough, because The Landing is the kind of place that unabashedly brags about its urban ambience, where little sanitized chunks of culture come housed in faux brick, and where little sanitized chunks of humanity come and go. But you're going to want to park there, and then, and I stress this, get out of your car. You drive into Renton, park in The Landing, get out of your car, see a pilgrimage of Blue, and belong.

You drive into Renton because the VMAC is in Renton. It's on Lake Washington. Near the stately center lies a practice field, and it spreads like Elysium from Renton's Underworld. The air smells good, in every direction there is a view, and the grass is always fresh, no matter how many cleats dug at it the day before.

You drive into Renton, but it gets better. You park, wend down the parking garage stairs, see a pilgrimage of Blue, and belong. You register. You wait on the curb and board busses and sit among the faithful.

On the bus, there is spirited conversation. Conversation about triumphs and casualties, and maybe you disagree about this and this, but the spirit is shared. Everyone just wants to win. Everyone bleeds Blue.

Off the busses you walk, and there's some fanfare, a gauntlet of sponsors, and a path that wends up a hill.

The other side is where the Seahawks hold training camp. Speakers blast top 40. Players split into small groups organized by position. Everyone is running drills.

To your left you might see blitzing and blocking drills. The defender charges, and the offensive blocker charges to meet, and the two collide—if the blocker is lucky. Some players are so quick they just run around the blocker, and that's embarrassing. As a fan you feel the embarrassment. There are no enemies at training camp. But you feel the triumph, too.

The receivers run routes and catch. They line up and run identical routes and run to the other side and line up again. It looks like high school practice. Just a bunch of grown-up kids running around and stomping and playing football. There's nothing professional about it but the money. Talent pops. There's the high-effort players, yessir-yessir-yessir, who do everything they're told, and they are typically the least talented players on the field. There are the veterans and the soon-to-be cut. There are the bad days for the players who cannot afford a bad day. It broke my heart to see Derek Walker, shoulders slumped, carrying four helmets into the locker room. So I yelled, "Stick with it, you're doing good out there!" and he turned and looked. Of course, he probably wondered, *Who the*

Discover the Next Great Seahawk

If you ever visit training camp, you have two basic options to get the most of it. The first is the sampler. You can walk around the hill and try to get a look at everything and everyone. This is the typical path. One might spend a little time seeing wide-receiver drills and then move on to locking and passing drills.

The other is what I suggest for anyone who thinks of himself as a true enthusiast. Instead of walking around and just breathing it all in, pick a player or two and just track them all day. See how they do in every attempt in every drill. It helps if this player is unestablished.

It might seem silly to wander around and scrutinize someone who is likely to be cut, but if someone did that in 1991, they could have been the first person to talk up Michael Sinclair. Discovery is probably the truest joy of the enthusiast. And championing a player from obscurity to stardom is something that just cannot be matched.

heck is that? But he made it. And if you think tracking a player from the draft to starting gives you a connection, try tracking a player from fighting for his job to making the 53-man roster.

Players line up and scrimmage. It's contact, but for the most part, no one wants to hurt anyone else. Every so often there's a scrap, and it erupts in predictable ways. The early-round picks who haven't established themselves but are safe chafe the practice fodder fighting for a job. You hate to see bad blood among teammates, but at training camp, teammate is battling teammate for a job.

If you take notes, you are going to get a little extra attention from security. I sat on the hill and recorded names and performances. An officer walked up to me and asked me who I was. And I said, "Nobody. A fan." He told me that they had to be on the watch for advanced scouts evaluating their schemes and talent. I guess I was, but I was reporting only to Seahawks fans. Attending is about the only way you'll ever know what happens in training camp. Along the sidelines you can see press hanging out, shootin' the shat, soaking up the sun, and when the day is done, they all file the same story.

Camp's fun, and none of it matters much. If you've never been, maybe you imagine a heated contest between veterans and up-and-comers, clashing of pads, scrapping in the pile, and epic match-ups that determine jobs. But it's nothing like that. Players run drills, and many of the players most adept at running drills are least able to play football. Some players practice well and get through an entire career by impressing coach after coach with their discipline and hustle, but when it's game time, the best players play. Training camp gives coaches a look, but it's preseason and innate talent that typically defines who sticks and who's cut.

It's harmless, wholesome fun like a '50s sockhop, and for the most part, your fellow 12 are good people who just want to talk Seahawks. A couple people come with an agenda, and that can be annoying. Circa 2009, my last chance to attend, one guy had a real bone to pick with Matt Hasselbeck. All day, he was slagging Hasselbeck, deriding his game, his baldness, his past failures, and at the top of his lungs. What's worse, he had a really confused impression of Seneca Wallace. He championed Seneca like he was doing Wallace and all of us a favor. Training camp lasts about two hours, and most people talk quietly among themselves, so anywhere you went, this guy could be heard. Somehow knowing we're all together in this irrational, somewhat arbitrarily decided pursuit softens opprobrium toward cranks and fanatics. Anyone that pays and travels to see professional athletes practice is a fool of some kind, and the foolish among fools attain a certain nobility.

Camp's fun, and it's over fast. If you stick around, players walk over and sign autographs. The veterans are friendly but impassive. Calloused to fan ardor, inured to fan scorn. When Red Bryant walks over, you understand just how huge Bryant is. He's not just tall or built, but every part of him is bigger and broader than a typical human. His head is big. His hands are big. And when he towers over everyone, he's not awkward or gangly, he's alien. The young players eat up the attention. The Max Ungers and Kam Chancellors of the world are still pretty unaccustomed to the fervent fans and star-struck kids, and you can tell it's still a thrill to thrill. Some players are shy, and that's lovable, too. Some are hammy and some are humble, but they're all human, and that sounds trite, but you can never appreciate that across a television set.

You get back on the bus and watch the VMAC fade behind the tree line and know you're going back to Renton and feel sad. Heady conversation percolates about the day and the season. Who impressed, who disappointed, and of course, *Who was that who did that? That was who who did that? I thought it was him. No, Logan Payne is white.* Most around you are not going to be back tomorrow, so this was their day. Enthusiasm fades into reverie for some, and others are already back into their lives, talking shop or making business calls. But for a few hours on a tortilla flat plot of green, green grass beside Lake Washington, the business of being alive took the fore, and we were kids and we were fans and we were fools for the Blue.

Cheney

The Seahawks held training camp in Cheney, Washington, 20 times. Cheney is one of those big small towns that people settle down in and doom their children to misery and alcoholism. It's bucolic and boring.

It's where Chuck Knox first connected with his men. Gave them water. Looked them in the eye and promised them they could be good, even if he knew he was fibbing.

It's where Jack Patera stole away. Suffered the media. Denied the players water because of outdated ideas about toughness and good football.

It's where Tom Flores first Raiderized the Seahawks. Undid Ground Chuck. Hatched the schemes that would destroy the Seahawks' offense.

It's where Dennis Erickson did whatever Dennis Erickson did.

It's where Holmgren looked out and first saw a champion. And where he eventually pieced it together.

It's where 2,500 fans first dreamed the big dreams of a new season.

After 20 seasons of Seahawks football touching down in eastern Washington, taking the field of Eastern Washington University, Seattle upgraded and moved their camps a little closer to home.

I have never been out to Cheney. Eastern Washington has that tough temperate climate I grew up on. It has mountains and desert and gorges and farmland packed into every space in between. There is no night life, I figure, but X-box Live and hard drinking. It probably was extra special when the Seahawks came to town.

There was a lot of sadness and nostalgia when the Seahawks moved to Renton. I guess Cheney became the kind of place that somehow contained not just land, but action, people, and memories.

 **Silver**

Warren Moon awoke in me a Seahawks passion. He brought exciting football to a moribund franchise. It wasn't all great. It never was once in Moon's career. And teenage me, full of contradiction and venom and discontent wanted Kitna. Jon Kitna was just 25, and Moon, he was a kind of old that I couldn't smell, see, or understand. Moon was 41.

Which was all part of the experience. Moon made me love the Seahawks, tune in to see him shell opponents, not grind and survive, but blow out the Colts and 49ers. The 13–3 49ers. Moon found Galloway for two long scores, Pritchard and McKnight for two more, and in a moment of portent and promise, Kitna substituted in, completed eight straight passes for 88, and scrambled for the finishing score.

False portent. False promise. Kitna proved less than stellar. But Moon, in his unintentional yet inestimable fashion, brought excitement and controversy. A quarterback controversy. Real football teams had those. Morton-Staubach. Montana-Young. Kitna-Moon. It put the Seahawks on *SportsCenter*, and *SportsCenter* was my lifeline to Seattle sports. I lived in New Hampshire and followed my love from afar. Like any long-distance relationship, moments of connection were wonderful, sun-kissed moments of profound agony that I played over until my heart was sore.

The Seahawks mattered again. After a retched stretch, Seattle had crawled from the primordial ooze and clawed itself toward relevance. A vestigial Unverzagt stuck through camp, but he was shed, too. This team was going to be good. Walter was beginning his legacy at left. Joey Galloway was straight running past defenders. The kids, Kevin Mawae and Pete Kendall, weren't getting it, but the talent was there. Dennis Erickson would teach them. Dennis Erickson would lead the way.

Moon was charismatic. He was big-business, big-city, wide-smiled, important, and legendary: a real living future Hall of Famer in the Silver and Blue. His passes escaped gravity and reentered the atmosphere with big plans and bad intentions for opponents. Moon to Galloway was football as it was never meant to be—easy and graceful, a rank affront to football's smashmouth origins. It was too beautiful to describe. It was too big to comprehend. It was American football at the apex of its evolution and was happening in the Kingdome.

If you were a kid like me, that is all it ever was. It never began and never ended but existed outside of time like a dream half-remembered. I never knew Seattle signed him, and I was not paying attention when he moved on. He retired a little while later, and maybe I remember that. Someone named "Warren Moon" does broadcast work for Seahawks radio, but that voice is a stranger to me. The Moon I know is still hanging 'em high over Joey's shoulder as regular and unstoppable as the tide.

79 Buy a Jersey

I was drunk. Not loaded, but not able to legally operate machinery, either. I was blasting "This Time Tomorrow." It's a habit when I've had a few. I was wailing, "This time tomorroooo*oow*!" It's a habit when I've had a few. I was inspired, by beer. Beerspiration. Now, that's just bad. It's the same way I got my first cat. I was drunk, sitting beside my future wife, and I said, "Let's get a cat!" and she said, "No way. You're drunk." She was right, but as Hemingway said, always do sober what you said you would do drunk. That'll teach you. The next day we adopted Houdini.

I was in front of my laptop. I was drunk. Not loaded, but optimistic. I was saying, "I should buy a jersey," and my wife said, "You should." Bad idea.

I was on NFL.com. I was in front of my laptop. I was drunk. I was wailing "This Time Tomorrow." Jerseys are crazy expensive. For the price of a jersey, you could attend a game, and games are

Jerseys from Goodwill

Goodwill is a great place to find Seahawks memorabilia and jerseys. I have a Ricky Watters, and my wife has a Deion Branch and Shaun Alexander, all authentic, that we got from Goodwill. Jerseys at the Goodwill cost less than $10, and if you are concerned about this kind of thing, look worn in.

Not only do I have two jerseys, but multiple Seahawks mugs, Seahawks glasses, Seahawks tees from different eras, a Chuck Knox–style ball cap, and some Seahawks sweaters. I think part of the charm is that it's cheap and supports a good cause rather than crass commercialism. That is what's kind of cool about buying anything at Goodwill, you know you are doing more than recycling, you are taking garbage and making it a treasure again.

The other part of the charm is that it's a bit like antiquing, I guess. Goodwill cuts across eras, and so you get the good, the forgettable, and the gaudy. My wife and I do not make a ton of cash, but leafing through the Goodwill lets us have a robust collection of Seahawks stuff. She is on standing order to buy me any jersey I can fit in.

crazy expensive. I was on NFL.com. The jerseys bored me. Matt Hasselbeck? No. Aaron Curry? Oh sweet merciful God! thank you, no. Shaun Alexander? You must be kidding me.

I was on NFL.com. I was in front of my laptop. I was drunk. I was about to buy a Brandon Mebane jersey.

And, man, I have never regretted it.

What compels a grown man to buy a player's jersey? It's all kinds of silly. It's juvenile. Walking around with a "Largent" or "Jones" or "Tatupu" on your back. It looks like a desperate grasp at lost glory. Pale dude, buck-sixty soaking wet, with a 'Tez jersey on—it looks foolish, incongruous, puerile.

But stupid has a calling. It plays in our hearts, it's charming and inviting and totally unlike smart, which is distancing, threatening. Maybe it's the Homer in the human soul, but embracing your dumb, your irrational, your primitive self, and boldly declaring,

"I am Seahawks! You can find me stuffing my face and screaming crumbs this Sunday!" has an undeniable savor.

And so I bought it and spent too much and maybe thought about that a little between the time of ordering and arrival, but mostly embraced a giddy anticipation. I pestered the UPS lady, and she reciprocated with a world-weary stare. I, 11:45 sharp, opened my front door and said, "Hello, Mr. Sun," with a smile, and he burned on hot and indifferent. When it arrived, I tore off the packaging like it were wrapping paper, saw the embroidery and the "Mebane" and the "92," and slid it on. It was cool and soft and lazily hung over my shoulders. I put on pants and walked to the store, and every few blocks I shouted out:

Me!

Bane!

80 Watch the Real Rob Report

Marshawn Lynch is sitting in his locker, checking his phone. Nothing could be more boring than watching someone stare intently at their phone. Fullback Michael Robinson, from behind the camera and in a tone that is a bit pitched-up and very non-threatening, says "Hey, Beast." Lynch doesn't even flinch.

"Everything going good today, Beast?" Lynch looks over and into the camera, showing no hint of recognition. He maybe says "shit" under his breath. He looks back at his phone, grins, stands, and begins walking toward the showers and stalls. Robinson pursues, asks, "Everything going good today, Beast?"

"Yep."

"You gonna talk to me today?"

"Nope," Lynch turns his back on Robinson, throws up a middle finger (which is covered by a "Real Rob" patch) and continues toward the showers.

"I don't even know if I have a blur spot that small," Robinson says. Lynch snicker-laughs, what sounds like leaking gas and lowers his head in amusement and frustration. "Where you going man?" Lynch walks into a bathroom stall. It's brushed steel and somehow both expensive-looking and yet institutional and utilitarian. "So now you're gonna go where the camera [muffled by the sound of Lynch slamming the door shut]. That's okay. I can do that." Robinson peaks the camera above the stall door. We see Lynch still unaware. From somewhere someone says. "Are you serious, man?" Lynch looks up, sees the camera, kind of smiles, and says, "Oh." The camera quickly ducks away, and we hear Robinson laugh.

If you've watched The Real Robinson Report, from here on referred to as the The Real Rob Report—which sounds much better, don't you think?—you know Lynch does not like to be filmed.

Now we're watching from the left aisle seat of an Airbus. Seahawks are settling in. Seahawks are finding seats, and stowing luggage. But something's wrong.

"What's up with your rookie, man?" asks Russell Okung.

"You forgot the apple pies!?"

"Hey."

"How do you forget the apple piiies!?"

"Hey, everybody man—"

"Turbo, that's the most important thiiing," Robinson admonishes Robert Turbin. Turbin is carrying a bright orange box of Popeye's. Turbin is Robinson's rookie. "I know," says Turbin. "I'm gonna have to get it to you…I'm gonna have to make it up to you, bro." Turbin is one of those guys whose hip-hop slang sounds kind of forced and awkward coming out of his mouth, like he's behind in his street-cred installment payments. His voice is a less wheezy Weezy, or Chris Tucker minus Tucker's overbearing, ahem, "funniness."

It's a simple idea. Take a player, give him a camera, have him film his teammates and produce a show from the footage. But what Robinson captures is fun and funny, and so humanizing and personal, it makes me rethink my long held belief that I just don't care about athletes as people (or, more specifically, I don't care any more about professional athletes as people than the billions of other people I do not know but am sure are cool and interesting, etc.) Because I am absolutely hooked on The Real Rob Report.

Give it a try. It's not human interest story garbage, nor is it debased reality television. It's more like guerilla journalism. Robinson has a natural talent for putting people at ease. Well, except Marshawn Lynch. Dude's got serious dead eyes.

81 The Jim L. Mora Guide to Never Failing, Ever!

I have never failed in my life.

—Jim Lawrence Mora

Thank you for purchasing this *Jim L. Mora Guide to Never Failing, Ever!* We at Mora & Mora strive to never be wrong, forget when we are wrong, and argue in such an exhausting, passive-aggressive, and outright insulting and rude fashion when accused of being wrong to deter any such accusations. It is our binding and lifelong desire to never fail, and to never fail, one must always succeed, and to always succeed, one must never fail. You, too, can both succeed and never fail, if only you follow these steps!

Step 1: Attaining Power

To never fail it is essential to attain power. A powerful enough man may write his own history, and through his words purge mistakes, missteps, misgivings, and mistakes—*that never happened!*

Infiltration

Mora Brand Guides require a special kind of power not readily found in a wall jack. It is not AC or DC but dodgy and BS. Before activating a *Mora Brand Guide*, it is essential to loom near your predecessor/victim/host organism. This loom phase should be long and drawn out to maximally undermine said host and best position yourself to pounce and feed off said host when said host is weakest and least able to defend himself. So we say at Mora Labs, "The best enemy is a close friend."

Ascension

Do not be hasty! We understand your need to thrive and replicate your successes, to exploit every opportunity for maximum gain. But consider the relative successes of two famed graduates of the *Jim L. Mora Guide to Never Failing, Ever!* One was indiscriminate and aggressive, barely able to infiltrate before taking over. It would start big, generate feverish excitement but ultimately leave others cold and hollow. The other was slow and selective. It spread over a series of months and years, and that spread was not clear until it had been shared with dozens of others. Both possess a real dirtbag will to do whatever it takes to win. But the former is so urgent to ascend, so impatient to attain power, it never gets far. It stays a regional phenomenon. The latter spread its influence the world over before anyone knew it existed! And its influence thrives to this day.

Mobilization

As the days grow shorter and your quarry nears his demise, it is essential you snap tight and spin and spin till success drowns in water stained by its own blood. Only then shall success be yours to devour.

This snap and spin, we call it a press conference! When it's your time, remember the five T's:

Token acknowledgment to your predecessors!

Take control of the room!

Talk down to the media!

Tiger Mountain!

Treat strangers as potential enemies!

Step 2: Establishing a Tyranny of Hooey
Team-building

Bizarre feats of quasi-fitness draw men together by giving them a shared enemy. Perhaps you run a start-up tech firm—those things seem to be everywhere! And suppose you dream of making a time-stealing, frustrating, and ultimately useless application for the iPhone or some other expensive piece of crap. But you've yet to succeed at forming an idea. Have you considered taking your entire staff to Tiger Mountain and having them wheelbarrow jars of fruit preserves to the top? You should! Soon all will be so worn out, injured, and confused as to why they're there (and on their weekend) that they will unite against not succeeding. You'll start the day with paunchy wusses and end the day with a tough, lean crew of fighters befitting the HMS Bounty. Real men of action!

Hectoring

Quite the opposite of the newly incarcerated, the newly successful must lay low until a weakling reveals himself. And when this poor, defenseless mare among stallions does reveal himself? You guessed it: wait some more! Because one day, when it seems not-success is closing in all around you, that mare may prove itself less than perfect, may prove itself successful a mere 67 percent of the time, and you can point a big, confident successful index finger at him, and say, "He did it! He did it! Blame him! He lost us the game!" And in this way, like J. Simpson's mighty warrior Hector, you will remain undefeated, and your name will stand for gallantry, fair leadership, and respect.

Enemy-making

So your men are united and through targeting the weak and defenseless, you have earned their respect. But how to direct their frustration and contempt for leadership toward a common foe?

In a word, make enemies.

The first step to making an enemy is constant paranoia and maddening hyper vigilance. Whoops! I succeeded a little too quickly there because the true first step is meet strangers. Strangers are great! Strangers are scary. And every stranger is just an enemy you haven't exploited yet. The stranger the stranger, the easier it will be to focus your team's hatred on that person.

Step 3. Cha!ch!ng!
Winning

Like water through the gills of a whale, winning may become so common you'll stop noticing it's there.

And

And what? Now I'm curious.

Losing? Never!

Phew. Had me worried.

Retirement

When the time comes and your superiors are deeply jealous of your continual, unceasing success—those cowards—and that jealousy forces them to protectively grant you success in your employment freedom, it may become time to consider retirement. It was surely a long path from your early days when you strove and fought for your first coaching job, never relenting, doubling your effort, and really whining at Dad before he gave in and said, "Jesus, Jim. I've already given you most of my name, what more do you want?" And tears of success welled in your eyes, and he said, "Okay. Okay. Cut the crybaby shit. I'll call Don and ask him if you can be a quality control coach or something. Myles says that's just a way to funnel money to friends and family anyway."

And you rose inexplicably fast on a wave of potential success and never failures. Until you were so close you could breath deep the cadavarine wafting off Dan Reeves' neck. And the day, the day you took over, the day you were entrusted to nurture the full potential of Michael Vick, not just as a quarterback, but as a human being. What a day! To the day you lifted the pall that had settled over the city of Atlanta and brought new hope to Falcons fans, January 1, 2007. It was a long journey of never ending, exhausting success. But even success must end.

So concludes your *Mora & Mora Guide to Never Failing, Ever!* Have you succeeded? Of course you have. Because failure is for the pitiful. And as we say at Mora & Mora, if you don't acknowledge it, it never happened!

82 Please Think of a Better Nickname Than Legion of Boom

What I am about to propose is an idea so right, so obvious, and which I can make such a compelling argument for, yet against something so entrenched, so repeated into truthiness, and so synonymous with the 2013 Super Bowl champion Seattle Seahawks, that I might as well be proposing campaign finance reform. But allow me to anyway.

The Gene Upshaw Oakland Raiders were known as the Legion of Doom. This fit the spirit of the city and the spirit of its football team. 1970s Oakland was indeed a place of doom, as squalor, death, hellfire, eternal damnation, and so forth, rode tall in the saddle. (What the hell's that a reference to?) And of course the Legion of Doom is a group of comic book super villains. This is a natural and fitting nickname. The Raiders are evil. The city of Oakland is a snake pit. Howie Long is indeed a megalomaniacal exile from Gorilla City.

Now consider this: we hate the Oakland Raiders. Deriving a name from one of their teams is not only beneath the Seahawks, but it's bizarro given the decades old rivalry. Further, Legion of Boom is not in fact anything at all. There's no Biddler, no Bex Buthor, no Bolomon Brundy.

But this foolishness cuts even deeper than all that.

The Seahawks secondary, the nominal Legion of Boom, is not a group of especially hard hitters. There's little boom in the Boom. Among the longtime starters, only Kam Chancellor is really known for the savagery of his tackling, and I've always been much more impressed with the way Chancellor is able to intimidate and bully without breaking the rules: verbatim or implied. He's not a headhunter. And he hasn't exploited a loophole to head hunt, like the New Orleans secondary did in the divisional round. (There is no prohibition against striking your opponent's head into the hard turf, but given the intention of supposed anti-concussion regulation, it's certainly against the spirit of the rules.) Chancellor blows suckers up, but the fear his quarry feel is not fear of someday forgetting their children's names. It's simple fear of pain and embarrassment. Good, natural football fear. If you've ever played, you've felt it, and you've felt the satisfaction of inspiring it in another.

Earl Thomas is a good, reliable tackler that hardly shrinks from conflict, but among safeties, he's smaller, more like a corner, and certainly not a hammer like say Ken Hamlin. Richard Sherman likes to intimidate, but he's built light and rangy like a wide receiver. He intimidates quarterbacks through his incredible talent and skill, not his hitting. Each is a great defensive back. None but Chancellor are particularly punishing tacklers.

So what the hell's with the boom? Where does the boom in Legion of Boom come from?

And if it's not even apt, what on God's Earth would motivate people to adopt a silly, nonsensical nickname derived from the nickname of a hated rival!?

What the Seahawks secondary is known for is not its hitting, but its ability to press receivers off the line, reroute them, knock the ball loose if it does reach the receiver, and, most of all, its ability to intercept passes. It would be tough to think of something that incorporates all of those skills, but the interception thing should be easy. After all, the Seahawk or osprey is a raptor, and raptor literally means to plunder or steal. (And osprey, you maybe know, literally means "bone breaker," meaning the no-funny-stuff name of the team is already much cooler than its "cool" nickname.)

So, here's an ultra-quick list of suggestions, each better than Legion of Boom, and each never likely to catch on:

The Velociraptors: means fast raptor, or basically quick thief. It's so good, plus *Jurassic Park*. Plus, plus, the name gives paleo nerds, and by that I mean eight-year-olds (and we eight-year-olds at heart) a chance to point out the inaccuracies that plagued *Jurassic Park*! Feathers! There should have been feathers!

The F-22 Fighter Jets: okay, that's lame in an '80s way, but, but, but the F-22 Raptor is a "stealth air superiority fighter"…eh, still: lame.

The Dead Zone: Named after an ecological disaster occurring off the Olympic Peninsula. Ha! We're killing the only known life-sustaining planet in the universe. But black humor aside, *this is so cool!* It's local, it's scary as hell sounding, it fits the team, it's contemporary, and it's original.

Actually, screw the rest of the list. I'm not gonna top The Dead Zone. The Dead Zone Defense. DZD.

Dead zones suffocate to kill. They are a place of no life.

Dead zone. Dead zone. Dead zone.

83 The Stage and its Actor

Football produces plenty of villains, but it's short on cartoonish super villains—players who talk big, have a bigger persona, and fail hard. Fail hard, then fail, fail again.

That is the unspoken charm of a super villain. For all their showboating, dash, and flair, they're losers. Bruce Wayne is a charming, billionaire playboy with talent, charisma, and connections to burn. The Joker is a deranged fool in a clown costume. Wayne is almost alien in his rectitude. The Riddler could run a puzzle shop at Pike Place Market.

The Boz, alter ego of Brian Keith Bosworth, was a late-'80s super villain and Seahawk—in that order. He touched down his helicopter in King County in the summer of 1987. The smoke machines billowed, the strobes flashed, and from the hull of Sooners football emerged the biggest joke of a bust in franchise history.

His hair was a joke: a bleach-blond flattop that melted into a straggly late-'80s mullet. It stood atop a manly visage—all chin and brow.

He looked football, as interpreted by a sugar-addled eight-year-old: huge pads, thousand-yard stare, jaw like a shovel, and body like an action hero.

Brian Bosworth and his mullet take a phone call from his agent, or possibly one of the coaches in the booth, during a 16–10 win over the Cleveland Browns in October 1988 at Cleveland Municipal Stadium.

The Boz was branded, patented, and sold. He hucked product like a second calling. He called out John Elway and then covertly sold "Boz Buster" shirts to angry Broncos fans. He challenged Bo Jackson and lost. Jackson ran for 221 yards and three touchdowns. You can still watch Bo drag Boz into the end zone on YouTube.

Of course, he wasn't dragged. Brian Bosworth hit Jackson at the 2, stood him up, attempted the strip, and held on as the two fell forward into the end zone. Strip off the hype, and it was just another slipped tackle. Bosworth wasn't dragged. He wasn't blown up or broken down. He hit his man square but lost.

Strip off the hyperbole, the caricature Bosworth wrought, and No. 55 was a promising young linebacker who played big as a rookie before breaking down and fading away. Bosworth hit hard and fast, played hard, and tried harder. In Week 14 of the 1987 season, facing the declining but still great Ditka-led Bears, Bosworth flew across the field, from outside the left hash mark to the right flat, smashed, stripped, and recovered a Neal Anderson fumble and returned to it to the 1. Curt Warner soared into the end zone on the next play. Seattle would never trail again.

He wasn't great. He wasn't likeable. He was polarizing, galvanizing, and good. The Boz was run over, through, and around. Bosworth had four sacks his rookie season and two forced fumbles. The Boz inflated his physique with 'roids. Bosworth twice won the Dick Butkus Award as the top college linebacker and deserved every cent of his 10-year, $11 million contract. The Boz adapted his look and shtick for a short and ignominious career as a Hollywood action hero. Brian Bosworth lost his career, his talent, and his passion on the operating table.

He retired after only 24 games in the NFL, all starts. His image collapsed on him. Bosworth's self-idolatry came to haunt him like a specter; the hype he created was used to retroactively define him as

A Star Is Stillborn

Chuck Knox talked about Brian Bosworth with the quiet patience of a father. The mainstream media finds ways to take potshots at the long-irrelevant athlete. I wonder if what would really kill Bosworth is if everyone just stopped talking about him?

His career was short and undistinguished. Apart from the hype, he had one good season, and two seasons of sudden and cataclysmic decline. He had one movie of note, *Stone Cold*, and it was of note because people still cared about Bosworth when it was released. If you have seen it, you are among the dozens. It's amazing what total crap $25 million can buy.

I had never considered Bosworth before writing this book, but the guy really does cast a long shadow. For someone who failed at football and failed at acting, he holds fascination like few ever have. I don't think Bosworth is evil or scum or anything as marginalizing as that, but I figure he is a heck of an egotist. He was a self-promoter of historic proportions, and it was his self-promotion that is his legacy. Instead of calling Bosworth a bust, perhaps the ultimate act of cosmic justice is to call him what he truly is: irrelevant.

a legendary bust. And so it was with some consternation that people read about the Boz rescuing a woman from an overturned SUV in 2007, and later, saving a man's life with CPR in 2009.

I mean, villains don't save. Cartoonish super villains like the Boz are crafty and despicable. Could it be that Brian Bosworth was just a man, and as any man faced with crisis, beholden to his humanity—his innate need to do right? Could it be the Boz was just a fiction, and like any fiction, as real as we need it to be? And that, where the two meet, there was nothing more than a good linebacker whose body never let him be great?

Nah. That's a terrible story. One not even the Boz would sign on for.

84 Let *Win Forever* Change Your Life

I hope Pete Carroll does not in fact "always compete." If Carroll did always compete, he would quickly become a David Brent-style satrap ruled by a compulsive need for one-upmanship. You know this guy. I've known these guys. *Saturday Night Live* ran a brief, recurring, mechanical sketch about this guy. No, "always compete" like most of *Win Forever* is the burped out phrasing of an idea that makes sense in the mind of Pete Carroll, but put into words, reads like inelegant sloganeering. And I think we can safely say Carroll is not simply compelling people to push themselves to be their best. Compete from Latin *competere* means to seek (*petre*) that which others (*com*) also seek. And that phrasing, however clumsy, is what preserves always compete from being yet another hamfisted way of saying "do your best." (Though always doing your best is also rare and probably not desirable. How often do we ever do our best? And how would we know that we had?) No, Carroll wishes you, himself, me, presumably, and his team for sure. Carroll wishes us to strive against others to always be the best. Not the best we can be—the best by besting others.

Win Forever is talky, conversational in a mostly unflattering way. The voice is good. There's a few splashes of psychology in a quote-gathering as cherry-picking sort of way. Carroll suffers setbacks, but every setback is made rosy with the retrospective wisdom that it all worked out in the end. One never reads the reflections of the man that passed up a watering hole before embarking through the Sahara. There's no "maybe I suffered and maybe I faced down death, but as sand scoured my desiccated cornea, I learned the true meaning of thirst." No. There is mistake and death, and so wisdom of a kind is always circumstantial and a hair's breath from damned folly. Carroll offers little in the way of concrete reflection on past failures. He doesn't quite—like Jim L. Mora did—say he has never failed, but when things go wrong, it's always because of some nebulous admixture of bad luck, bad relations with a superior, or other unfortunate circumstances that are not really his own fault.

The faults gang up on you. You may begin to feel foolish for reading on. You're liable to discount Carroll's ideas wholesale. *Win Forever* reads like hogwash and hucksterism, the superstitions of the lucky rather than the methods of the skilled. Yet bit-by-bit something ameliorating seeps through. Something that requires, I don't know, decoding. It's subtextual. It's common sense. Its value is only limited by how willing you are to believe. Carroll has a message to share about success, and it is try hard, enjoy yourself, and do not concentrate on the goal but the process.

So I finished *Win Forever* and sorta laughed, you know? Of all things, it actually kind of fizzles at the end. There's this cartoonish enthusiasm. This through-line of "Go! Go! Go!" that's almost breathless in parts, so breakneck in its rah-rahs and affirmations. I finished *Win Forever* and later that night went to the gym and swam. I'm built like a lead fishing weight and taught myself what little of swimming I know, so swimming's always been a clumsy, splashy exercise for me. But for once in my life, I did two things I do not think I've ever done before. I stopped thinking about finishing the lap and concentrated on finishing the stroke, and upon concentrating on finishing the stroke, I tried to stroke better, with less wasted motion and more skill. Stroke by stroke, I was a little better until my fingertips grazed the edge of the pool and I ducked under and pushed off toward the next lap.

It didn't take me but part of an afternoon to plow through *Win Forever*. And all my arch smugness, all my too-sensitive BS receptors, were fatigued past exhaustion. Maybe it was in that state of too exhausted by bullcrap to fight it that Carroll's message seeped through. I don't know. Life had been in a funk. Then Coach

Carroll got in my head and reminded me joy's in the doing. Life never goes no place, but there's fun in climbing, fun in navigating rocks and roots and joy in that rare moment the path levels and you chin up and see ancient Redwoods outspread, clotting every inch and avenue of open wilderness.

85 The Richard Sherman Fiasco, Part 1

To understand the resonance and staying power of Richard Sherman's 15-second rant to Erin Andrews, following Seattle's win over the San Francisco 49ers, many other things must be understood, perhaps least of which is Sherman himself.

The NFC Championship Game brought in 55.9 million viewers, and those viewers were overwhelmingly middle-classed and light skinned. Over the last 20 years, light-skinned middle-class people have become increasingly terrified of being thought racist. That is a bit of an oversimplification. Some people are terrified of their own racism. Some people are terrified of the professional and social consequences of being perceived as racist. Celebrities like Mel Gibson, and, recently, Paula Deen, have had their careers all but destroyed through public shaming and censure because of their racism or because of their perceived racism.

All of these people were put into a really puzzling situation by Sherman's rant, what's called cognitive dissonance. Here's someone shouting at them, someone doing something we'd normally criticize. But he's black, and so the situation becomes dangerous, delicate, and complicated. We're a long way from talking about Sherman, but let's for a second talk about Sherman's actions in the abstract. Media are often trying to trap athletes and celebrities into just this kind of spontaneous blunder—this show of emotion. And it was a blunder. Athletes, Sherman included, are trained to say as little as possible when being interviewed, substituting instead a string of clichés known colloquially as "Bull Durham," to avoid just this kind of distraction. Had Sherman not been a handsome, young, intelligent, and Stanford-educated black man but an ugly, 30-something, poorly-spoken white southerner, I think reaction would have been more or less polarized against him. After all, as a culture we are still very much prejudiced. Our prejudices have just migrated, moved to safer grounds. But prejudice doesn't even have to factor into how people viewing at home felt, nor does Sherman's skin color.

Viewers have a right to feel a little uncomfortable when someone suddenly and without warning begins shouting at them through their television. It's not common. It's not pleasant. It's not how postgame interviews are done. Sherman's slip-up is very much a tempest in a teapot, but the media loves such minor but public outrages because the viewing public is fascinated by such minor but public outrages. I am not sure exactly why, but I guess it has something to do with blowups like Sherman's being well-known, novel, indicative of some larger social trend, and mostly safe to talk about. Opinion is the stuff conversations are made of, and since the set of subjects so heated and polarizing as to be untouchable grows ever larger, it's nice when some little news item comes along to talk about and argue about but not lose any friends over in the process. Thus, the media, which is primarily comprised of market-driven, profit-making corporations, gives people what they want. Once the ball got rolling on this whole Richard Sherman fiasco, it wasn't going to stop, it would pick up steam, and eventually snowball into a self-sustaining media event. And that is exactly what happened.

Now let's get back to our ambivalent light-skinned people for a second. They're interested in this fiasco, for whatever reason, but they're uncomfortable with slipping up themselves, and because

Sherman is black, they know taking a stance is walking into a minefield. Or so they believe, and all things considered, you can't entirely blame them. They are, after all, just a bunch of individuals, too, with particular workplace environments, and friendships, and family relationships, etc. Just a bunch of individuals that do not want to lose something important to them because of some really, really trivial but noteworthy happening on their television sets. In these kinds of situations, a special subset of the media mobilizes to start staking out particularly promising-seeming places on the battlefield. This is big business. Every person that can be deemed a pundit, from the satirical-like Stephen Colbert to the dead serious like Bill O'Reilly must offer some opinion, some "take." There was money to be made and no choice but to make it. Whether your business is measured by viewers, readers, or page views; whether you are slave to ratings, subscribers, or SEO; and whether you really gave a damn about Sherman or football, participation in this media event was all but forced.

Some opinion mongers were overtly racist, and that worked for them. Some were covertly racist, and that probably worked for them. Some were apologetic, pointing out the particular situation in which Sherman's tirade took place and that though he yelled, he didn't swear, and I assume that worked for them. And seemingly throngs and throngs of people actually sung the praises of Sherman...because he acted like an ass?

Well, yes or indirectly yes. Because those overtly racist and covertly racist people are such a ready-made straw man, and if there's one thing ambivalent light-skinned people afraid of being thought racist know works well enough, it's to venerate anyone even perceived to be the victim of racism. So almost as quickly as racist buggers could slip out from under their rocks and spew their hate, the greater "tolerant" news media, or at least that part employed in the manufacturing of opinions, stood atop their rocks and professed loud and clear "Sherman is smart! Sherman is well-spoken! Sherman is authentic!" and "Look how far he's come! And from Compton!"

There is a scene in the satirical cartoon *The Boondocks* in which the Freemans are invited to a rich man's garden party, and Huey Freeman attempts to freak out the rich squares and challenge their status and entitlement. At the party he engages all the nice and well-to-do people and says Jesus was black, Ronald Reagan was the devil, and so forth. As the episode progresses, a bigger and bigger circle of rich people throng around him and comment on just how well-spoken he is. None are bothered, none respect him enough to fear or be hurt by anything he has to say.

This is almost exactly what happened to Sherman. He was patronized. He was exploited. People were prejudiced against him by assuming, among other things, that he was some kind of novelty, like a latter day Hottentot woman to be eyeballed and poked at, that it was truly admirable of him to overcome the extreme disadvantage of being poor and black and learn to speak well enough to shout an angry tirade across the airwaves. And because the often pernicious quality of flattery is harder to tease out and censure, this "Isn't he well-spoken?" "and a Stanford graduate!" rhetoric flourished.

Back on ground level, back to Sherman the human being, the football player, the man ranting wildly into Erin Andrews' microphone, we can maybe strip away the prejudice. The bad, the bad masquerading as good, the favoritism and knee-jerk excusing of his actions, it can be all cast away, and the fact of the matter can be seen. And the fact of the matter is that Sherman screwed up. He immediately shifted attention away from the glory of his team's victory and toward himself. He opened a can-of-worms controversy right before the two biggest weeks of sports media coverage all year. He motivated a rival, a fierce and dangerous rival, which needed no further motivation. He didn't represent the Seahawks franchise very well—which is a sports team but ultimately a product, too.

And he ceded high ground so rapidly that he was left standing in a sinkhole. Unknown in all this is what the heck Michael Crabtree said or did to so anger Sherman. I wouldn't be the least surprised if whatever it was—was far worse than what Sherman did, but what Sherman did we witnessed, and whatever Crabtree did, remains at best hearsay.

So Sherman screwed up, in a very, very minor but very, very public way. The relevance of that screwup snowballed, and for all sorts of unavoidable reasons, and not because the media are a bunch of hacks or scavengers. And because of a strange admixture of real prejudice and stifled prejudice, a real need to have acceptable opinions among friends and coworkers, a real fear of being thought racist and the real prejudice that feared racism sometimes creates (in the form of lowered expectations, mostly), Sherman's wounded and indignant freak-out at rival Michael Crabtree became something of an event.

We'd probably all have been better off laughing, and forgetting about it. It *was* pretty funny.

86 The Richard Sherman Fiasco, Part 2

To understand Sherman…well, I do not pretend to know Richard Sherman in a deeper sense. We've never met, never talked, he doesn't know I exist, etc. But I am going to try to relate to him because I think maybe we have a lot in common.

Sherman's one of those people that feels an indefatigable need to prove himself. If you grew up poor like Richard Sherman, this maybe's totally understandable. Envision 16-year-old Sherman: poor, living in Compton, California, and still very, very far from

Shortly after deflecting this pass from Michael Crabtree in the NFC Championship Game, Seahawks cornerback Richard Sherman ranted to Erin Andrews, where he notoriously ripped the 49ers wide receiver.

anything like a good chance at making it in the NFL. Sherman is smart. He's doing well in school. There's some chance of earning a scholarship, academic or athletic, but no guarantee. Without a scholarship the chances of entering a good school and avoiding crippling debt, of taking the risks it will take to better himself and escape the cycle of poverty become less likely, maybe remote. So he's poor, not counted even to be counted out, passed over, and disrespected, and doesn't live so much with a chip on his shoulder as a yawning chasm beneath his feet. He's making his identity. He's learning that to do more than survive, to excel, to fulfill his potential, he's going to have to work harder, take bigger risks, and never let anyone ever take a piece of what's his.

Two years later, Sherman's a three-star recruit. This means that he's athletically gifted but among his peers, mediocre or thought mediocre. Rivals rates him the 93rd best football player in California for 2006. He signs with Stanford, which is a big step up and gives him an avenue to success should he never develop into a great football player but also means he has to work that much harder. Sherman is a steady, not even remotely standout receiver for the Cardinal his first two seasons before switching to play cornerback full time before his senior season. He enters the NFL Draft. He runs a 4.56 at the NFL Scouting Combine, which is borderline bad. He waits and waits until the fifth round when the Seattle Seahawks draft him 154th overall.

Then Sherman begins to break out, makes a Pro Bowl, earns himself distinction as one of the best corners in the NFL but continues playing on his rookie contract. That means all the praise is just praise and should something terrible happen, his brief time at the peak of his profession will have earned him almost no long-term security.

Crabtree says something offensive to Sherman at a charity event, something that wounds Sherman. That insult may stay forever hidden, but like the never-known slight that motivates

Poe's protagonist in "The Cask of Amontillado," we know its gravity by its effects on Sherman.

Prior to the NFC Championship Game, Crabtree's head coach and Sherman's former head coach at the college level, Jim Harbaugh, singles out Crabtree for praise, saying Crabtree has the best hands in NFL history.

Sherman's survived the depths but hasn't fully escaped. He knows, surely he knows, of the exceptionally high rate of bankruptcy among former NFL players. Sherman was born into the clutches of poverty. Pity the man or woman that dare try and put him back there.

That's what Crabtree did. That's what Colin Kaepernick did. Not literally, no, but in a way that felt every bit as intense and dangerous as if it were. Because with 28 seconds left in the fourth quarter of a 23–17 game, Kaepernick targeted Richard Sherman's receiver, for what would have been the game-winning touchdown for the San Francisco 49ers. And Richard Sherman's receiver, Crabtree, positioned himself in the corner of the end zone, ever so slightly free of coverage. And had Richard Sherman not leapt at just the right moment to tip the football down and away from Crabtree and to Malcolm Smith for the game-sealing interception, had Crabtree somehow caught it, it would be Richard Sherman that took the fall. But Sherman did tip the pass, he did cause the game-winning interception, and he did excel during the very crucible of his young career. The chasm of failure and poverty beneath his feet, Richard Sherman stretched to the very limits of his ability and succeeded.

The game over but for a few kneel downs, Sherman walked over to Crabtree and maybe offered an innocuous "good game," and maybe taunted him—who knows? Crabtree pushed Sherman in the facemask and said...something.

When less than five minutes later, Sherman stood beside Andrews and began his now notorious postgame interview. He was still nuts on testosterone, adrenaline, androgen, and he acted kind of asinine really. He lost his cool and later he apologized, broadly and to Andrews specifically. Okay. But money was to be made, and for all sorts of reasons, everyone in the commentary game needed to comment, needed their own spin on the hot take. Some of us didn't like it, but that didn't stop us, did it? It's the classic non-paradox: the commenter criticizing the subject matter of the story he just read. Sometimes we stumble into hypocrisy, all ass over teakettle, and don't realize we've funded what we supposedly hate until it's too late. But it happened. I read the stories. Maybe you read the stories, watched the news, clicked the link. You've read this essay, anyway.

All our venial sins, all our missteps, all the sorta dodgy and embarrassing, morally compromised and professionally required blunders we, we the media, we the viewers, we the fans, we including Richard Sherman, committed since that pristine tip, that foolish tirade, are all gone, are all irrelevant now. Sherman has his commercials. The Seahawks have a championship. The 49ers have their billboard material. The press found another way to saturate the 24-hour news cycle, just like their viewers demand.

87 Sea Hawk

Seattle is named after the osprey. The osprey is a beautiful bird of prey that Seahawks fans can truly be proud of. Loving your mascot is a small but important thing. I would be horrified to have to root for the Redskins or Chiefs. Both are old teams, teams that were founded before it seemed taboo to name a team after a racial epithet, but both are nevertheless stuck with an offensive and ignorant team name. I guess like so many things, fans become inured. Certainly the name does not make the fans or the franchises themselves racist, but "Redskin" and "Chief" are nevertheless unsavory.

The osprey is a fish-eating raptor. Raptors are noteworthy for hunting in flight, and when you combine hunting in flight with fishing, you have one of nature's great coordinated acts of grace. The osprey is actually the only species of the genus Pandion and is found all over the world. One place it is not often found is Seattle.

The most Seahawk-like Seahawk of all-time is Dave Brown. *Raptor* derives from *rapacious* and Brown was a true ball hawk. The all-raptor team for Seattle would include Brown, Eugene Robinson, Kenny Easley, and John Harris. That is actually very close to the starting secondary for the 1985 Seahawks.

The modern game is turning airborne, and though the name is incidental, something derived from a contest, it is cool to be a fan of the Seahawks. They are not dogs, not miners, not sheep, never will be victim to changing mores, but something elegant, skillful, and predatory, like a great football team.

 # Husky Stadium

For whatever reason, Husky Stadium inhabits a terrifying nook in my subconscious. I remember thinking it was ugly and intimidating. The seating looked too steep. It made me think of El Castillo in Chichen Itza. There, the steps are high and must be climbed on hands and knees. It was built for ritualistic sacrifice, the bodies cast down its steep sides.

When I started researching this book, a few things stood out to me. First, Husky Stadium is widely considered beautiful and scenic.

That baffled me. Well, it didn't, because I knew my memories were irrational, but on a gut level, it did. The other thing that really startled me were black-and-white pictures from the 1987 north deck collapse. The sound of twisted metal is horrifying. Seeing the bent and collapsing structure reinforced my foolish fear.

Husky Stadium housed the Seahawks for three regular-season games in 1994 and two seasons before the completion of Qwest. Seattle finished 10–9 in Husky Stadium. It was loud like every good Seahawks stadium should be. Maybe if I could see it as a haven from the Kingdome, something that let Seattle find a better home, I could love it, too. But I don't. I fear and hate it and assume I always will.

Superstitions die hard.

89 Concrete Cobain Cries Bacon Tears for Beast Burger

Of all the suggestions my editor gave me in the making of this book, and there weren't too, too many, one recurred to him again and again: try the Marshawn Lynch Burger. I'd laugh about this with my wife. And for the longest time, like one does, I just didn't acknowledge his request.

My innocence, by way of ignorance, was torn to bits when my wife decided to actually find out what the heck the Marshawn Lynch Burger is. I assumed: burger + Skittles. I guess the burger could pay tribute to Marshawn Lynch in some more subtle way. It could be bison tongue to commemorate Lynch's time in Buffalo. And, because he's such a bruising runner, the burger could be made not with pre-ground burger meat, but bison tongue, tenderized on site and freshly ground—you get me. My wife told me it is a burger topped with ham and bacon and served with a side of packaged Skittles.

Around the same time my wife was pouring gasoline onto the smoldering embers of my misanthropy, the abandoned logging mill known as Aberdeen decided to honor its favorite son and potentially profitable moldering skeleton, Kurt Cobain. Hologram technology may lend a new terror to death, but good old fashioned poured concrete suffices for poorer, less ambitious grave robbers, and so mayor Bill Simpson dedicated a memorial statue to Cobain. It's a terrible likeness, probably due to the extreme anonymity of Cobain (who was a "well-known heroin addict who shot himself nearly 20 years ago," in the words of KING 5 News' Dennis Bounds, for anyone who is unaware of the singer's legacy). This likeness is immortalized, strumming a chord that for some reason requires him to flip the bird, wearing torn jeans that reveal a smooth melon-like patella, and uh appears to be crying. Oh and his lips are ringed in a craggy, scabby thing—maybe a burn? Maybe Cobain had drank a particularly hot cup of coffee all at once and without opening his mouth. Now we know the wellspring of his pain. Artists court such odd muses.

Simpson said of Aberdeen and his recent attempts to monetize its incidental and bitter relationship with Cobain: "We hope this is just as big as Graceland, eventually."

This Skittles thing...and Marshawn Lynch...it's...how to put this as delicately as possible...it's like a beloved but very private athlete had a totally innocent and lovable tradition, right? He ate Skittles Brand Fruit Chews to amp himself up for a job that is frankly unnatural and surely kind of terrifying. That tradition was leaked and then shared, and it put the greater public's interest in a fricken headlock from which it could not escape even after like three years. So like every Skittle I've ever eaten, it's now very stale, and one can't help but wonder if Lynch even likes the attention anymore. It's a better, more marketable reputation than the athlete's misadventures on the roadway, sure, but it's Skittles—*Skittles!*

But, well, this novelty has some staying power. And now that the Seahawks are *merde chaude*, people to which profit is reason enough are climbing over each other to exploit that popularity. (Hell, look at me!) Does Lynch profit from this Skittles burger? I sincerely doubt it. Does food provider Delaware North profit from this burger? Oh God, you know it does. The thing costs $15.

The last book had an essay entitled Be a Fan but Never a Completist or something like that. So here's an update: do whatever the hell you want. It's your money and your time. What do I know what makes you happy?

90 Josh Brown

You won't find too many kickers listed among a team's all-time great players, but you won't find too many kickers who did what Josh Brown did.

Brown was a star athlete in high school. He was a letterman in basketball, football, and track for the Foyil Panthers in Oklahoma. It is a subtle reminder that the oddball kickers we love to revile are in fact gifted athletes. He finished Foyil with 9,136 all-purpose yards and 51 touchdowns, but Brown's future lay in kicking.

He attended Nebraska and distinguished himself as an NFL prospect. Brown was a heck of a kicker. Of course, that's a bit of a matter of perspective. Brown only converted 69.4 percent of his kicks in college, including a sophomore season in which he was 5-for-10. That's enough to get someone run out of the league in the NFL, but in college long snappers are less skilled and hash marks wider. Further, Brown kicked 'em when they counted, or whatever. He was carried off the field after a 29-yard field goal to beat Colorado, and that win kept Nebraska in bowl contention. The Cornhuskers would finish the season stomping the piss out of Northwestern in the Alamo Bowl. Brown made the embarrassment of a million Wildcats fans possible. He helped turn the Alamo Bowl into an unwatchable travesty of entertainment.

It was all about good timing and better luck for Brown. There's little evidence that a kicker can control when they're accurate and when they're off. Retrospective psychology applied by beat reporters and fans invented concepts such as "clutch." Brown got lucky at the right time. It would propel him to NFL millions. It would save the season like a kicker never should.

Seattle drafted Brown in 2003, and for his first few years, he was an ordinary kicker of little distinction. Then came 2006. Seattle was cursed. The Super Bowl losers' curse. It dragged teams to their graves, fans to the bottle, coaches to their antacids, and reporters to their thesauruses. The curse was booming in 2006, supported by the unimpeachable proof of recent history, believed by the unimpeachable intellect of Joe Sports Fan, Esq.

The Seahawks avoided this cosmic curse because they didn't actually lose the Super Bowl. The Steelers watched their quarterback motorcycle his face off. Good times. A correction of sorts. An IOU from God, delivered six months too late and a few dollars short. Sort of a "Sorry I ran over your dog, but here's a gerbil."

By ordinary stats, the 2006 Seahawks were ordinarily bad. They were outscored by six points. They ranked 19th in offensive yards and defensive yards allowed. They lost the turnover war 34–26.

Ordinary stats neglect quality of opponents, and the NFC West was brutally bad that year. The 49ers, Cardinals, Rams, and Seahawks combined were outscored by 209 points. Seattle squeaked out an NFC West title on the leg of Brown.

Brown kicked four game-winning field goals. To get what that really means, let me use Brian Burke's win-probability metric. Burke broke down years of data to determine how much every play, in every situation, time, score, etc., is worth. Brown's first kick, a 42-yard strike to beat the Lions in Week 1, was worth 16 percent. Seattle went from an 84 percent chance of winning to a 100 percent chance of winning. Minor drama compared to what would come.

Brown's next feat was a 54-yard, game-winning field goal against the St. Louis Rams. Kickers convert about half of all attempts from 50-plus yards. Brown nailed it, adding another 40 percent to his win total. He again beat the Rams four weeks later, but this was a chip shot from 38, so only worth 10 percent. Brown notched another 50-yard game-winner against the Broncos. The 50-yard shot broke up a tie and so was less valuable than his dagger against the Rams, thus 26 percent.

All told, Brown's four field goals accounted for 82 percent of win probability, or a bit less than two wins. Ignoring home-field advantage and team quality, both teams start with a 50 percent chance of winning, and so 50 percent must be gained to achieve victory. Brown's two wins carried Seattle, and that those two wins came against the division-rival Rams proved decisive in the NFC West. Seattle finished 9–7. The Rams finished 8–8. Brown became a cult hero, was franchised, eventually signed to the Rams for *way too much* money, and became the enemy. But for a season, Brown was chicken bones and slumpbusters and salt over the shoulder.

91 The New Prototype: Prologue

It was inductive reasoning that sold me down the river against Russell Wilson. He was a rookie. Rookies fail. He was a third-round pick. Third-round picks rarely ever develop into franchise quarterbacks. And, bordering on the personal, Wilson is short. The kind of short that gets brought up, over and over, that in the recesses of the television broadcasters' mind, feels of urgent importance, to be mulled over, to develop graphics about, to openly speculate as to the accuracy of. Russell Wilson, all season, was 5'11" going on pipsqueak. The play-by-play guy would say it in that detached, damning way television journalists can. The color guy would take you the viewer into his confidence and share, I don't think this kid's even 5'11". He's 5'11" with a high-top fade and on stilts.

So there was a case. A popular, hackneyed case you could feel the grooves of without any kind of independent thinking, but a case. And that's good, because hobgoblin of the feeble-minded as they may be, stereotypes are a good bet. And I was wagering on being right.

Because of his height, maybe, Wilson didn't play like a successful quarterback. And even now I can not totally silence my fear that his success is built on a gimmick that will steadily produce diminishing returns. Will his madcap scrambles behind the line of scrimmage forever succeed? And if not, can Wilson develop conventional football skills? Can he become a pocket passer?

But there was more, at least personally. Wilson was 2012's "it" sleeper. Not the only, but a prominent one—perhaps inordinately popular. And if you've ever attempted prospect analysis that rises above reading other people's opinions and offering your spin, you know how damnably hateable are draftnik know-it-alls and their hunches and sleepers and insights. If loving player over team, or hating player over team, is an eddy of fandom, draftniks are Charybdis, dragging the whole of human reason to its watery grave.

And there was something vogue, something pseudo-scientific in the love of Wilson. Something will-over-talent, 10,000 hours, wanting it, Horatio Alger about why he would succeed in a way no one else had succeeded. I have a conflicted relationship with the Puritan work ethic. There is a poisoned bootstrap quality to it, but then there is a meritocratic quality to it, too. It may be a nightmare for the poet to be appreciated by being misunderstood, but purveyors of pop nonfiction are probably not so picky, and so Malcolm Gladwell probably doesn't cringe when hopeful proletariat folk opine they are just time and commitment from being pro golfers and rock musicians and pop nonfiction writers, but I do. There is talent, ineffable, beautiful talent. There is hard work, and there is luck. And without any one, there is no greatness.

NFL quarterback is a queer, trivial kind of greatness but greatness nonetheless. And people seemed to think Wilson could get there because he wanted it so damned much, which isn't just insulting to the hundreds of other fiendish workers in the NFL, but the thousands, millions of people that exerted beyond reason and never even neared greatness. His narrative of hard work was an affront to hard work like Lance Armstrong's narrative of survival, perseverance, and recovery is now an affront to those people praying for survival, learning in their marrow what perseverance really is, and envisioning a recovery that is realized attending a grandchild's birth, a daughter's graduation, a son's wedding. Wilson getting there because he "wanted it," was not a testament to the power of hard work and belief; it promised results, big, unprecedented results, and now.

Or maybe that's only how I see it through my just scraping by, no success, out in the wilderness of my dream and it's getting dark, aperture.

But I didn't like Wilson, didn't think he would succeed, saw the very worst in whatever he did, and hoped, and I say this ashamed, hoped he would fail big enough that the whole team failed with him. And poor Matt Flynn replaced him. Because Matt Flynn was my guy. And I had invested my pride and my hopes in Flynn. What's more, I identified with him.

Ultimately however much I wanted to be right, however much I had invested time, hope, and credibility into Matt Flynn, my loyalty for the Seahawks is much older, much stronger, and much more important than my loyalty to my opinions. If I didn't want to be wrong, if I didn't want to believe in something bigger than myself or my ideas, if I didn't desperately need to belong to something so much bigger than myself, I would have never become a sports fan. And so for all my "hate," some stifled part of myself cheered Wilson on. Little by little he won me over. He became first good, then capable of greatness, and now great.

I admit to my nasty apostasy for a reason. There were a few weeks in his rookie season in which the difference between Wilson's performance and his reputation were so great, I couldn't help but think of Rick Mirer. Even his good plays, his improvised plays, seemed in danger of disaster (a disaster very much like the disastrous strip-sack fumble Aldon Smith landed on Wilson to start the NFC Championship Game). And I was sort of right in my skepticism. But what blackness there is in being right about someone else's failure. This being right, finding the self-serving thrills of an essentially communal experience is part of how I will forever enjoy sports. But it's nothing compared to being neither right nor wrong, of having no ego at stake, and just joining in and cheering along.

Labor

I was a Teamster for a little over a year and managed Teamsters for about that same amount of time. *Manage* is the technically correct way to put it, but I imagine what I did is a lot like coaching million-dollar athletes. You can attempt to intimidate, you can befriend, you can just try to do right, but you are never truly in control. You motivate, hopefully, and you assign jobs, sure, but control, discipline, authority—all essential qualities of management—those are more or less out the door.

When you're a Teamster, there is a true camaraderie unlike anything I have experienced outside of sports. You meet complete strangers, and all the friction and awkwardness of being new or strange is just not there. That might sound idealistic, and maybe it is a little polished by memory, but it felt that way. I think it was a combination of factors that made everyone so tight. Pay was pretty good where I worked, and there were benefits. It was the first time I had health insurance in about a decade, and it wasn't scummy state insurance, but good, honorable insurance—and dental. People felt safe in their jobs. Removing competition between workers removes a lot of the mistrust. More than anything, I think when you are in a union you have a common enemy. You have a common enemy, you are in a constant state of near to total-war, and friendship among allies is fast and easy.

When you are managing a union, no matter how fair you try to be, or just or tolerant or respectful, you are that enemy. It's not subtle, either, or misguided: the union thinks you're their enemy, and fellow management reminds you that you are. Over and over I was reminded that union employees are not your friends and could not be your friends, no matter what. The management

mistrusts union members implicitly, and union members recip-
rocate. The management thinks the union is lazy, entitled, and
slow. The union thinks the management is crafty, greedy, and
dishonest. Both sides work toward fulfilling their rivals' stereotype of them. Some union members revel in displays of laziness
and defiance. Some management seem almost liberated by the
assumption that they are ruthless, treacherous, and inhuman, and
become all that and worse.

*O God, that men should put an enemy in their mouths to steal away
their brains! That we should with joy, pleasance, revel and applause
transform our selves into beasts!*
—Cassio, *Othello*

If you try to walk the line, not take sides, you become a man
without a country.

That is pretty much what I did. I joined management because
my wife wanted to go back to nursing school. Without the union
protecting me, I was almost immediately transferred, and where
I landed I was viewed with hostility. I was put on the kind of
job assignment upper management puts you on when they want
to promote you or want you to quit. It was all old-school union
guys, and they didn't have any reason to respect me, but they had
plenty reason to assume the worst. I worked it out with them the
best I could and won respect, if never trust. I wouldn't trust me.

The Seahawks were affected by two strikes. The first was in
1982. Labor unrest probably cost the Seahawks Sam McCullum.
McCullum was the team's union rep, and the team's first true deep
threat. The position of union rep can seem esoteric to anyone who
hasn't been in a union situation, but let me translate: to a union
member, the rep is the go-to guy for complaints and, as such, the
buffer between you and management. There is no one you have to
trust like the union rep, and when you have a good one, it's a true

godsend. For management, the union rep is the face and body of your frustration. They are the hardest employee to work with, and the one who corrupts the most. Jack Patera made waves by cutting McCullum prior to the labor-charged 1982 season, and even with what little I know about Patera, I understand that he would hate a union rep. That decision probably cost him his team, their trust, and ultimately his job.

Before the 1982 strike, Steve Largent and Jim Zorn cited Matthew 5:36–37 as the reason they would not strike. That might be a convoluted and convenient interpretation of that isolated passage, and it surely did not win friends among their teammates, but they were far from alone. Terry Bradshaw and Joe Montana were opposed, and Montana quit the NFLPA. It weakened the union's position, but not enough to destroy it.

Largent crossed picket lines in 1987 and played among the Sea-Scabs. If you are union, there is no greater betrayal than an employee who crosses the picket lines. That Largent was honored and established certainly made his action that much harder for others to swallow. Not only did he have less to lose from breaking the picket line and weakening the union, but because he was so prominent, his decision reflected weakness throughout the Players Union.

The 1987 strike started after Week 2 and lasted until after Week 6. Players returned for Week 7, and Seahawks fans booed the returning Seahawks. Sports fans do not tolerate when their team stops playing because the players want better wages and more equitable treatment. The how and why of the strike probably cost the team Kenny Easley, but also probably saved Easley's life. Easley succeeded McCullum as Seahawks union rep. When the team walked, the Seahawks scrambled to field a scab team. They enlisted a bouncer, and two players who flew in on Sunday and departed on Monday—not even NFL hopefuls, really. But members of the CFL's recently shutdown Montreal Alouettes, former USFL players, and so-so former college players long past their glory years. The replacements got a ringer in their third week when Largent broke ranks a second time and took the field to dominate scabby scrubs, scrubby scabs, or whatever. That was a major thumb in the eye to Easley. He was fighting to convince Zorn not to return to football and take the field. He convinced Zorn, only to be betrayed by Largent. So Easley demanded a trade before the 1988 season, which trade and corresponding physical probably saved Easley's life.

Abolitionist, hero of mine, orator, great man of letters and master of the parted fro, Frederick Douglass, long stressed how the institution of slavery debased the slave and the slave master. Overall, and historically, I am a fan of the labor movement and what unions have done for this country. I am not one of those people who think professional athletes are overpaid. The NFL makes billions in revenue, and not because of the stadium owners or PA announcers. The Players Union has helped ensure players receive an equitable portion of that revenue, and huzzah and so forth. But if union-management relations in the NFL are anything like union-management relations where I worked, it is an institution that debases player and team. An institution in need of a revision.

93 The Hasselbeck Exit Strategy

Heading into the 2011 off-season, the Seattle Seahawks organization had a bit of a fix on its hands. Now, from a fan's perspective, from a Seahawks fan's perspective circa 2011 especially, this was just a chance for everything to become convoluted and stupid. The good, kindly, and most literate city of Seattle is known for its sports snafus: lost teams, kidney damage, the Mariners—yet...

Matt Hasselbeck was set to become a free agent. One has to be a Seahawks fan to understand how beloved Hasselbeck was in and around Seattle. He personified a certain gentle but firm, modest yet confident, underestimated but never counted out Pacific Northwest masculinity. 'Beck was from Boston, but Beantown is sorta kindred and at least demographically similar to Seattle.

He was just 35, which is kind of football old but also kind of prime age in the modern NFL for a quarterback, and a lot of people still believed in him and a lot of people maybe had plausible reasons to believe in him. I want to emphasize plausible because I do not think we should call those, ahem, good or at least *the best* rationales. The case against Hasselbeck was definitely stronger, but alas fandom dies hard even for individual players. What muddied all this that much more is that he was coming off his best season in a few years, and that seemed to corroborate a strong notion that Hasselbeck was

Leaf It Be

Seattle flirted with one of football's greatest busts when Mike Holmgren signed Ryan Leaf in 2002. Leaf was probably the most famous bust of our time. He was the loser in one of the great pre-draft quarterback controversies of all-time, when leading up to the 1998 draft pundits debated who had the better potential, Leaf or Peyton Manning. The funny thing is, most actually thought Leaf had the higher ceiling. Manning was the safe pick.

He not only busted and busted in the shadow of perhaps the greatest quarterback ever, but he did so publicly and embarrassingly. Holmgren signed him, thinking that with time to heal and the pressure off, Leaf could finally reach some of his potential. He attended Seahawks minicamp and was finally producing something he hadn't since his rookie year: good press. But just a few weeks later, Leaf called it quits. One has to wonder what Matt Hasselbeck thought about the signing.

not the problem. The surrounding talent was the problem. General relativity is better understood than the interdependence of quarterback, receiver, offensive line, and offensive coordinator. To this day smart people quote "individual" stats to defend Tony Romo, never wondering aloud whether Romo is ship or anchor. Hasselbeck's surrounding talent was a problem but not the only problem by any stretch. He had exploded in the Beast Quake game, and though entirely in garbage time, performed respectably against the Bears and on the road. That season Chicago's pass defense was like *half* as good as Seattle's pass defense in 2013—which is pretty damn good.

Plus, and it should be noted that I have no idea if these so-and-sos actually swing such a big bat opinion-wise, but certain local journos and sports personalities were all in the bag for this guy, and Seahawks fans so long beaten down were afraid dropping Hasselbeck before he was surely and truly done might instigate another decade-plus of desperate, foundering quarterback play. There's no arguing the intuitive brain when it comes to this kind of thing, and the intuitive brain of any longer term Seahawks fan has to access the idea of "quarterback" through a nuclear waste repository marked Kelly Stouffer-Dan McGwire-Rick Mirer. This is a fan base that has a rather warm place in its heart for now Tacoma high school math teacher Jon Kitna.

To start the off-season and much to my terror, Pete Carroll announced that re-signing (note the grim hyphen between "re" and "signing" and its horrible implications) Hasselbeck was his No. 1 priority. But it wasn't. It wasn't. It never was. This announcement was a way to get the goofy local media wholly off his back, which would be handy when the team made the hard to understand move of signing Tarvaris Jackson four days after the end of the 2011 NFL lockout.

This flimflam is part of being a professional head coach—especially in the media-saturated NFL. Here are two facts and an opinion: the NFL season, including the playoffs, is the shortest among the five major professional sports, both in number of games and total duration. But football is also the most popular professional sport in the United States and by a good margin. The NFL has become so popular and so pervasive in American culture that citing statistics about revenue or Super Bowl ratings is rote, yet still impressive sounding, and still doesn't capture the monetary or cultural impact of football. This book, the local media, blogs, television networks, etc. exploit this popularity to make money, and nothing's ever quite so interesting as big opinions. Whereas there is debate over exactly who the best baseball player is or what constitutes truly valuable performance in basketball, media seem honestly perplexed about most of football. Most do not understand the strategy, most do not understand those qualities that make a player good, and seemingly almost all of us are helpless to project with any accuracy which team will be good any given season. Winning is panacea, but in those six long months between season's end and another chance to win, winning the battle of opinion and hype has to suffice.

Jim L. Mora, in a moment of authenticity and honesty, singled out Olindo Mare for criticism after Mare missed two field goals, and the Seahawks lost 25–19 to the Chicago Bears. This was Week 3 of the NFL season, and the Seahawks were 1–2 with a +9 point differential—i.e. no time to panic or lose your cool. This rankled fans for all sorts of reasons. Mare had converted four of his six field-goal attempts. Field-goal kicking depends on multiple players, including snapper and holder. A kicker never intends to miss a field goal, and if you've ever seen a kicker warm up, you know they are near automatic in non-pressure situations. It's worth wondering if Mare really deviated at all from what he's done thousands of times or if maybe one of the snapper, holder, or blockers had something to do with his miss. (The kicker is least opposed by the defense and most sensitive to the ways that defense opposes his teammates.) But most importantly, Mora singled out a player for blame and took that blame to the media. A good football team is as thick as thieves and would rather severe punishment administered privately to public shaming. It's destabilizing and divisive, but maybe above all, it's embarrassing. Much the way top players wish to be paid top money to dignify their position as top players, all players of substance loathe and dread playing for a team that itself is embarrassing.

Carroll lied, conned, kept it in-house, and when Seattle signed Tarvaris Jackson and Hasselbeck signed with the Titans, not but a peep of protest was heard. (Well by me anyway.) We may never know the exact ramifications of winning the media game, but if you can win, why ever lose?

94 Make Your Own All-Seahawks Team

Thirty-five is a strange number to celebrate. It looks somewhat like a prime number but obviously isn't. It is not a quarter century or half century or third of a century, or a fraction of any meaningful milepost save 700—which isn't terribly meaningful but for being an even 100. It is a number of little distinction, neither relevant in human years nor football franchise years, and in fact, as far as I can tell, no other football franchise has bothered to celebrate its first 35 years.

No, not required nor asked for, instead the Seattle Seahawks organization's celebrating its 35th anniversary evinces two not ignominious but surely ignoble facts: the human mind has a clockwork tic when it comes to counting by fives. And the Seattle Seahawks franchise, at 35, was looking for something to celebrate, something to show for its 35 years of life.

That the franchise's highpoint to that point was an embittering Super Bowl loss, that the Seahawks had been consistently bad but for two grasps at above-average in the '80s and '00s, and that the franchise seemed to be spiraling back toward turmoil, shame, and irrelevance, probably *ahem* inspired the Seahawks organization to throw its own kind of siege party.

But how does a good, professional, sure-handed, and able move tight end, who will never make a Pro Bowl—save some miracle union with Peyton Manning—still on his rookie contract, off a dramatic decline in performance, and with fewer than 2,000 total yards receiving, how does that player end up on an all-franchise team? And on a franchise old enough to be price-shopping Miatas?

Well...what we have is a tale of woe and Mike Tice, of a position as deficient as other positions like slot receiver, fullback, and offensive tackle were strong. What we also have is a bit of a fun proposition. After all, this team is nearing its 40th anniversary, and with so many good receivers and so few good tight ends through its history, why even worry about filling up the traditional positions? Why not make an all-time Seahawks team dictated by talent and coaching, rather than a generic, forced sense of what positions matter and what position do not?

My picks are directly below with some elaboration where I think it's needed. But to me this is more like a good conversation starter at a sports bar. Who's the head coach? How about the right tackle?

Head Coach: Pete Carroll
Offensive Coordinator: Mike Holmgren
Defensive Coordinator: Chuck Knox
Quarterbacks Coach: Jim Zorn
LT: Walter Jones
LG: Steve Hutchinson

C: Max Unger
RG: Steve August
RT: Russell Okung
QB: Russell Wilson
Backup Quarterback: Matt Hasselbeck
FB (yes, fullback): Max Strong
RB: Curt Warner ca. '83
Backup Running Back: Marshawn Lynch ca. 2012
Third-down Back: Shaun Alexander ca. 2003
Flanker: Steve Largent
Split End: Joey Galloway
Slot: Bobby Engram
(Did you expect otherwise? Seahawks fans know the three wide, I-formation was Holmgren's bread and butter.)

DT/DE: Jacob Green
NT: Brandon Mebane ca. 2013
Strongside End: Cortez Kennedy
(Holy crap, that sends chills...)

LEO/OLB: Julian Peterson ca. 2006
ILB: Lofa Tatupu ca. 2005
ILB: Bobby Wagner
OLB: Chad Brown
RCB: Richard Sherman
LCB: Marcus Trufant ca. 2007
SS: Kenny Easley ca. 1984
FS: Earl Thomas
K: Josh Brown
(I'm tempted to write Olindo Mare here, as I have an immense respect for Mare and his ability to force touchbacks, but the modern rules diminish that ability, and Browny's the sentimental favorite.)

P: Jon Ryan
KR: Percy Harvin
PR: Nate Burleson

Subs:
TE: Zach Miller
Move TE: John Carlson
Jumbo Package TE: Itula Mili
Second Slot/4ᵗʰ WR: Darrell Jackson
5ᵗʰ WR: Benny Blades
Nickel: Josh Wilson
Dime: Dave Brown
(It may seem as if I am slighting Brown, but consider: Sherman is surely the best cornerback in Seahawks history, if only for peak value. I am stubborn in my belief that Marcus Trufant was a very good cornerback habitually victimized by poor pass rush and poorer-still safety play. Wilson is simply a better nickel, maybe should he ever settle into the position, a great nickelback. And so Brown mans the rear, so to speak, as the skilled generalist you need to cover the wide assortment of fourth wide receivers but also first depth should Sherman or Trufant be injured.)

Big Sub: Kam Chancellor
The Big Sub is a sorta linebacker-strong safety hybrid, mostly deployed in college football. Brian Urlacher played the similar Joker position at New Mexico. The Seahawks employed a Big Sub in 2011.

So…what'd I get wrong? Who'd your gunner be?

Futility

The Latin *futilis* means "pouring out easily" as like a cup, and, in this context, a vessel that pours out easily is leaky and unsound. And from this we get the French word "futile." Thus futility is not like hitting your head into a wall or—as Derek Millhouse Zumsteg of USSMariner.com once compared the Mariners franchise to— Sisyphus rolling a boulder uphill for eternity. The first is simple stupidity. The second is laborious, noble punishment for a divine crime.

No futility is much more common even vulgar than all that. It is anything that bears a semblance of soundness, but which is undermined (and often subtly) by a fatal flaw. A glass tumbler need not a very large hole to be worse than useless. Futility is tying wings to your back and jumping from the Eiffel Tower. It is punting on fourth and 11 from the Seattle 39, down 29, but attempting an onside kick one quarter later, down 28. It is the very concept of distinct human "races." It is the plausible but false—the illusion and the painful disillusionment in one. Futile is not the same as unsuccessful. Futile is not the same as noble but doomed. Futility is something at once more appealing than obvious failure and therefore much, much more dangerous.

Is this an essay about Tim Ruskell? you ask. This is an essay about Tim Ruskell, I answer.

* * *

It would be wrong to characterize Tim Ruskell as a fiend or a fraud or a fool—at least in the flattering sense of the word. Ruskell certainly meant no harm. Up to his final big moment as decision maker, the 2009 NFL Draft, he did something selfless so sure was he that it wasn't selfless. Seattle, without complication really, traded its second-round pick in 2009 to the Josh McDaniel-cursed Denver Broncos. Denver drafted Alphonso Smith, but had Ruskell kept the pick, he would have likely drafted someone like Eben Britton, Mohamed Massaquoi, Glen Coffee, or maybe even Max Unger (and I write this with confidence, so formulaic was Ruskell's approach to drafting). In exchange Denver traded its 2010 first-round pick. In McDaniel's wild fantasies, this would become the 34th overall pick after the Broncos defeated the Ravenous Bugblatter Beasts of Traal in the first ever trans-universal Super Bowl. But as cruel fate would have it, that pick became the 14th overall pick in the 2010 draft—a much better class it seemed at the time and has all-but proven to be now. Seattle selected Earl Thomas, and Thomas is easily the most essential not-Russell Wilson Seahawk: essential to how Seattle's schemes its defense, essential to that defense's success.

Ruskell was a well-meaning and not totally incompetent general manager. However much as we may want to, there is no extracting Ruskell from what, when I started writing this, was the pinnacle moment of the Seahawks franchise: 2005 and the run to Super Bowl XL. Let us not confuse competent, conservative, and fatally flawed for total idiocy or outright failure. Little suggests Ruskell is or was an idiot. And were he an outright failure, what then would be Matt Millen? Some necrotic force, that cannot be credited with success or failure, can only be described in terms of duration and extent?

Tim Ruskell insisted on a certain stereotype of player. If you were attempting a least squares type analysis, the only two inputs necessary would be starts and conference. I write that only half-jokingly. Of his 37 picks, only four (John Carlson, Tyler Schmitt, Courtney Greene, and Mike Teel) were drafted from a conference outside the ACC, Big 10, SEC, or Pac-10. Schmitt was a long snapper (with a debilitating back condition that ended his career before it began). Carlson played for Notre Dame. And Greene and Teel played for Rutgers—a smaller but by no means small school. Still...maybe ultimate arbiter of manliness and true soul-of-the-gridiron, then Rutgers coach Greg Schiano, now fired and defamed former head coach of the Tampa Bay Buccaneers, gave Ruskell his kneel-down blitz of approval.

You can sort of compare this to building a baseball team entirely from top performers in Triple A, and patching holes with expensive free agents. Basically, what Ruskell would contend are talents tempered by the highest level of competition and proven to be pro-ready. But maybe then the futility of this kind of process begins to show through, too. In formal logic, the first damning part of this process is what's called a "conjunction fallacy." That is, a subset cannot contain more than the set it belongs to. Then we have the matter of starts, of perceived polish of all kinds that so haunted Ruskell's analysis.

I was certainly seduced by the simplicity and common sense of Ruskell's method to an extent anyway. Good, motivated players strive to excel wherever they go. (It might send a shiver up the spines of some, but I maintain Russell Wilson would have been a Tim Ruskell player, one Ruskell may have drafted, one that could have possibly saved his career. Wilson started a combined 50 games and had the Ruskell two-fer of starting in the Big 10 and the ACC.) The average number of college starts for a Ruskell pick was 33.6. The average number of college starts for a Carroll-Schneider pick is 26.4. And if starting were a feat worthy of recognition, starting and excelling in the most competitive conferences, was a feat that to Ruskell indicated future success. Seems sensible. Sort of.

Much economic analysis and particularly prospect theory has investigated so-called "risk aversion." Many people as they age and become settled and content (in *The Merchant of Venice* way) become almost paranoid of risk. There was a time in their teenage years, maybe, they weren't so, but little by little it crept up on them, and their lives became smaller and smaller, like the mouse who is afraid of the possibilities of life until eventually he sees the converging edges of the wall he is running toward, in that famous Kafka parable. I've justified/apologized for this tentativeness by mocking up a pseudo-evolutionary biology interpretation: thousands of years ago, life was once much more dangerous with much less to be gained through risk. And people stick at jobs they hate and in relationships they hate and live in places they hate, etc., because of a healthy impulse misplaced. There may be no great danger to quitting a dead-end, modestly paying but unfulfilling job, but our minds weren't designed to navigate the complexities of updating a resume, transferring a 401K, etc. Instead we magnify possible worst-cases, like an uncivilized man might were he to consider moving from a place of adequate but not good foraging. Where we should rationally "fear" inconvenience, we instead intuitively *fear* starvation. The end of that Kafka parable, if you know or remember, is the mouse, seeing the end of his journey and the "trap [he] must run into," delays, and is at once eaten by the cat we never knew till then was chasing it. Life feels like that sometimes: narrow, inherently doomed, and haunted by unseen evils. It can be hard to adopt the calm and general optimism the luxury of civilization has made, really, the most rational mode of thinking. It's not that bad things do not happen. It's only that most of the worst things you're never really prepared for anyway. So why bleed an ulcer fearing the unforeseeable?

Ruskell overcompensated to avoid foreseeable failure and thus hamstrung his chances at real success. He seemed to overestimate the damage done by busted draft picks. I don't know why. Teams that do not retain much of their draft class are often good teams—teams talented enough that it's difficult to upgrade many positions, and so a drafted player may be cut simply because he is not as good as the incumbent. This selectivity is part of the maturation of a

From End to End

Julian Peterson was a defensive end at Michigan State but became a linebacker in the pros. He started his career in San Francisco and was best known there for his cover skills. That's remarkable when you think about how little experience he likely had. It wasn't until he rejoined Seattle that his skill as a pass rusher was rediscovered.

Normally, Peterson is the kind of talent teams do not let get away. He became a Seahawk after rupturing his Achilles tendon in 2004. When he returned to San Francisco the next season, some thought he had lost something. Tim Ruskell signed Peterson in his first big free-agent spree. Right away, defensive coordinator John Marshall saw the end in the linebacker.

Peterson would play end on obvious rushing downs, and he became a terror against left tackles. He was long-limbed and agile and could turn the corner at a speed most 270-pound ends couldn't imagine. He had 10 sacks his first season and another 9.5 his second.

Free agency: how bad teams become mediocre.

roster. Teams in rebuild may retain every bit of their draft, year after year, like Seattle did under Ruskell, but good teams do not. Ruskell emphasized those qualities that seemingly best ensured longevity within the NFL.

During Week 16 of the 2013 NFL season, Ruskell's seventh-round pick of 2007, Steve Vallos, suffered a concussion. This was news to me, news that Vallos still played in the NFL, and for the 13–3 Broncos. But Vallos takes blows protecting punters and kickers. It's presumably those Ruskellian qualities of dutifulness and discipline and so forth that keeps him employed but at a position of maximum fungibility. Vallos is n-deep offensive line depth, a problem few anticipate will ever happen. A guy that may as likely be retained by Denver because he's a nice guy that does what's asked of him and sets a good example for more-talented but less-disciplined players instead of for his absolute value on the gridiron.

This minimization of risk was not "half-assed" in regards to work—Ruskell and his team seemed hard working. It was a poor idea, obviously, but in what way it was too easy and thus futile is not easement of effort but easement of fear. He didn't simply emphasize well-coached players at or near their athletic potential. He demanded well-coached players at or near their athletic potential. But through this pernicious fixation on low-risk, low-upside talent, he ensured eventual failure.

To me the quintessential Ruskell pick was Kelly Jennings, a cornerback out of The U—which in the early oughts was a powerhouse that eventually graduated guys like Andre Johnson, Vince Wilfork, and Frank Gore. That's two five-time Pro Bowl selections and a receiver, still just 31, within 500 yards of surpassing Steve Largent. Also teammates with young Jennings were, like, almost a dozen more NFL talents: Sean Taylor, Greg Olsen, Jonathan Vilma, Antrel Rolle, Eric Winston, D.J. Williams, Devin Hester... With almost 10 years of hindsight, it's pretty clear Jennings was one of the worst Hurricane players among those likely to be drafted.

Jennings was a good college player that showed well at the 2006 NFL Combine, at least in those categories that can be readily quantified. But he was stick thin and for all his polish and consistency, his ball skills were among the worst I've ever seen. The quintessential play of this quintessential player happened...well, I don't remember the game. But Jennings was in perfect position in the end zone, and the quarterback's pass descended down, down through his outstretched arms before colliding with his facemask. The case for why Jennings could be good was replete with circumstantial evidence. But he wasn't good, and rather than develop like most young, talented corners do, he regressed as his weaknesses were exposed. All coaches and all sensible quarterbacks fear the interception. Jennings was a corner that could cover but not cover, that could be close but never to the pain. And now he's three years removed from playing professional football. Pete Carroll traded him to Cincinnati for (useful) situational defensive tackle Clinton McDonald. Contained within that minor roster move is the DNA of the diverging legacies of Ruskell, and Schneider and Carroll.

Here's a cliché, but a cliché apt enough that it would be tacky to end around it to appear fresh: Ruskell built his teams within the superstructure of his fears. He feared his players would bust and he mortgaged potential for an often false sense of security. When all was said and done, he had still drafted Aaron Curry, a famously "safe" prospect, and among the biggest busts in franchise history. Schneider and Carroll have built the contemporary Seahawks upon the foundation of their hopes. Sometimes, silliness ensues as in the case of CFL project Ricky Foley. And maybe, though results make us think otherwise, had Carroll and Schneider failed, their failure would be quicker and of a greater magnitude than Ruskell's. Had Chris Clemons' injury problems persisted or the Leo concept not worked, had Russell Wilson been drafted by another team or failed to develop; had Walter Thurmond III never recovered; Richard Sherman proven to be anything but an All-Pro corner; had the NFL chosen to flag rather than mostly allow the borderline holding and interference Seahawks DBs commit almost every snap; had oft-suspended third-string running back Marshawn Lynch never regained what made him such a special talent; etc.

Or what if Seattle won Super Bowl XL?

It's okay to be afraid. No one, not even the boldest, ever stop being afraid. Only they fear more never trying. Of never failing, and so never even having a chance to succeed. Carroll and Schneider shook futility, and took a path toward noble failure, finding along the way something Ruskell never could: success.

96 The Science of Churn

It came to be called churn. It could be interpreted as the final, damning case against Tim Ruskell. It could be called "always compete" applied to the executive level of football operations. Whatever it was, starting in January of 2010 the Seahawks organization conducted a level of roster turnover unprecedented in NFL history. From that time and to the eve of Super Bowl XLVIII, the Seahawks made 1,105 roster moves. The most in the NFL, and over a 100 more than the second place New England Patriots. Much of that was done early, and we have since (mostly) left the churn era of roster construction. Seattle is back to a more traditional practice of adding and retaining talent. But the sheer vigor of the cycling of talent, the sheer number of names known and unknown connected with the Seahawks, and for so many months, was both thrilling and scary.

New head coaches and general managers are expected to audit a roster, be more rational in assessing existing talent, and "streamline" a team with the ruthlessness and efficiency of the Bobs. Maybe you believe that. New head coaches and general managers are—likely as not—prejudiced against existing talent, force a mismatched scheme on otherwise useful players, and strip a team bare, catalyzing an often unnecessary rebuild. Or maybe you believe that.

Those would be the rough polarities of opinion circa August of 2010. Opinions that seem to generate from genetics: skepticism or orthodoxy; a fear of or belief in power. Were Pete Carroll and John Schneider exhausting every opportunity to improve the Seahawks roster, or turning Virginia Mason Athletic Center into a mockery? Were these tryouts the show trial version of roster development? Emphasizing the "optics" of progress while accomplishing little?

Obviously it worked, or this book wouldn't exist, and Triumph Books would be readying a new edition of *100 Things 49ers Fans...* or that would be a facile, neat, halo-effect indebted explanation following the Seahawks' first Super Bowl win. But did it really work? Did Seattle benefit from all this dogged cycling of fringe talent? And who could know?

Let's start with one assumption: it is very hard to build a winning football team. Maybe this isn't true. Maybe a reasonably intelligent person with a reasonably good understanding of football and no damning character flaws could have outperformed five-time Executive of the Year award winner Bill Polian, so long as that person started his career with the first overall pick of the 1998 draft. But let's assume it is difficult and that, though the former players and scouts that have typically populated front offices rarely ever impress with their reasoning, scope, or depth of intellect, they like so many are very good at a very specialized profession reliant on a kind of hard bitten intuition. Intuition that even they do not wholly understand, but an intuition that is real and reasonably reliable and only earned through lots and lots of time and effort. Okay.

Auditioning as much talent as possible, giving every eligible person a chance to prove themselves capable, and thus simultaneously challenging the entitlement of every entrenched starter on Seattle's roster seems like a great decision. Or it seems facile, cutting the proverbial Gordian Knot, and totally clueless to the realities of running a football team.

How quickly can anyone know if a player is good or not? And did the Seahawks risk losing good talent undermined by a bad audition? If you want to stretch this even further, did Seattle risk staking too much on the audition, and not only stocking the roster with something akin to "workout wonders," but in the process anger and motivate a lot of better players? Players that did not or could not properly perform in an irrelevant and misleading trial? I mean, doesn't anyone and everyone—professional scout, professional draftnik, general manager now and former—do they not all point to "the tape," as Holy, Gospel and Witness all rolled in one?

What does constant turnover do to the chemistry of a football team? And before you "Chemistry? Ha! Pfft," me, keep in mind chemistry has not been disproven in football the way it's been more or less disproven in baseball. That at least the trust, timing, cohesion, and collaboration parts of chemistry are all but inherit to the way football is played (i.e. quarterbacks throw to a spot rather than a receiver, option routes require receiver and quarterback to read coverage identically, offensive linemen must be able to coordinate and account for free rushers against a blitz, blitzing defenders must likewise coordinate to create the spacing or "overload"—which = defenders > blockers at any given space on the line—the offense, etc.)

Given the multimillion dollar process by which teams in the NFL already scour for and assess talent, how likely is it that useful players are just lying around, awaiting an opportunity? After all, the overlap of 300-plus pounds and good at football is slim to vanishingly small.

What really was the sum product of the great roster churn of 2010–2014?

Well…maybe great and minor. Maybe.

Of Foleys and Browners

Around February of 2010, the team signed this Canadian fellow named Ricky Foley. Some—I don't want to say cynical because cynical doesn't mean that, no matter how desperately it's been bullied to (stand tall little ancient eponym)—paranoid schizophrenic part of me (but fun-loving) thinks Foley was signed to make good with the local media. I mean, guy was-a Sunday features dream. Just not that good at football, but hard working, of a ripe-for-Hollywood undermining father, storybook of a corny sort origin. My mind's eye envisions him flipping tractor tires. I do not think he ever actually flipped tractor tires, but you get the point. Foley, it turned out, was this administration's Nick Reed. (Editor's note: immediately after writing this sentence, John realized that it was true.)

And April that same year, the team signed Mike Williams. The Williams story is a bit more layered than the Foley story. But that's for another book or at least another essay.

Williams, Foley, Brandon Browner—this is more or less what all that churn brought in, as far as talent.

100 Times Gravity

While it was almost universally praised by press and fans, a plausible argument could be made against Seattle's extreme roster turnover, which is why saintly football is ultimately not about plausibility of rhetoric but winning on Sunday and Monday (and Thursday and sometimes Saturday).

The Seahawks didn't add much talent, and that talent that was added was of limited value or soon gone. But though I doubt anyone involved in the great churn process would admit so, it may have been the churners rather than the churned, who benefited most from this high speed, hyper-engaged, and surely grueling process of constant tryouts. Because while athlete after athlete performed and was assessed and subsequently was rejected or signed, the people assessing were (unwittingly) involved in the kind of breakneck, all-consuming practice regimen required of an Olympic athlete. With every tryout, Schneider and Carroll understood better what it really took to be a great football player. With every no, they refined their ultimate standard of what the Seahawks should become. And with the very few yeses, that standard received positive reinforcement.

For two people both experienced and new, accomplished and aspiring to accomplish much, much more at the very peak of their respective professions yet starting all over again, the churn was the implied arduous and soul-searching path of enlightenment Kung Fu movies show as a training montage.

There is no absolute way to prove this, mind you. But if churn is essentially the process of cycling fringe players, players without a team or even a market for their services, and efficiently analyzing why they could or could not be of use to the Seahawks, perfecting that analysis should show in success from late-round picks. Late-round picks in the NFL Draft are, after all, the churn candidates of tomorrow.

What counts as a late-round pick can be debatable. Surely the seventh and final round is "late," but how about the fourth? And what of the beginning of the fourth versus the end? (Doing a very poor job of) extrapolating from Kevin Meers' work at The Harvard Sports Analysis Collective, I am going to call the 95th pick and on "late." Because, in Meers' words, "The 94th pick is a close to [...] normal pick, having a draft value of 100.3 and a CAV of 15." Picks occurring before 94 are thus above average in value, and picks occurring after 94 are below average in value.

Who then are our churn superstars? Kam Chancellor (133) and Richard Sherman (154) have both made the Pro Bowl. K.J. Wright (99), Walter Thurmond (111), Byron Maxwell (173), and J.R. Sweezy (225) all started in Super Bowl XLVIII. Malcolm Smith (242) may have done something you heard about. Robert Turbin (106), Luke Willson (158), and Jeremy Lane (172) contributed. Throw in undrafted free agents Alvin Bailey, DeShawn Shead, Doug Baldwin, Jermaine Kearse, Lemuel Jeanpierre, Mike Morgan, and 16 of the Seahawks 46 active players on Super Bowl Sunday were late-round picks or undrafted but immediately signed by Seattle.

Compare that to the Broncos, a team opposite of Seattle when it comes to roster turnover. Over the same time span as above, while the Seahawks were making a league-leading 1,105 moves, the Broncos made only 689—26th in the NFL. The upshot: an inferior team comprised of high-round picks and free agents. Denver netted one Pro Bowl player from the selection criteria given above: Julius

Thomas. He started the Super Bowl as did Danny Trevathan and Duke Ihenacho, who had been benched mid-season. David Bruton, Omar Bolden, Aaron Brewer, and Virgil Green played but mostly on special teams. Brewer is a long snapper. Wesley Woodyard and Chris Harris subbed in defensively, and C.J. Anderson got some late, ultra-garbage time snaps at running back. He's fourth on the depth chart. That's 10 of the 46 active and maybe three real contributors. (And two of whom were marginal contributors to the league's 22nd ranked defense.)

Truth be told, no general manager in the NFL would trade Sherman for all 10 Broncos. In that sense numbers and names do not accurately represent the discrepancy between Seattle and Denver when it comes to talent acquired through the late rounds and undrafted free agency. It's an absolute blowout.

Now an Anecdote

For some throwing back Red Hooks at Sluggers, the deep philosophical argument is the goal. Krieg was better than Elway, Warner a bum knee from enshrinement in Canton, and Seneca Wallace should've been converted to wide receiver his rookie season. Sports fans like the deep philosophical argument. Sports fans are protective of the deep philosophical argument. Some sports fans are even antagonistic to anything that might threaten the deep philosophical argument. Stats, for instance, are sometimes said to take the fun out of being a sports fan by being *too accurate*. Facts get in the way of the monology, shouting matches, and "Lord Palmerston!"-"Pip the Elder!" preambles to fisticuffs, which soundtrack that modern symposium known as the sports bar.

Certain front offices of certain sports teams seem forever mired in the deep philosophical argument. I like philosophy, but it wears its age poorly. Plato championed Sparta, its asceticism, aggression, low-culture, and slavery. Nietzsche advocated war and conquest and thought Napoleon an almost ideal human being. Schopenhauer was said to be a terrible tipper. Though intellectually akin, science and philosophy are near opposites in method. The great reliance on semantics make philosophy ever mutable, ever debatable, and never able to resolve much of anything. Metaphysics, it seems, cannot help an airplane to fly.

Science depends on trial. Atoms must be smashed, double blind studies must be conducted, wombats must be tagged and tracked. There is room for error and bias, but because information is attained, some kind of resolution of trial is possible. I doubt anyone at the VMAC considered their work to be science, and it wasn't. But it was scientific in method. Decisions were not made based on high-sounding ideals, or an inflexible idea of what the team must become. Churn is trial and error, a somewhat controlled study of available talent. That Schneider and Carroll churned and churned maybe never resulted in much talent added *directly*. But it surely indicates a modern, progressive approach to roster construction. Data is substantial. Data can be rethought, recontextualized, and shared. Conclusions derived from data can be challenged. It isn't private and ephemeral like a hunch, or plausible but incapable of being tested like a philosophy.

From these careful experiments in talent acquisition, Pete Carroll and John Schneider built a Super Bowl champion.

97 Danger B-Russ

It's hard to pin down when I first came to hate Brian Russell. And I write "hate," meaning that particular neologism we wield against pop musicians and actors, etc. I didn't hate the signing; I misinterpreted it. Maybe I hated that I misinterpreted it. I thought

Russell was signed to provide depth, but he became a starter. And he started two years, nary a missed snap nor a criticism.

See: in the years I hated Brian Russell—that loathsome joyful hatred of the komodo dragon for the ox dying from sepsis, salivating at its festering wounds, shortening my distance as it stumbles and becomes too weak to fight, famished for its demise—I thought I hated the corruption he represented to me. He was walking inefficiency. A player whose press connections, his ability to speak coach to coaches, be assignment correct, and disastrously conservative covered up his athletic insufficiency, his badness as a football player. I was struggling to get a foothold as a sportswriter and felt trapped behind some older scribes, many of whom mailed it in, many of whom seemed almost put out to cover the Seattle Seahawks for a living. Russell became the hobbyhorse for my bitterness, my resentment. My team was struggling to be good again. Russell was corruption come inefficiency, a player who played for the wrong reasons and so doing, hurt his team's chance of winning. A 6'2" beady eyed personification of all my privilege and woe.

The expression "catch lightning in a bottle" comes from former Dodgers manager, the late Leo Durocher, but its meaning is obvious enough without origin or elaboration. Russell caught lightning in a bottle his second season in the NFL. He intercepted nine passes in 2003. By extra points added, a no-funny-stuff metric that simply converts box score information like "sack for a loss of six" into a number representing how many points that play is worth, he excelled among free safeties. Ranking eighth, the sum of plays that season accredited to Russell was worth a bit under eight touchdowns. So exceptionally valuable are interceptions. And football coaches know this. Pete Carroll speaks of turnovers with the fear and reverence of a shaman for a rain god.

Maybe I didn't hate Russell because he was some walking symbol of corruption, an inefficiency. Maybe Russell wasn't an inefficiency. Maybe Russell was no worse than the 32nd best free safety in the NFL, a true one-in-a-thousand talent, only relatively bad—but quick, coordinated, strong, focused, competitive beyond my wildest aspirations, your wildest aspirations, all but a vanishingly small percentage of the population's wildest aspirations. Maybe I didn't hate Russell because he was bad. Maybe I hated Russell because of the inadequacy of merely good.

When someone is an amateur—consider: woman in a coffee shop: strumming heartfelt, inobtrusive in her quietude, working in a respectable cover of Joni Mitchell here and Woody Guthrie there, and altogether a nice break from piped-in pop music—we relate, and this ability to see ourselves in this amateur badly biases us to their ability. We're desperate for genuine, not slick, not corporate, but genuine is slippery, corrupting; our captive coffee shop ingenue propped by our good will; our experience warped, adrift on ingenuous goodwill for a fellow unremarkable; in hot denial that art means artfulness, and artfulness means craft, and craft means artifice, and Shakespeare wasn't bearing his soul. He was making a play for an audience, so that audience may tell others of their delight, and others may pay, and Shakespeare may eat, may wear nice clothing and buy leather-bound books.

And Russell, Brian Russell, B-Russ, the man of slapstick tackle attempts, and bad angles, and meaningless tackles 30 yards downfield, he would school you so hard at any sport you dared play against him (most likely), and it would be the kind of big brother sort of massacre that, to the onlooker, can be funny, can be pitiable, and is undeniably both. He would make you look slow and tired and hobbled, and it would be YouTube gold. It is YouTube gold. Google Uncle Drew. And such is the gulf between us in our billions and they in their hundreds. Men like Brian Russell are not better people, not smarter or happier, kinder, or harder working, but they do one thing exceptionally well, and that one thing, for all sorts of reasons, is in exceptional demand. Thus: they are rich and famous. Thusly thus: it is that much easier to despise them.

For eight years Brian Russell played in the National Football League. For two of those years, he played for the Seattle Seahawks— my favorite team, presumably your favorite team. In those eight years, he was absolutely excellent and relatively awful—that too customary word that literally means something creating wonderment in its terribleness. Those Seahawks defenses were once good and once bad, but bad both years at preventing yards. Russell had been brought in to prevent long, touchdown-scoring plays, and in his first season, the Seahawks in fact did do that. He succeeded, at life, in football. By being so good people expected him to be better, being among the so-good he couldn't seem much worse, a bad idea with inertia, a marvel of human achievement vastly inferior to so many of his kind, that sort of sticks around because he does one thing someone needs, and, because for reasons irrational, we're all innately scared of change.

98 A Threat with His Legs and Hands

Before he became a Seahawk, Seneca Wallace was an Iowa State Cyclone. His success there tells us a lot about the difference between the college and pro game. On one famous play, affectionately known as "the Run," Wallace ran left, then right, then back, then forward, then left all the way back across the field, and then forward into the end zone. Wallace's scurry is estimated to have covered 135 yards vertically and horizontally but managed only 12 yards net. Seahawks fans can attest: that nonsense doesn't work in the pros.

Wallace would take long drops that made it very hard for his tackles to block the edge. He has only averaged four yards per attempt and has only run for one touchdown. Matt Hasselbeck has averaged 3.8 yards per attempt and rushed for five touchdowns.

Watch any game that Wallace started, and the announcers are sure to tell you that he is a threat with his legs, but Seahawks fans learned his legs were a greater threat to his team. He fumbled 17 times in his Seahawks career. He also had a habit of running out of bounds behind the line of scrimmage instead of throwing it away. That meant Wallace was essentially sacking himself. He just is not fast enough to regularly outrun professional linebackers.

99 The City of Seattle Wants to Apologize for the 1992 Season

The 1992 Seahawks were the kind of team commentators felt free and in fact actively enjoyed making fun of. This actual exchange between the three-man *Monday Night Football* booth of Al Michaels, Dan Dierdorf, and Frank Gifford gives you a sense of how frightfully awful and unwatchable this assemblage of Raiderized football runoff truly was.

Dierdorf: "I wonder if…[boos of crowd] I wonder what would happen if you took the 11 defensive players and taught 'em a couple plays."

Gifford: "With Cortez Kennedy as the quarterback."

Dierdorf: "Could it…Could it be any worse?…I mean…let's go through this now. Eugene Robinson, he could be the quarterback. Rufus Porter, now is he a running back or what? 6'1", 225."

Gifford: "I want Kennedy."

Dierdorf: "And I'd run right behind Kennedy every time."

Tube Boobs

I was watching a game commentated by Merle Harmon and Jim Turner, and there were quite a few really funny foibles. Both seemed very uncomfortable being on the television. When they introduced themselves, Harmon held a mike to Turner, only for Turner to reveal a second later that he himself had a mike.

There was a real radio feel to the announcing. It was rich and full of detail. It makes me feel that much more frustrated with modern booth crews that are often incompetent, and sometimes worse. Nothing grates quite like hearing Joe Buck make it perfectly clear he is not excited or invested in the game.

One thing Buck would never attempt is to completely mischaracterize the action. On one down, Harmon attempted to credit John Harris for a play he was clearly nowhere near. When they showed the replay, he credited the player who actually made the tackle, but then credited Harris again. Makes me wonder what it was like when you had to listen to a game and trust what the announcers were telling you was true. I bet I would have never realized that it wasn't the line's fault but Shaun Alexander's.

Michaels: "Robert Blackmon is my tailback after his interception return."

Gifford: "Harper and Hunter as WRs, why not?"

Dierdorf: "Why not? Bryant, Nash, Kennedy, Woods, up front. We got to work on this."

Gifford: "Stamina might be a problem."

Dierdorf: "This guy plays where he wants to play [on Tez]."

Michaels: "I think Nash would be my wrangler."

Gifford: "Al, ooh…that is…that just ruined the entire thing."

Dierdorf: "You know Al, that is…that is beneath you…or so I thought."

This re-envisioning of the Seahawks very talented defense as its offense was but one of a long series of insults volleyed at the Seahawks that day. It was obvious that Seahawks-Broncos, with Elway out because of a tendon injury, was entirely beneath the

Monday Night crew, and they were all too comfortable voicing it. Usually, this Joe Buck-like entitlement angers me. But, one, the team really was some kind of awful. And, two, sometimes I think Buck is the real loser. The guy seems to hate sports but seems duty bound to uphold his dad's legacy.

Here are some more timely insults for what may very well be the least watchable team in NFL history.

The Explicit

Michaels: "That may have been the ugliest offensive series in the history of football: two timeouts, a six-yard sack, a false start, and a terribly thrown pass for an interception."

Dierdorf: "They could have saved us a lot of time and effort and just thrown the interception right away."

Dierdorf: "The bad new is, [Maddox] threw an interception. The good news is, Seattle's offense comes back on the field."

The Metaphorical

Dierdorf: "They're awash in a sea of numbers…and they're gurgling."

The Subtle

Michaels: "The jury is out, at least according to Flores, on Stouffer."

Michaels: "Tom Flores, he wanted to change the offense here."

Dierdorf: "At this stage in his career, [Stouffer] will not win the game throwing."

The Non Sequitur

Michaels: "Guys, ready for the cartoon?"

The Insightful

Dierdorf: "That might be the problem, Frank. They're trying too hard to put the defense on the field."

The Sarcastic
Dierdorf: "I wouldn't award [the Broncos] a victory too soon. This is quite an offensive machine [the Seahawks] have here."

100 A Fictional Account of Franco's Half-Season in Seattle

"Mr. Harris! Mr. Harris!"

"Oh, hey, Mikey. What's on your mind?"

"I just think it's real neat you're on the team, Mr. Harris."

"Well okay, but you told me that yesterday and the day before and—"

"Oh I'm sorry, Mr. Harris. I—"

"Franco. Call me Franco."

"Shucks, I'm sorry Franco Harris, it's just we're a young franchise without much winnin' and it's just such an honor to be aroun' a legend like you."

"Well okay, son. That's real nice. Now listen, it's my snap so I better suit up and—"

"Of course. I'll just..." and Franco Harris snapped on his silver helmet and trotted out to the huddle.

"Mike, leave the man alone."

"Sorry, Mr. Knox. It's Mikey, Mr. Knox."

"You're a goddamn grown man, Mike, and I'm not calling no goddamn grown man Mikey. Now do something useful for a change and get the starters some water."

Mikey scampers over to the cooler. Chuck Knox looks out from the sideline at his offense, his arms crossed, his face relaxed and dispassionate. Offensive coordinator Ray Prochaska walks up beside him. Snap. The click of pads, the wet thud of flesh striking flesh, and the mixed grunts and groans of large men desperately battling for an inch resounds from the gridiron. Prochaska's face twists and contorts as if he's looking on at a car crash.

"Why'd we sign this puddle of crap?"

"That's Franco Harris, Chuck."

"I know his goddamn name."

Sources

Books

Carroll, Bob, Pete Palmer, and John Thorn. *The Hidden Game of Football.* New York: Warner Books, 1988.

Gay, Timothy. *The Physics of Football.* New York: HarperCollins, 2005.

Jeffery, Keith. *Field Marshal Sir Henry Wilson: A Political Soldier.* New York: Oxford University Press, 2006.

Knox, Chuck, and Bill Plaschke. *Hard Knox: The Life of an NFL Coach.* New York: Harcourt Brace Jovanovich, 1988.

Moody, Fred. *Fighting Chance: An NFL Season with the Seattle Seahawks.* Seattle: Sasquatch Books, 1989.

Raible, Steve, and Mike Sando. *Tales from the Seahawks Sidelines.* Champaign, Illinois: Sports Publishing, 2004.

Twain, Hank. *Following the Equator—A Journey Across the World.* Hartford, Connecticut: American Publishing Company, 1897.

Magazines

People magazine

Sports Illustrated (Peter King, Bruce Newman)

News Services

The Associated Press (Rachel Cohen, Barry Wilner)

Newspapers

Boston Globe (Will McDonough, Michael Vega)

Chicago Tribune

Ellensburgh Daily Record (Daryl Gadbow)

Milwaukee Journal

Moscow Pullman Daily News

New York Times (Samantha Stevenson, William N. Wallace)
Rock Hill Herald
San Diego Union Tribune (Jim Trotter)
Seattle Post-Intelligencer (Steve Kelley, Danny O'Neil)
Seattle Times (Greg Bishop, Clare Farnsworth)
Spokane Chronicle (Dan Weaver)
Spokesman-Review (Dan Weaver)
St. Petersburg Times
Sun Herald
Tacoma News Tribune (Mike Sando)
Tri-City Herald
USA Today (Denise Tom)
Washington Post (Leonard Shapiro)

Websites
Advanced NFL Stats (AdvancedNFLStats.com)
Alabama.com (Kevin Scarbinski: Al.com)
Becky's Seattle Seahawks Fan Site (Beckys-Place.com)
ESPN (ESPN.com)
Etymonline.com
Football Outsiders (FootballOutisders.com)
Google News (news.google.com)
Pro Football Hall of Fame (profootballhof.com)
Pro-Football-Reference.com
San Francisco Gate (SFGate.com)
Sports Illustrated (SportsIllustrated.cnn.com)
The Official Site of the NFL (NFL.com)
The Official Site of the Oakland Raiders (Raiders.com)
The Official Site of the Seattle Seahawks (Seahawks.com)

Television
NFL Game of the Week: Bo versus Boz (NFL Films)
NFL Game of the Week: 1999 Seahawks @ Dolphins (NFL Films)